FLYING
to GLORY

Patrick Stephens Limited, a member of the Haynes Publishing Group, has published authoritative, quality books for enthusiasts for more than twenty years. During that time the company has established a reputation as one of the world's leading publishers of books on aviation, maritime, military, model-making, motor cycling, motoring, motor racing, railway and railway modelling subjects. Readers or authors with suggestions for books they would like to see published are invited to write to:
The Editorial Director, Patrick Stephens Limited, Sparkford, Nr Yeovil, Somerset, BA22 7JJ.

FLYING
to GLORY

The B-17
Flying Fortress
in war and peace

MARTIN W BOWMAN

PSL

Patrick Stephens Limited

First published in 1992

British Library Cataloguing in Publication Data

Bowman, Martin
    Flying to glory: The B-17 Flying Fortress in war and peace.
    I. Title
    623.7

    ISBN 1-85260-328-3

Patrick Stephens Limited is part of the Haynes Publishing Group P.L.C., Sparkford, Nr Yeovil, Somerset, BA22 7JJ.

Printed in Great Britain by J. H. Haynes & Co. Ltd.

Contents

Not for Glory – then for what?
Those hours of waiting, pain and cold?

Not for Glory – then for what?
Those youths once vital, bright and bold?

Not for Glory – then for what?
Those acts of horror, death and strife?

Not for Glory – then for what?
Those born for Justice, Peace and Life.

© S.M.P. 1989

'. . . The Air Force kind of grew up with the B-17. It was as tough an airplane as was ever built. It did everything we asked it to do, and did it well.'

Gen Curtis E. LeMay

'Without the B-17, we might have lost the war.'

Gen Carl A. Spaatz

'The B-17, I think, was the best combat airplane ever built – it could sustain more battle damage. You wouldn't believe they could stay in the air.'

Gen Ira C. Eaker

Acknowledgements

I would particularly like to thank the following people for their help and expertise in making this book possible:

Mike Bailey; B-17 Combat Crewmen & Wingmen; Richard E. Bagg; Gp Capt Antony J. Barwood OBE; Richard Bing; Gp Capt Roy Boast CBE, DFC; Robert Browne; Steve Carter; William M. Cleveland; Bob Collis; Mrs Diane L. Cook; Howard K. Corns; Wayne E. Cose; Clyde Crowley; Colin Deverell; Jack P. Dorfman; Sandy Ellis; Kenneth W. Fields; Reuben 'Ruby' Fier; Jim French; Robert M. Foose; C. E. Ben Franklin; Harry Friedman MD; Capt Al D. Garcia USAF; Larry Goldstein; Andrew Height; John A. Holden; Col E. C. 'Ned' Humphreys; John L. Hurd; Air Cdre Tom Imrie; Pete Hardiman; Col Raymond F. Hunter; Loren E. Jackson; Lawrence Jenkins; Antonio Claret Jordao, Museo Aeroespacial; Michael W. Kellner; Arthur Lange; Bernal 'Rusty' Lewis; Jerry Linderman; Ped G. Magness; Ed Maloney; Ian McLachlan; Gus Mencow; Richard C. Muchler; Ralph J. Munn; Musée de l'air; Charles M. Nekvasil; Tony North; Air Cdre Christopher Paul; Ralph E. Reese; Sue Reilly; Wilbur Richardson; Hans Heiri Stapfer; George Stebbings; William B. Sterrett; Frank Thomas; Geoff Ward; Brig-Gen Robert W. Waltz; Angela Westphal; Richard Wynn; Larry D. Yannotti.

Introduction

The early fame of the Boeing Airplane Company was earned as a result of its position as the leading American supplier of single-seat fighter aircraft from 1924 to 1936. In the early 1930s production switched to the more lucrative transport business. Boeing Air Transport was formed to operate the San Francisco–Chicago airmail route which had been bought in 1927. The success of this venture encouraged the company to design larger, passenger-carrying aircraft and the airline was expanded into the Boeing Air Transport System.

In 1929 the Boeing airline and aeroplane operations merged with other manufacturers in the American aviation industry including Pratt & Whitney, a leading manufacturer of aircraft engines, and the Standard Steel Propeller Co, to form United Aircraft and Transport Corporation. The airlines operated under their own names within a holding company called United Air Lines.

In 1934 Congress passed legislation which forced aircraft and engine manufacturers to sever the links with airline operations. The Boeing Aircraft Company resumed independent operation and moved into the bomber business. On 14 April 1934 the US Army's General Staff issued a request for design proposals for 'Project A', an aircraft capable of carrying a one-ton bomb 5,000 miles. Boeing proposed the Model 294 or the XBLR-1 (experimental bomber, long-range) as it was known initially. On 28 June 1934 it won a contract for design data, wind tunnel tests and a mockup. The XB-15 resulted, complete with a 149-ft span, four Allison V-1710 inline engines and weighing some 35 tons. The only other contender, the Martin XB-16, became too expensive to build.

While Boeing wrestled with the problems associated with the experimental monster, on 18 July 1934 the US Army Air Corps (Air Corps) at Wright Field issued a specification for the next production bomber to replace the Martin B-10. This new 'multi-engined' four to six place bomber had to be capable of carrying a 2,000 lb bomb load at a speed of 200-250 mph over a distance of 1,020-2,000 miles.

On that same day Boeing learned that competing manufacturers were to build prototypes at their own expense. They also stipulated that a flying prototype had to be available for trials in August 1935. Since the winner could expect to receive an order for some 220 bombers on 26 September, Boeing President Clairmont Egtvedt and his board – after first making certain that 'multi-engined' also permitted four, as well as two, engines (because Boeing were already working on a new concept for a four-engined bomber called the Model 299) – decided to risk $275,000 of his company's capital on the new venture. Egtvedt's decision was based on the knowledge that the Model 299 was already in the design stage. Eventually, the project to build a prototype would require over $600,000.

The Model 299's lineage could be traced back to the B-9 monoplane bomber of 1931 and the Boeing 247 transport of 1933 and further data was available as a result of the work on the XB-15. E. G. Emery had been appointed project engineer with Edward C. Wells as his assistant. (In December 1935 the 24-year-old Stanford graduate was promoted to the post of project engineer.)

Unlike its predecessor the B-9, the Model 299 would carry all bombs internally. Defensive armament was provided by four streamlined

The Model 299, shown here at its roll-out at Boeing Field, Seattle on 17 July 1935, was flown for the first time on 28 July by the company test pilot, Leslie Tower. The clean lines of the Model 299 owed much to the sleek Model 247 airliner which was scaled up into the much bigger Model 299 by using many of the engineering innovations that had been developed on the earlier Model 294 (XB-15) project. (Boeing.)

machine-gun blisters on the sides, top and bottom of the fuselage and a nose gunner's station. The prototype was powered by four 750hp Pratt & Whitney R-1690 Hornet engines and could carry 2,500 lb of bombs 2,040 miles. Rushed to completion in only a year, the Model 299 was flown for the first time on 28 July 1935 at Boeing Field, Seattle, by the company test pilot, Leslie Tower.

Richard L. Williams, a *Seattle Times* reporter, wrote: 'Declared to be the largest land plane ever built in America, this 15-ton Flying Fortress, built by Boeing Aircraft Company under Army specifications, today was ready to retest its wings . . .' While the role of later versions was to be offensive, the Model 299 was conceived for a purely defensive mission: the protection of the American coastline from foreign surface fleets. It was this designation, and not the later, formidable defensive machine gun armament,

which suggested the famous name 'Flying Fortress'.

On 20 August only a month after the roll out – Tower, his assistant and co-pilot Louis Wait, with C. W. Benton as mechanic and Henry Igo of Pratt & Whitney on board to maintain the engines, flew the Model 299 from Seattle to Wright Field at Dayton, Ohio, to begin service trials in competition with the twin-engined Martin 146 and the Douglas DB-1. The Model 299 completed the 2,100-mile trip, much of the way on auto-pilot, in a record breaking 9 hrs non-stop with an unbelievable average speed of 233 mph. A delighted Egtvedt and Wells were on hand to tell the crew that the Air Corps did not expect them to arrive for another 2 hours.

Air Corps pilot Lt Donald Putt was assigned to the Model 299 as project test pilot. Competitive testing soon proved that the Boeing aircraft was in a class of its own and it went on to exceed all the Army specifications for speed, climb and range. Maj Ployer P. Hill (Chief of Wright Field's Flight Testing Section) took over the final tests from Putt.

Testing was almost complete and the Air Corps about to confer the title XB-17 to the aircraft when on 30 October 1939 Hill took the controls for yet another flight. Putt sat beside him in the right-hand seat and Leslie Tower stood behind them on the flightdeck. The Model 299 raced down the runway and began its climb before appearing to stall. It crashed and burst into flames. Putt, Benton and Igo scrambled clear of the wreckage but Hill and Tower, who were trapped inside, were bravely pulled clear by Lt Robert K. Giovannoli. Maj Hill never regained consciousness and died later in the day. Tower died a few days later.

The subsequent investigation revealed that the crash was a result of the tail controls not having been unlocked prior to take-off. No blame could possibly be attributed to the aircraft design; it was clearly pilot error. Before the crash the Air Corps had been considering an order for 65 B-17 bombers. In January 1937 however, production contracts were awarded to Douglas for 133 twin-engined B-18 Bolos while Boeing received

only a service test order of 13 flight articles and a static test model under the designation YB-17. This was changed to Y1B-17 shortly before the first one was ready for test flying on 2 December 1936. The major significant change from the Model 299 was the introduction of Wright 1820-39 Cyclone engines in place of the earlier Hornets. The landing gear was also changed to a single leg arrangement instead of the earlier double legs and minor changes were made to the armament systems.

The YB-17 was flown for the first time on 2 December 1936. Five days later the aircraft was flown by Air Corps representative Capt Stanley Umstead at Boeing Field. Everything went according to plan until the landing. Umstead applied the brakes too forcefully and turned the bomber over. No one was hurt but Boeing had to endure a nerve-biting Congressional investigation. No action was taken but any further accidents in the tale of bad luck which seemed to dog the new bomber would have resulted in its ultimate downfall.

The first Y1B-17s went into service during January 1937 with the 2nd Bombardment Group, which had earlier taken delivery of the sole XB-15. By 4 August 1937, 12 Y1B-17s had

Boeing Y1B-17A 37-369 which flew for the first time on 2 December 1936. (Boeing.)

been delivered to the 2nd Bomb Group's base at Langley Field, Virginia. Lt-Col Robert Olds' 2nd Bomb Group pioneered the early use of the B-17 and it gained a well-earned reputation for rugged construction and safe operation (there were no serious mishaps during three years of strenuous flying). Pre-flight check lists were introduced to prevent a repetition of the Model 299 crash. Many men who were to become synonymous with USAAF achievements in World War Two, such as Harold L. George, Curtis E. LeMay, Robert B. Williams, Neil Harding and Caleb Haynes, served in the 2nd Bomb Group.

In February 1938 six B-17s led by Col Olds made a very successful goodwill trip to South America. Apart from confirming the 2nd Bomb Group's navigational skill and airmanship it also reminded any would-be aggressor that the Air Corps now had the ability to fly bombers over long distances.

Despite this wonderful achievement (for which the 2nd was awarded the MacKay Trophy in 1939) the War Department chose to ignore the earlier words of GHQ Air Force Commander Gen Frank Andrews who, in June 1937, had urger the War Department that all future bombers purchased should be four-engined. Twin-engined bombers meant the Army would be tied to a support role for the ground troops in any future battle. Andrews, like Gen Billy Mitchell before him (who had been court martialled as a result of his beliefs), was convinced of the need for a genuine strategic bomber which could destroy America's enemies before they reached the battlefields. Instead, in May 1938 the War Department declared that for the fiscal years 1939 and 1940 experimentation and development would be confined to aircraft 'designed for the close-in support of ground troops'. It also stated that aircraft production would be restricted to 'medium and light aircraft, pursuit and other light aircraft.'

In an attempt to fully ram the point home about the need for a strategic bombing capability, and at the same time fire a warning shot over the US Admirals' bows, in May 1938 three B-17s were given a 'navigational exercise;' to intercept the Italian liner 'Rex' some 725 miles off the coast of America. Olds and his navigator, Lt (later Gen) Curtis E. LeMay, completed the task and dropped a message onto the deck of the liner. This brilliant feat of navigation proved that an invasion force at sea could be intercepted before it could harm coastal defences. This startling fact was not lost on the Admirals. In a futile response the US Navy tried to limit the AAC's area of operation to not more than 100 miles from the American shore!

Meanwhile, the 13th Y1B-17 was delivered to the Matèriel Division at Wright Field for experimental testing. A static test aircraft was also ordered for use in a controlled experiment to discover just how much stress the aircraft could take before it disintegrated. However, the experiment was deemed unnecessary after a 2nd Bomb Group Y1B-17 emerged intact after being thrown onto its back in a violent thunderstorm during a flight in the summer of 1938.

As a result, the static-test aircraft was converted to a flying model and used to test exhaust-driven turbo superchargers which would be needed for high altitude flight. It flew for the first time on 29 April 1938 with the turbos installed on top of the engine nacelles. The experiment was a failure but confidence was restored when the Y1B-17 flew again on 20 November with the turbos operating, successfully mounted under the nacelles. The Y1B-17A, as it was re-designated, was delivered to the Air Corps on 31 January 1939. Incredibly for the first time, it was able to reach a top speed of 295 mph at 25,000 ft. Not surprisingly, turbos now became standard on the B-17B and all future B-17 models.

The B-17B also had Wright R-1820-51 Cyclones giving 900 hp up to 25,000 ft and a new, more streamlined nose, 7 in shorter than that of the Y1B-17. The kinked forward fuselage and small rotating turret on the nose were deleted and replaced by a Plexiglass nose with flat bomb-aiming panel with a simple socket for a .30 calibre machine-gun. The navigator-bombardier was moved from behind the pilots to a more practical position in the new nose section. In addition, the flaps were enlarged and a Plexiglass dome added to the cabin roof. External bomb racks could be added to carry a further 4,000 lb of bombs.

The Air Corps was anxious to proceed with the B-17B and prove the strategic bomber concept but financial implications soured relations. Boeing had spent $100,000 on the supercharger development and wanted payment. Although the Air Corps had previously agreed to pay $205,000 per aircraft it now offered only $198,000. Not only was Boeing faced with a bill for the superchargers, it was also losing money on each air-

Boeing B-17B which flew for the first time on 27 June 1939. The first models were delivered to the 2nd and 7th Bomb Groups between October 1939 and 30 March 1940. (Boeing.)

craft! Eventually, a compromise was worked out where the Army would pay $202,500 per aircraft. Altogether, contracts were received for thirty-eight B-17Bs but problems with the super-chargers meant that the first aircraft did not fly until 27 June 1939.

These were delivered to the 2nd and 7th Bomb Groups during the period October 1939 – 30 March 1940. In October 1940 the 2nd Bomb Group's original B-17s were transferred to the 19th Bomb Group at March Field, California.

A B-17B belonging to the 41st Reconnaissance Squadron, 2nd Bomb Group in Newfoundland, was the first US Army Air Force bomber to drop its bombs in anger when it attacked a U-boat on 27 October 1941. In 1940-41 many B-17Bs were revamped and fitted with new devices such as flush-type waist windows for .50 calibre guns.

The first B-17B was retained at Wright Field to test new armament installations intended for the B-17C. The B-17C, which flew for the first time on 21 July 1940, was a more combat worthy

Boeing B-17C which was supplied to the RAF as the Boeing Fortress I. (Boeing.)

model following recommendations made by Britain and France as a result of their experience with bombers in air combat. The two limited vision gun cupolas on the sides of the fuselage were replaced with streamlined Plexiglass teardrop shaped windows, while the top gun blister was replaced with a sliding Plexiglass hatch. The under gunner's blister was replaced with a large 'bath-tub' containing a single .50 calibre machine gun. A .30 calibre gun could be fired from any of six ball sockets in the nose. Armour plate and self-sealing fuel tanks were fitted but the bomb load remained the same (4,996 lbs) as on the B-17B.

Thirty-eight B-17Cs were ordered on 10 August 1939. The first flew on 21 July 1940 and was retained by Boeing for test purposes. In the spring of 1941 the first of 20 aircraft (designated 299U) from the 1939 contract were diverted to Great Britain where the type was converted for service as the Fortress I. These aircraft were intended as trainers pending deliveries of the B-17E and were not to be used operationally. However, the aircraft situation in Britain at this time was acute and in June 1941 five Fortress Is were delivered to No 90 Squadron at Polebrook for high-altitude bombing operations. Three aircraft from this unit took part in a daylight raid on Wilhelmshaven on 8 July and a further 23 operations followed during the summer of 1941.

By September it was decided that the Fortress was unsuitable for further operations with Bomber Command. Although it was an extremely well built aircraft, operational experience revealed that its defensive firepower of five .3 in and .5 in machine-guns was totally inadequate for flights over heavily defended targets in Europe. The RAF operated the Fortress I at altitudes approaching 30,000 ft. In 51 sorties, 26 were flown with no bombs being dropped: bomb aimers did not feel able to drop their bombs accurately (the then top secret Norden bomb sight had been deleted from all 20 models supplied to the RAF and replaced with the Sperry sight).

A further 42 B-17Cs which had been ordered on 17 April 1941 required so many modifications as a result of the RAF experience that they had been redesignated B-17Ds on 6 September 1941. Outwardly, the 'D' differed from the 'C' by the addition of engine cowl flaps and twin-gun installations in the belly and upper positions. Internally, more armour plate was added, a new self-sealing fuel tank system installed and changes were also made to the bomb release, oxygen and electrical systems. In May 1941 21 B-17Ds were flown to Hawaii and the remainder were sent to the 7th and 19th Bomb Groups.

Results of the European combat experience and lessons learned in the Pacific were incorporated into the extensively improved B-17E which was ordered on 30 August 1941. The rear fuselage from the radio compartment on was extensively re-designed to provide more space for the gunners, and greatly enlarged tail surfaces gave better control and stability for high-altitude bombing. A new tail gun position with two .50 calibre Browning M-2 machine-guns fired by the gunner in an uncomfortable half-kneeling, half-

Boeing B-17D pictured at Seattle in June 1941. The 'D' incorporated many design changes as a result of the experience gained by the RAF in Europe. (Boeing.)

Boeing B-17E which first flew on 5 September 1941. Note the power-operated Bendix gun turret. (Boeing.)

sitting position was fitted.

The ventral bathtub was deleted on the first 112 B-17Es and replaced with a new Bendix power-operated gun turret with twin .50s fired by a gunner using controls and a periscope sighting arrangement in the fuselage. The turret proved troublesome to operate and was subsequently replaced with the Sperry ball turret with the gunner squeezed inside. A Sperry electrically operated turret with twin .50s was installed behind the cockpit just in front of the bomb bay which still carried the normal .50 calibre machine-gun. The single .30 calibre machine-gun in the nose was retained as it was thought no enemy fighter pilots would attempt a head-on attack with such high closing speeds between fighter and bomber.

Boeing received orders for 812 B-17Es but material shortages delayed production and the 'E' did not make its maiden flight until 5 September 1941, four months behind schedule. About 100 B-17Es had been delivered to the Air Corps by the time of the Japanese attack on Pearl Harbor on 7 December 1941. Fifty more on hand were the older 'C' and 'D' models. A handful of bomb groups fought the Japanese in the Philippines and Java and the survivors retreated to India. The B-17 continued to operate in the Pacific Theatre until 1943.

Beginning in March 1942, the first of 45 B-17Es known as Fortress IIAs was delivered to Britain. Many gave sterling service in RAF Coastal Command where they helped close the mid-Atlantic 'gap'. The first B-17Es of the 97th

B-17E 'Yankee' during training in the peaceful days just prior to America's entry into World War Two. (USAF.)

B-17F-10-DL, one of 600 built by Douglas Aircraft at Long Beach, California. (Douglas.)

Bomb Group landed in Britain in July 1942 and this unit flew the first American Fortress mission on 17 August.

After 512 B-17Es had been built the remaining 300 aircraft on the contract were converted to B-17F production standard. The 'F' was the first Fortress model to enter really large scale production. The B.V.D. pool was created when Boeing agreed to let Lockheed-Vega at Burbank, California and Douglas Aircraft at Long Beach build the B-17F under licence. Lockheed had first approached Boeing about building the B-17 under licence in April 1941 when it feared that gathering war clouds would severely limit the need for passenger transport aircraft.

The 'F' appeared to be similar to the B-17E, save for a frameless Plexiglass nose which gave the bombardier the better all-round visibility. However, no less than 400 changes and modifications were made to the B-17 design, most of them being carried out on the production line itself. New Wright R-1820-97 Cyclones with wider Hamilton Standard 'paddle' propeller blades, meant that the standard 1,200 hp could be raised to 1,380 hp ('war emergency' power) to give a top speed of 325 mph. The leading edge of the engine cowlings had to be re-shaped and

shortened so that the blades could clear the cowling when feathered. The installation of 'Tokyo Tanks' in the wings and an 820-gal tank in the bomb bay increased the tankage to 3,630 gals. Maximum bombload was 9,600 lb, but the normal combat load was nearer 4,000 lb.

The first B-17F-1-BO was delivered to the Army Air Force (the Air Corps had become the US Army Air Force in June 1941) on 30 May 1942 and after August that year, 19 B-17Fs went to RAF Coastal Command as the Fortress II. Originally, the British had signed a lend-lease contract in June 1941 for 300 Fortress IIs for the RAF but these aircraft were diverted to the USAAF when Britain decided not to use the B-17s as bombers but only for maritime operations.

At the beginning of 1943 the 8th Air Force in Britain had only four B-17F groups totalling some 200 aircraft. On 27 January VIIIth Bomber Command bombed Germany for the first time when B-17Fs of the 306th Bomb Group attacked Wilhelmshaven. During mid-July hundreds of B-17Fs were used in a week of attacks beginning on 24 July which came to be known as 'Blitz week'. Despite high losses the B-17s were despatched to Schweinfurt and Regensburg a month later, on 17 August. Sixty B-17s were lost and many other written off in crashes in England; an unacceptable 19% loss rate. On 6 September 45 B-17s failed to return from a raid on Stuttgart. The worst day, 'Black Thursday', occurred on 14 October, when another 60 B-17s were lost, again on a mission to Schweinfurt.

Altogether, B-17F production totalled 3,400. Boeing built 2,300 and starting in July 1942, 600 and 500 each were delivered by Douglas and Lockheed-Vega respectively, in new factories built specially for the purpose. Many modifications were phased in during assembly and considerable confusion developed in the war zones when it was discovered that although each manufacturer used the same block numbers in production, not all the aircraft were similarly equipped. Differences often occurred in nose armament but generally the B.V.D pool was a great success and greatly speeded the flow of Fortresses to the war zones.

Meanwhile, in August 1942 it was suggested that bombers be accompanied by 'destroyer-escort' aircraft, since existing fighter escorts did not possess the range to accompany the bombers deep into Germany. So the only logical proposal was a heavily armed Flying Fortress. In November 1942 Boeing converted the second production B-17F-1 into the XB-40 'destroyer-escort'. Two additional gun turrets; a Martin in place of the radio compartment guns and a Bendix chin turret, were fitted, and the single waist guns were replaced by twin .50s, making a total of 14 guns in total. Both the waist and tail guns were hydraulically boosted for improved control. Although it was still capable of carrying a bomb load it was seldom carried because of the added weight of the guns, armour plate and 11,275 rounds of ammunition.

Some 22 YB-40s were built by Douglas (although they were identified as Vega-built aircraft) and 12 were flown to England in January 1943 for operation by the 92nd Bomb Group at Alconbury. The first raid involving YB-40s took place on 29 May 1943 when four accompanied the Fortresses to St. Nazaire. It was evident after the first few weeks of operations that the YB-40 did not add materially to the combined firepower of a group and it could not protect stragglers from a concentrated fighter attack. The YB-40 was only used in very small numbers and flew the final mission on 28 July.

One tangible benefit that resulted from the abortive YB-40 project was the chin turret which was adopted in the last 86 Douglas-built B-17Fs and the final production version, the B-17G. The early B-17G retained the nose window configuration of the early B-17F. Bulged cheek windows were added at various stages of production by all three manufacturers. Beginning with the Boeing B-17G-50-BO, the waist gun positions were staggered to allow the gunners more freedom of movement in combat. An all-new tail turret with enlarged windows and a reflector gunsight in

The second production B-17F-1-BO 41-24341 which in November 1942 Boeing converted into the XB-40 'destroyer-escort'. Some 22 YB-40s were built by Douglas and were identified as Vega-built aircraft. (Boeing.)

Above: B-17G-45-DL in flight. Altogether, Douglas built 2,395 'G' models. (Douglas.)

Below: B-17G-5-VE models under construction at the Lockheed Vega plant, California. (Lockheed.)

place of the ring and bead sight was designed by the United Air Lines Modification Centre at Cheyenne, Wyoming. The 'Cheyenne' turret provided greater gun elevation and a completely re-designed gunners enclosure. It was installed during various stages of production at all three B-17G plants.

The B-17G flew for the first time on 21 May 1943 and first began to equip bomb groups of the 8th Air Force in England in September 1943. The arrival of the P-51 Mustang enabled 1,000-plane raids deep into Germany. During March 1944 the first American raids on Berlin took place and by April the 8th could call upon almost 1,000 B-17Gs; the number was to double by August that year. By the time hostilities in Europe finished in May 1945, almost 300,000 Fortress missions had taken place from Britain. Eighty-five B-17Gs went to the RAF as the Fortress III where they were used by Coastal Command and in 1944-45 by two radar countermeasure squadrons.

Altogether, some 8,680 B-17Gs were built. Boeing built 4,035 B-17Gs and Douglas and Lockheed built 2,395 and 2,250, respectively. At the peak of B-17 production in June 1944, the Boeing Seattle factory was rolling out 16 Fortresses every 24 hrs. The last B-17G rolled off the Lockheed-Vega production line on 29 July 1945.

The B-17G enjoyed a short but colourful post-war career. In 1946 a B-17G set the world altitude record for a four-engined aircraft of 43,499 ft. Three civilian-owned B-17Gs purchased by Israel were armed in Czechoslovakia, where they took off and manually bombed the Cairo area on 14 July 1948 while en-route to Israel. They flew about 200 sorties in the Arab-Israeli War and served the Israeli Air Force for 10 years.

Meanwhile, in America Boeing specially modified some 180 B-17Gs to B-17H specifications for the US forces. The B-17H was developed to carry a 27-ft long droppable lifeboat. Initially, the

B-17F under construction at the Douglas, Long Beach, California plant. (Douglas.)

One of 'Rosie's Riveters' cleans the Plexiglass nose of a newly constructed Lockheed-built B-17F. (Lockheed.)

'H' retained the B-17G armament except the ball turret, but gradually all armament was deleted to save weight and accommodate a radome in the former chin turret position. The B-17H was used in the air-sea rescue role from 1945 to 1956. At the outbreak of the Korean War (1950-3) B-17Hs were re-armed and re-designated SB-17 for the search bomber role. The 2nd and 3rd Rescue Squadrons based in Japan, which were the only air rescue aircraft available to Far East Air Force, used the SB-17 until it was quickly replaced by the SB-29 Dumbo as a result of the appearance by MiG 15 jet fighters in November 1950.

A number of B-17Gs were diverted to the US Navy as PB-1W for airborne early warning, anti-submarine and weather reconnaissance flights, and to the US Coast Guard as PB-1G rescue aircraft. Wartime reconnaissance versions, originally converted from B-17Fs and known as F-9, were re-designated RB-17G reconnaissance bombers. The first mission flown during the Korean War took place on 25 June 1950 by aerial mapping RB-17Gs of the 6204th Photo Mapping Flight based on Clark Field in the Philippines. VB-17G VIP Transports also saw service in Korea where they were re-armed with the top turret and tail guns.

Some B-17Gs were converted to radio-controlled QB-17 remote piloted drones, initially for use in the Bikini atomic bomb tests to collect data after the explosion. Controller aircraft for the drones were designated DB-17. QB-17s were also used as target aircraft in missile test. The last B-17 in US military service, a QB-17 drone, was destroyed in 1960 – ironically, by a Boeing Bomarc missile.

Altogether, some 12,371 B-17 Fortresses were built. Today only a handful are known to survive. Some B-17s have been used as 'Borate' bombers, extinguishing forest fires throughout the USA while others have found their way into museums and some have even been restored to flying condition after years of neglect. It is all a far cry from the B-17 pioneering days of 1941 when the RAF first used the Fortress in combat over Germany.

CHAPTER 1

Boeing Boys in Blue

Fortress pioneers of No. 90 Squadron (RAF)

On 5 May 1941 a group of bemused young airmen arrived at a bleak Norfolk airfield to be confronted with an aircraft they had never seen before, and one which they were to fly in broad daylight and at high altitude. Most of the men were veterans of RAF night bombing or low-level daylight operations and recent graduates of a rigorous de-compression test (which consisted of 'climbing' at 3,000 ft/min to 35,000 ft, and remaining there for 5 hr) at Farnborough.

The aircraft in question was the Boeing B-17C Model 299T. Early in 1941 the United States Government offered 20 Boeing B-17Cs to the British Purchasing Commission, together with the necessary personnel to instruct and assist in bringing the aircraft into RAF service. The B-17C possessed an impressive top speed of 325 mph at around 29,000 ft and could cruise at 230 mph at 30,000 ft. These speeds were only achievable because the lack of armour plate

(which was only installed in the tail behind the waist positions) and power operated gun turrets, meant there was no excess weight. Nevertheless, the B-17C was considered well armed, with one or two .30-in nose and six .50-in pannier-fed guns (two in the waist, two in a ventral cupola and two in the dorsal position).

The B-17C's range was poor and only American bombs, up to 1,000 lb, could be carried. The top secret Norden precision bomb sight, developed by the US Navy and able to place a bomb in 'a pickle barrel', had been deleted and replaced by the Sperry sight. Depending on one's point of view, it was either a very bad bomb sight ('one needed a bloody big barrel') or an excellent device but limited because it was only calibrated for automatic operation to 25,000 ft and bomb aimers had to 'guestimate' by feeding in pre-set calculations supplied by Sperrys at higher altitudes.

Boeing Fortress I AN530 of No 90 Squadron over England in 1941. (Charles E. Brown.)

Despite the B-17's limitations, some of which would only manifest themselves in combat, the need for operational aircraft for daylight operations by the RAF was so great that despite the Americans' suggestion that the aircraft be used only for training until a more fully developed type was available for operational flying, it was decided to modify the B-17Cs in the UK to an operational standard. The 20 Fortress Is, as they were known in RAF service, were serial numbered AN518 to AN537.

The first aircraft to arrive flew the Atlantic Ferry Route on 14 April 1941 with Maj Walsh USAAC, who was to head the American advisory personnel, at the controls. AN521 crossed the Atlantic in the then record time of 8 hr and 26 min, but for security reasons the news was not released. It was intended that the new type equip No. 21 Squadron but as this would mean taking a first-line squadron off operations, on 7 May 1941 No. 90 Squadron was officially reformed at Watton in Norfolk under the command of No. 2 Group, whose headquarters was at Huntingdon. No. 2 Group was unique in RAF Bomber Command in that it specialized in daylight bombing. Four days later the squadron took delivery of two B-17Cs, AN534 and AN529.

While the American contingent came from all parts of the USA, the RAF personnel came from all corners of Fighter and Bomber Commands. The squadron CO, Wg Cd J. MacDougall, or 'Mad Mac' as he was known, had previously commanded No. 110 Squadron (Blenheims) at Wattisham. He was Anglo-Argentinian by birth, often appeared pompous and airmen recall he wanted everything done 'at the double' which was probably a result of his earlier time in the army.

Sgt Tim (Mick) Wood, an Australian, had recently completed seven Wellington operations with No. 115 Squadron from RAF Marham. 'I was on the land in Australia jackerooing when the war threatened. I always wanted to fly and could never afford it, so 1939 came as the chance to get it for free.' Nineteen-year-old Sgt (later Air Cdre) Tom Imrie DFM, was already a veteran of 34 operations as a WOAG (Wireless Operator-Air Gunner) on Whitley bombers with No. 51 Squadron at Dishforth, Yorkshire.

On 7 May, AN521 – now called 'K-King' – was flown to Burtonwood near Liverpool by Maj Walsh with Roy Boast (later Gp Capt CBE, DFC) as navigator, for modifications. Boast, who had previously flown on Whitleys and, more recently, the Halifax, had 'foolishly' volunteered to go to Farnborough for a day's high altitude test 'to get a night in London' only to find himself posted to No. 90 Squadron forthwith. Like many other old hands in No. 90 Squadron he yearned for a return to night 'ops'.

Also on the 7th, AN534 arrived at Watton to become the squadron's first Fortress I. On 11 May Maj Mike Walsh, accompanied by Tom Imrie and others, flew AN529 to Watton from Burtonwood. The only incident occurred when the 2nd pilot forgot to lock the throttles and the Fortress began heading for the barrage balloons over Liverpool.

Next day flying training was started from Watton's satellite airfield at Bodney. It proved a very short sojourn, lasting only two days, for the undulating grass runways proved most unsuitable for Fortress training. On 13 May Mick Wood made his first Fortress flight on conversion to type in AN534 with Capt Connolly USAAC, and followed it on 14 May with an intercom test in AN529, again with Capt Connolly. Wood and the other pilots also received instruction from Maj Walsh and Lt Bradley, son of US General Omar Bradley. Altogether, the Air Corps provided five experienced airmen while other American advisors included Franklyn Joseph, an expert on the Sperry 01 bombsight; a number of Boeing representatives including Bob Crawford and Tex O'Camb – an expert on Wright Cyclones and superchargers and Air Corps reservist who joined the RAF as a flight lieutenant on condition that he could transfer to the USAAC if America entered the war.

On 15 May Fortress training flights continued, this time from Great Massingham, a satellite of RAF West Raynham, while Fortresses went for overhaul at West Raynham. Despite the constant upheaval, training was beginning to pay dividends and Wg Cdr MacDougall chose Mick Wood as his second pilot and Tom Imrie became one of his gunners.

A young medical officer, Flg Off Antony J. Barwood (later Gp Capt Barwood OBE), was posted to No. 90 Squadron in May to deal with the problems of high altitude flying. He had been sent to Farnborough where he had been exposed to a routine 'bends test' in the decompression chamber. The Fortress was expected to fly at heights well in excess of 30,000 ft, an altitude not achieved by operational RAF bombers (except for

Antony Barwood (centre wearing sunglasses) leaves the scene as a No 90 Squadron crew prepares for take-off. (IWM.)

the pressurized experimental Wellington Mk V/VI). Tony Barwood recalls:

'I was still very young but much older than most of the aircrew. Later, my job became selection of aircrew at Polebrook where we operated a mobile pressure chamber, which could take six men to a simulated 35,000 ft, driven by a Coventry Victor single-cylinder engine. Crews were young, keen and declared fit to fly B-17Cs after they had passed the decompression test. I always flew with them on their first training sortie. Wg Cdr Noel Singer, Senior Air Staff Officer to the AOC, Air Marshal Pierce, at 2 Group HQ, came to Polebrook to fly in a B-17. I said he had to be bends-tested first. He didn't pass and was not allowed to fly.

'Sqn Ldr Edgar Bright (another aviation medicine specialist who retired as Air Cdre Bright AFC) came in as Station SMO at Polebrook and did some of the training. Before each sortie we always checked every crew's oxygen supply to make sure that the cylinders were correctly filled and the regulators at each crew position was fully functional. We also briefed the crews on oxygen systems and clothing and attended operation debriefings to see if there had been any problems.'

There were many problems with the oxygen and intercom systems which needed sorting out before the aircraft could be operated at altitude.

'We started with American Oxygen system, A8 individually controlled regulators and BLB re-breather bag masks with hand-held carbon granule microphones. The regulators seized up, the masks froze and the microphones became progressively more useless above 15,000 ft as they depended on air density to excite the carbon granules within the diaphragm of the microphone. We then changed to British Mk VIII oxygen regulators and Type "E" masks with an incorporated electromagnetic microphone, which also required amplified changes in the aircraft. The masks still froze and were modified with an additional valve. I covered the diaphragm on the microphone with a French Letter to prevent it freezing.

'An oxygen economiser, which had been invented by Prof – later Sir – Brian Matthews KBE, was introduced. It stored the oxygen flowing through the regulator while the user was not breathing in, which is only about one-third of the breathing cycle. The original economisers were hand-made by "metal bashers" within the Royal Aircraft Establishment and

No 90 Squadron ground crews pose before the camera at Polebrook. (Antony Barwood.)

at the Physiology Laboratory, as the IAM then was. They effectively reduced the weight of oxygen cylinders which the aircraft had to carry by 50% and produced a more effective oxygen system. The final change was to a Mk 10 regulator controlled centrally by the captain delivering oxygen to each crew position.'

The bitter cold at altitude was made far worse by the aircraft having to fly with all four of the rear fuselage blisters off so that high air blast affected all the rear crew, rendering effective flying clothing of vital importance.

'At first we used electrically heated one-piece suits made by Seibe-Gorman with electrically heated gloves and boots. The suits restricted movement which was so essential for the gunners, were bulky and not very reliable. In August the "Taylor" suit became available, again one-piece but much more easily donned, with an electrically heated lining, glove lining and socks. These were used with fleecy-lined flying boots and soft leather gauntlets. The suit also provided built-in flotation. It was reliable and much easier to move in.'

There were technical problems to contend with, too. Tom Imrie recalls:

'We had constant engine oil problems caused by the pressure differences. The oxygen system and the intercom were bad. Armament was prehistoric with free-mounted .5s in the waist and one .300 in the nose. Ammunition was contained in heavy 50 lb containers and it was a hell of a struggle trying to lift them onto the mountings at 30,000-ft+. The guns jumped around all over the place and hosepiped on the free mountings. Often they didn't fire. They iced up at altitude and we had to wash them in petrol. The windscreens iced up too and eventually had to be double-glazed.'

By 26 May four crews had converted successfully

to the Fortress and now there were five on squadron strength. Training took on a new importance with regular cross country, bombing and altitude flights being made throughout East Anglia and, on occasions, further afield.

'We moved about so much we hardly ever had time to unpack, but morale always remained high. At West Raynham we shared the station with two Blenheim squadrons which at that time had suffered high losses in attacks on the Channel ports.

Imrie for one, was finding the transition from night operations to very high altitude daylight operations 'terrifying'.

'It was nerve wracking flying in broad daylight and on one test flight, over Cornwall on 4 June we even got the B-17 up to 41,000 ft. We could see the earth's curvature and the sky had turned a dark purple colour instead of blue.'

However, there were welcome features which were absent on RAF aircraft.

'On one occasion, at Abingdon, we were visited by HRH King George VI and Queen Elizabeth and the two princesses. The young Princess Elizabeth enquired about the incongruous dark grey carpets throughout and thermos flasks on the bulkhead. These were a left over from the Fortress's early role on long over-water operations when crew comfort was important.'

Tony Barwood adds:

'My first training sortie was to be a routine training flight from West Raynham on the afternoon of 22 June. I was fully briefed and kitted by Sqn Ldr D. A. H. Robson, the Station Medical Officer as West Raynham, and himself a pilot. The flight was delayed as Flt Lt William K. Stewart (later Air Vice-Marshal

CBE, DFC, Commander of the RAF Institute of Aviation Medicine) and a test pilot, Flt Lt Henderson, were on the way from Farnham to gain experience of a Fortress sortie so I was turned off. The Fort, AN522 "J-Johnny", flown by Flg Off Mike Hawley with Lt Jim Bradley as Instructor pilot. At high altitude the aircraft hit some cumulo nimbus at around 30,000 ft over Catterick, Yorkshire and broke up. Flt Lt Stewart was trapped in the tail section which broke away from the fuselage. It fell 12,000 ft but he managed to bail out at about 3,000 ft. He was the only survivor.'

During 27-29 June MacDougall and his available crews flew to Polebrook, their new permanent home near Peterborough. Much of the base was still under construction and crews, used to prewar brick-built barracks at other bases, were taken aback to find themselves billeted in highly uncomfortable wooden huts little better than the leaky nissens with their iron stoves used on other bases. The airfield tended to flood but at least the concrete runway was a vast improvement over grass.

The squadron's new tenancy was marred by the loss of AN528 on 33 July when "B-Baker"

burst into flames during an engine test on the airfield. Gradually, 12 aircraft were gathered at Polebrook but maintenance problems often reduced the available number of Forts to just three. Meanwhile, bombing practice continued at a pace and by 6 July bomb aimers were deemed to have reached an acceptable standard of proficiency. However, as Roy Boast recalls, practice bombing only took place at low altitude, well below that required for operational bombing. 'We did not do any practice bombing above 25,000 ft during training. I logged the dropping of 33 practice bombs from altitudes between 8,000-20,000 ft.'

Meanwhile, calls were mounting for an operation over Germany and at 15.00 hrs on 8 July three Fortress Is, each carrying four 1,000 lb ground burst bombs (armour piercing were not yet available) taxied out at Polebrook for the first RAF Fortress operation, to the docks at Wilhelmshaven. The outcome was awaited with great interest by RAF and Air Corps personnel alike. MacDougall piloted AN526 'G-George' while Flt Sgt Mick Wood flew as second pilot.

Prime Minister Winston Churchill is accompanied by RAF and American officers during an inspection of a No 90 Squadron Fortress I. (IWM.)

The rest of the crew consisted of Flg Off Eddie Skelton, the squadron navigation officer, Flg Off Barnes, the squadron gunnery leader, and Sgts Tom Danby, Danny 'Mophead' Clifford, both gunners, and Tom Imrie, who flew as signaller. Skelton and Barnes had been in MacDougall's crew in Blenheims.

Behind them came AN529 'C-Charlie', piloted by Plt Off Mathieson and AN519 'H-Harry', flown by Sqdn Ldr Andy MacLaren and Plt Off Mike Wayman, both ex-Blenheim pilots, with Roy Boast as navigator/bomb aimer. Despite the small size of the operation, crews never questioned whether this and subsequent raids did any good. Roy Boast recalls, 'I had been in single aircraft operations in Whitleys so the attitude was, "Let's do the job and get out".'

The loose vic formation cleared the coast and halfway over the North Sea began climbing on 27,000 ft. With light armament and little armour plate, the Fortress Is relied almost entirely on height for protection against Bf109s and Bf110s. Roy Boast recalls, 'We started losing oil from the breathers in two engines at 25,000 ft. It streamed back and started freezing on the tailplane and the aircraft began vibrating very badly. MacLaren was forced to abandon the attack and I aimed our bomb load on an airfield on Nordeney.'

Meanwhile, McDougall dropped all four demolition bombs on Wilhelmshaven but two of Mathieson's bombs 'hung-up' and were released over the Frisians on the return journey. Both aircraft climbed to 32,000 ft as two Bf109Es rose to intercept, but the German fighters lost control at such high altitude and failed to close the attack. It was just as well because the RAF gunners reported that all guns and mountings had frozen. Bombing results at Wilhelmshaven could not be determined because the cameras had also failed to function. Tom Imrie was 'pretty relieved' to get back 'Condensation trails were a dead giveaway at our height of 28,000 + but fortunately we did not encounter any fighters. We were on oxygen for almost the entire flight.'

On 23 July Winston Churchill the Prime Minister planned to make a speech in the House of Commons to coincide with a raid by Fortresses of No 90 Squadron on Berlin. Because the Fortresses would be operating at their extreme range, additional fuel tanks were installed in the bomb bay at the expense of two of the bombs, which reduced the high explosive load to just 2,200 lb. Even so, engine and throttle settings would be critical. Meanwhile, a blackout was imposed and crews were confined to camp at Polebrook much to the chagrin of Tom Imrie and the other airmen, who felt 'boot-faced' (fed up) about it.

Despite the grandiose scheme, once again only three Fortresses were available for the raid which began at 09.00 hrs. Wg Cdr MacDougall was at the controls of AN530 'F-Freddie' with MacLaren' in AN523 'D-Dog' and Mathieson in AN529 'C-Charlie'. MacLaren's navigator/bomb aimer, Roy Boast, recalls:

'It was a beautiful summer's day; "gin-clear" without a cloud in the sky. We had been told to stick to the throttle and engine settings as briefed but we tended to exceed them. Even so, we could not keep up with the other two aircraft and by the time we crossed the Dutch coast we were only at 23,000 ft. Mike Wayman and "Mac" didn't want our aircraft to arrive over Berlin on our own and at such a low altitude, so after "Mac" had checked the fuel and found we had used more than we should have, and we were making vapour trails anyway, he decided to abort. MacLaren dived for the deck and we flew home at 100 ft (being ex-Blenheim pilots, "Mac" and Mike were used to this). We were alive but we thought the other two would get their posthumous VCs.'

However, increasingly thick cloud had forced MacDougall and Mathieson to abort. MacDougall instructed Imrie to radio base. Churchill was presumably warned to change his speech in the Commons. All three aircraft returned safely but Sgt Denny passed out through lack of oxygen and experienced frostbite to the side of his face. The New Zealander was saved by Tom Danby who attached a walkaround oxygen bottle. Generous tots of rum helped completely to revive him and the Kiwi gunner suffered no lasting effect apart from a huge hangover!

The following day the same three crews were required as part of Operation 'Sunrise', an all-out attack by Nos. 5 and 2 Group squadrons on the battle cruisers *Gneisenau* and *Prince Eugen* which were berthed in harbour at Brest. MacDougall and MacLaren began the attack, dropping their 1,100-pounders from 27,500 ft. Although bursts were seen on the torpedo station and the outer corner of the dry dock, targets of this nature really required armour piercing bombs if they were to cause any lasting damage.

Five Bf109s rose to intercept the Fortresses, but they soon gave up and veered away to attack the incoming stream of 90 lower flying Hampdens and Wellingtons. The Fortress crews had not been briefed that a large RAF formation would be inbound after they came off the target. One of MacLaren's gunners saw the formation at 10,000 ft, mistook the twin-tailed Hampdens for Bf110s and shouted that 100 Messerschmitts were below them. MacLaren bolted for home. Nine bombers were lost and no hits were made on the ships.

The Brest raid was the last MacDougall flew with No. 90 Squadron. He handed over his crew to Mick Wood and Wg Cdr Peter F. Webster DSO, DFC, took over as squadron commander. On 26 July Sgt Mick Wood flew as first pilot of 'F-Freddie' and with 'C-Charlie', flow by newly promoted Sqn Ldr Mathieson, headed for Hamburg. Thunderstorms prevented an attack on the primary so Wood dropped his bombload on Emden. Mathieson returned to base with his bombload intact, but Wood's aircraft developed engine trouble and he was forced to land at Horsham St. Faith near Norwich.

Two days later the squadron's second flying accident occurred and claimed AN534, which crashed at Wilbarston, Northants, after encountering turbulence during a test flight. Flt Sgt Brook and Lt Hendricks USAAC, and crew were killed. Once again, Tony Barwood escaped certain death. He was briefed to make the flight but was delayed after an airman on a routine chamber test developed the "bends" during a session in the mobile pressure chamber and he had to cope with his descent and possible after effects.

On 2 August AN529 'C-Charlie', flown by Sqn Ldr Mathieson and AN530 'F-Freddie', flown by Plt Off Frank Sturmey, took off to attack Kiel. After 20 min into the flight Sturmey was forced to abort with engine problems and brought his bombs back to Polebrook, only to burst his tailwheel tyre on landing. Mathieson carried on to the target alone and successfully dropped all four 1,100 lb bombs.

At 17.15 hr, his tailwheel tyre repaired, Sturmey took off again and this time headed for Bremen. However, thick cloud made bombing impossible and he headed for the seaplane base at Borkum in the Frisian Islands. Roy Boast dropped his bombs from 32,000 ft. On the way home two Bf109s intercepted the Fortress at about 20,000 ft over the North Sea and one began attacking the nose while the other concentrated on the beam. Roy Boast, who hastily

Boeing Fortress I of No 90 Squadron in flight. (Antony Barwood.)

manned the nose gun, recalls: 'I fired one round and the machine-gun jammed. The fighter came round for another head-on attack and I crouched behind the bombsight. Fortunately, he did not fire (probably out of ammo) but kept on doing head-on attacks while the other carried out beam attacks. We had about 20 holes in the fuselage. I think he was trying to put the beam gunners out of action.' Sturmey lost them after some violent evasive action and made it back to Polebrook without sustaining any casualties.

Apprehension was growing about the B-17C's ability to remain immune from attack on high altitude but operations continued. On 6 August Sturmey in AN523 'D-Dog' and Mathieson in AN529 'C-Charlie' set off for another crack at Brest where the battle cruisers *'Gneisenau'* and *'Scharnhorst'* were in harbour. Aboard 'C-Charlie' the pilots could only wait, hands off the controls, while Roy Boast took over lateral control of the Fortress through the Sperry auto pilot system linked to the bombsight, to place the cross hairs on the target and keep them there while the bombsight calculated the wind velocity. Suddenly, the intercom crackled in his ear. Sturmey said, "Where are you going?" Boast replied, "Nicely on the run", only to be interrupted by a shout, "Look out to starboard!" The bombs were going down into the sea, proving that the bomb sight was way off. Mathieson bombed the target from 32,000 ft and claimed hits.

On 12 August four Fortress Is were ordered to take part in diversionary operations to draw Luftwaffe fighters away from Blenheims of No. 2 Group which would be making an attack on the Knapsack Power Station near Cologne. Because of increasing doubts about the proficiency of bomb aimers and/or the bomb sight, both Roy Boast and Plt Off Tony Mulligan (who did the setting) flew as bomb aimers with Plt Off Sturmey in 'D-Dog'. Sturmey was briefed to bomb De Kooy airfield in Holland but the target was covered by 8/10ths cloud and an airfield at Texel was bombed instead. Mulligan released his bombs from 32,000 ft after Boast had checked his settings.

Boast adds: 'The Sperry was a very good bombsight, in advance of its time. Our problems arose because we tried to use it outside its design capabilities. Sperry's preset calculations had not been fully tested and though they worked well in certain wind conditions they did not in others.'

Meanwhile, Plt Off Wayman in AN532 'J-Johnny' bombed Cologne through cloud from 34,000 ft and Plt Off Taylor in AN536 'M-Mother' also bombed through cloud over Emden from 33,000 ft. Mick Wood in 'C-Charlie' suffered an engine failure over Oxford (to reach altitude before crossing the coast the aircraft had to fly west turning over the Midlands, as a loaded B-17's rate of climb was so slow), and was forced to return to Polebrook after only 27 min.'

Flushed with the success of actually getting four B-17Cs into the air, No. 90 Squadron was assigned two targets on 16 August. Mick Wood and Plt Off Taylor were allocated Düsseldorf

Boeing Fortress I of No 90 Squadron in flight. (Antony Barwood.)

while two others attached the *Scharnhorst* and *Gneisenau* at Brest again. Bad weather forced Wood and Taylor to abandon their operation and they returned to Polebrook with their bomb loads intact.

Frank Sturmey and Plt Off Tom Franks in 'D-Dog', together with Plt Off Wayman in 'J-Johnny', made a successful attack on Brest but on the return Sturmey's Fortress was intercepted by seven enemy fighters at 32,000 ft. For 25 min Sturmey and Franks carried out a series of violent evasive manoeuvres all the way down to 8,000 ft.

Tony Mulligan, the bomb aimer, recalled later on the BBC:

'Three minutes after our bombs had gone Flt Sgt Fred Goldsmith, the fire controller, called out that there were enemy fighters coming up to us from the starboard quarter, 1,000 ft below. They closed in and there was almost no part of the Fortress which was not hit. A petrol tank was punctured, bomb doors were thrown open, flaps ware put out of action, tail tab shot away, tailwheel stuck half-down, brakes not working, only one aileron any good and the rudder almost out of control. The centre of the fuselage had become a tangle of wires and broken cables; square feet of the wings had been shot away.'

Fred Goldsmith had been badly wounded by shrapnel during the first attack but he continued to call out the enemy positions to Sturmey so the pilot could take evasive action and even attempted to cross the open bomb bay to give first aid to the gunners. He was prevented from doing so and an attempt by Mulligan also failed. Unfortunately, the gunners were already beyond help. Sgt H. Needle, the WO/AG, had been hit in the stomach by cannon fire as he tried in vain to fire his frozen dorsal gun.

Sgt S. Ambrose, the beam gunner, had also been killed during the fighter attacks and Sgt M. J. Leahy, the ventral gunner, had been seriously wounded. The Luftwaffe pilots only broke off the attack as the English coast came into view. Sturmey decided Polebrook was out of the question and put the badly damaged bomber down at Roborough airfield near Plymouth but he overshot, hit a tank trap and the aircraft caught fire. A Marine sentry sheltering behind the tank traps was killed in the crash. The survivors evacuated the Fortress but Leahy died later in hospital.

Düsseldorf was again targeted on 19 August but bad weather, freezing guns and tell-tale contrails forced Plt Off Wayman and Sgt Wood's crews to abort. Plt Off Wayman also had trouble with a turbo. Throttling back was critical at higher altitude as the engine exhaust drove the turbo superchargers. If exhaust pressure flow dropped the turbo would 'stall' and could not be restarted. Wayman's signaller alerted No. 2 Group that they had, in RAF parlance, 'dropped a turbo'. Group radioed back, 'Where did it fall and could it be recovered because it was classified!'

Another attempt was made on Düsselforf two days later when three crews were despatched. Sqn Ldr Mathieson led the operation with Mick Wood in AN518 'B-Baker', a new aircraft, and Plt Off Wayman in 'J-Johnny'. Mathieson was defeated by frozen guns in heavy cloud over Flushing and Wayman was forced to jettison his bombs in the North Sea after developing engine trouble. Mick Wood's guns also froze and after producing massive contrials at altitude, he too decided to abandon the operation.

Düsseldorf continued to elude No. 90 Squadron when on 29 August Mick Wood failed to get airborne in AN533 'N-Nan' and AN536 'M-Mother', flown by Flg Off Wayman, took off but returned early after producing heavy contrials at altitude.

On 31 August No. 90 Squadron opted for individual sorties and three Fortress Is were despatched to Hamburg, Bremen and Kiel. Mick Wood successfully attacked Bremen in AN518 'B-Baker' with four 1,100-lb bombs but Mathieson, who bombed Spikerooge, and Wayman, who bombed Bremen, returned with oil and turbo-supercharger problems respectively. Operational problems were now developing at an increasing rate and the shortage of trained ground personnel did not help the cause. The biggest let down though, appeared to be the continuing failure of the bomb sights.

Mr Vose, an American civilian who had been involved in the design of the Sperry bombsight, had taken to heart RAF jibes about the dubious accuracy of his bombsight. The old First World War veteran donned RAF uniform and acted as bomb aimer for Mathieson on the operation to Bremen on 2 September. Sturmey and Wood returned with intercom and engine failures respectively, but although Mathieson made it to Bremen, Mr Vose unfortunately placed his bombs wide of the target. At Polebrook he was last seen leaving the Mess, heading for the USA

Mr Vose, the Sperry bombsight specialist who participated in the operation to Bremen on 2 September, is pictured far left with RAF crewmembers at Polebrook. (Antony Barwood.)

– it was said, to modify his bomb sight!

In the back of crew's minds was the fear that now the Luftwaffe could engage them at altitude, something had to give and they thought it would be sooner rather than later. At the beginning of September No. 90 Squadron was alerted to provide four Fortresses for a raid on the German battleship *Admiral von Scheer,* which was sheltering in Oslo Fiord.

On 5 September four Fortresses with Wood, Sturmey, Romans and Mathieson as pilots, were bombed up at Polebrook before flying to Kinloss in northern Scotland. Sqn Ldr MacLaren, the detachment commander, flew a reserve Fortress, AN535, 'O-Orange' with ground personnel and spares on board. Next day four Fortresses set out to bomb the *Admiral von Scheer.* 'O-Orange' aborted with supercharger problems and the other three crews were prevented from bombing a heavy layer of cloud and smoke which shielded the battleship from view. All three bomb loads were dropped on targets of opportunity from 30,000 ft.

Crews were told to stand by for another raid on 8 September while bombs were brought from Polebrook for another attempt. Alex Mathieson tried to convince his friend Roy Boast that he should fly with him, as he recalls. 'His bomb aimer was older and Alex said, "Come on Roy, my chap will stand down. It's wonderful over the mountains of Norway." I said, "No, I don't think I want to." ' At 09.10 Plt Off Sturmey took off and headed for Norway. He was followed 5 min later by Mick Wood. Flg Off David Romans followed but Sqn Ldr Alex Mathieson in 'N-Nan', was delayed. Again he tried to convince Boast that he was 'missing a great experience' but although Boast was 'half tempted' he did not go. Mathieson and his crew were never seen again. Next day Sturmey and Boast carried out a sea search for Mathieson's crew but it was in vain.

Sturmey, in 'J-Johnny', carried on to the target but encountered heavy cloud and was forced to return early to Kinloss without dropping his bombs. At 11.27 two Bf109s from 13/JG.77 intercepted Romans at 27,000 ft. The Canadian's gunners shot down one fighter before Uffz Alfred Jakobi, whose aircraft was damaged by return fire, shot down the Fortress. It erupted in flames and crashed in the Norwegian mountains. It was the first Fortress to fall in combat in World War Two. Mick Wood in 'O-Orange' was about one mile astern when the attack started. He immediately jettisoned his bombload and climber sharply at maximum throttle to 35,000 ft in an effort to outclimb the fighters. He gave the order for all crew to be prepared to bail out, but in the rarified atmosphere the pilot's vocal chords failed to vibrate sufficiently. One of the gunners misunderstood the instruction and switched to his emergency oxygen supply and then passed out when it was exhausted. A waist gunner who went to help him, disconnected from the aircraft oxygen supply but did not connect to his portable oxygen bottle, and he too passed out.

Wood, who could not contact his gunners on the intercom, asked his wireless operator to investigate. When he was told of the gunners' plight he immediately dived the aircraft but at 29,000 ft the enemy fighters attacked again and riddled the aircraft with machine-gun fire. Flt Sgt Tates was hit in the arm and Sgt Wilkins was mortally wounded. The wireless operator slipped into

Sgt Wood's crew (left to right) Danny Clifford, gunner; Tom Danby, gunner; Tom Imrie, WOp/AG; Harry Sutton, navigator/bomb aimer; ?, gunner; Mick Wood, captain; Dave Hindshaw, co-pilot. (Antony Barwood.)

unconsciousness when his oxygen lead was severed by a piece of shrapnel. The fuel tank was punctured and began streaming heavy smoke. Fortunately for the Fortress crew the enemy pilots probably assumed that the smoke meant that the Fortress was finished and broke off the attack.

The bomb bay doors had remained open all this time and now that the fighters had gone one of the gunners attempted to hand crank them up. He soon passed out when he lost his oxygen supply but Dave Hindshaw, the second pilot, went to his aid and quickly connected him to another supply. Wood nursed the ailing Fortress across the North Sea, one engine was out and he had no aileron control, but the Australian managed to reach Scotland only for another engine to fail. Wood told the crew to take up crash positions and managed to put down without any further casualties.

No. 90 Squadron were to get involved with the *Admiral Scheer* again, as Roy Boast, who shortly after Oslo got his wish to rejoin a Halifax squadron, recalls. 'On 9/10 April 1945 I was bomb aimer in the Deputy Master Bomber aircraft – No. 405 (RCAF) Squadron, PFF – on a raid on Kiel. Part of the job was to mark the target for the Main Force of nearly 600 aircraft including Lancasters of No. 90 Squadron (then in No. 3 Group). The Master and Deputy stayed in the target area throughout the raid directing subsequent waves of aircraft. The *Admiral Scheer* was hit several times and capsized. I like to think that perhaps No. 90 Squadron had some revenge for Oslo.'

Only four more individual sorties were flown after the Oslo debacle. Of these only Sturmey's attack on Emden on 20 September was successful. His bomb aimer, Tony Mulligan, recalls:

'We lost sight of our aerodrome at 2,000 ft and never saw the ground again until we were off the Dutch islands. Foamy white cloud, like the froth on a huge tankard of beer, stretched all over England and for about 30 miles out to sea. The horizon turned – quite suddenly – from purple to green and from green to yellow. It was hazy but I could see Emden 50 miles away.

'I called out to Sturmey "Stand by for bombing, bombsight in detent, George in. OK I've got her." As the cross hairs centred over a shining pinpoint in Emden on which the sun was glinting, the bombs went down. We were still two miles away from Emden when we turned away. Almost a minute later one of the gunners told us through the intercom, "There you are,

bursts in the centre of the target," and back we came through those extraordinary tints of sky.

'During the whole sortie I only had one thrilling moment. I saw a Messerschmitt coming towards us, it seemed an improved type and I looked again. It was a mosquito which had got stuck on the Perspex in the take-off and had frozen stiff. Otherwise, it proved a typical trip in a Fortress, with the temperature at minus 30°C.'

Sturmey flew another sortie to Emden five days later but the operation was aborted when his aircraft began producing the tell-tale contrails at 27,000 ft. To all intents and purposes No. 90 Squadron's brief career on the B-17C Fortress was at an end, although on 26 October four Fortresses each with two bomb-bay tanks flew to the Middle East as No. 90 Squadron detachment, leaving five in England to continue operations with No. 90 Squadron.

The four Fortresses flew to Portreath and then out into the Bay of Biscay, over the Pyrenees and the Mediterranean to Malta. Each aircraft carried one additional man. Sqn Ldr Andy MacLaren flew as CO with 'Junior' Jim Taylor as second pilot, Kendrick Cox as spare pilot and Tom Imrie as Fire Controller. Flt Lt Tex O'Camb, the Engineering Officer and his assistant, Crew Chief Fly Sgt Murray, flew with Plt Off Freddie Stokes and Flg Off Frank Sturmey and Barwood, travelling as the specialist flying doctor, flew with Flt Off James Stevenson with Flt Sgt Ken Brailsford as his No. 2 and Flg Off Struthers RCAF, as navigator.

The next day they flew on to Fayoum, south of Cairo and later went on to Shallufa after the customary 'flying the flag' over Cairo, on 31 October. Operations began on 8 November when Stevenson and Stokes in AN529 'C-Charlie' carried out a daylight raid on Benghazi from 20,000 ft. As the bomb bay doors were open throughout the bombing run the vented hydraulic fluid from the operation of the auto-pilot swirled up into the bomb bay and froze the lower bomb releases. Tony Barwood, who was on board to experience high altitude operations under desert conditions, recalls:

'It was the passenger's job to be ready with two screwdrivers to manually operate the lower releases if the bombs failed to come off. On this occasion manual release under the direction of the bomb aimer over the intercom was necessary. It did not contribute to the accuracy of the bombing!'

Above: No 90 Squadron Fortress I at Shallufa, Egypt, late in 1941. (Antony Barwood.)

Below: AN529 'C-Charlie' which Stevenson and Stokes crashlanded in the desert about 200 miles southeast of Tobruk, on 8 November after a daylight raid on Benghazi.

Above right: Officers and men of No 90 Squadron, Shallufa. Back row (left to right) Flg Off James Stevenson; Frank Sturmey; Cox; Sqn Ldr Andy MacLaren; Tom Franks; Tony Mulligan; 'Digger' Spademan (naval observer); Antony Barwood. Front row (left to right) Flg Off Struthers; Tom Imrie; 'Junior' Taylor; Freddie Stokes; J. J. 'Bunny' Moffatt (Taylor's navigator); Tex O'Camb; Flg Off 'Tiny' Nisbet (Stokes' navigator).

Below right: Wreckage of AN521 'K-King' which crashed in the desert on 8 January 1942. (Antony Barwood.)

'There was some flak, which was a shock as we weren't expecting any. Shortly after turning for home the aircraft progressively ran out of fuel, engines 1, 2 and 3 being feathered in turn. The crew prepared to bail out but a convenient wadi came up and Stevenson effectively crashlanded about 200 miles south east of Tobruk, then under siege by Rommel's army, and about 200 miles from the wire at the Libyan-Egyptian border. Apart from some sand in the eyes, nobody was injured.

'We were not trained in desert survival so we stayed put with the aircraft for about 36 hr. It was extremely cold at night. Struthers, the Canadian navigator, took photographs as we destroyed the Sperry bombsight by machine-gun fire. We then opened 500 rounds of ammunition and, using oil and cordite, set fire to the aircraft and then hurriedly beat it. We walked hard during the next three nights as it was so cold, then laid up best we could during the day.

'We saw several unidentified patrols but we were not sure whether they were theirs or ours and one patrol actually passed between us as we walked in pairs at distance. We had sufficient water for at least 14 days which could have been extended by more severe rationing. We saw what we thought were Ju88s approaching but as they came nearer, we identified them as South African Air Force Marylands and fired off a Very signal cartridge. They signalled us to stay put and later returned to drop four canisters, three of which fell away from their parachutes and we arrived in time to see the water being sucked greedily into the desert. They had called for ground rescue and we were later picked up by an armoured unit of the Long Range Desert Group and dumped back on an advance desert strip.'

From about December 1941 the three remain-

ing B-17Cs in the desert operated with the Royal Navy from Fuka satellite on the North African coast between Mersa and Alexandria against shipping in the Mediterranean. A Naval observer was attached to No. 90 Squadron for ship recognition purposes. One aircraft flown by Freddie Stokes with Flt Lt 'Tiny' Nisbet attacked an Italian cruiser and the fourth bomb in a stick of four very nearly hit the target, but the vessel turned at the last moment. A Bf110 attacked and badly damaged one of the B-17's engines. Stokes made it back safely to Shallufa where 'Chief' Murray and Tony Barwood, bereft of spares, repaired the inlet manifold with elastoplast and Plaster of Paris!

The second Fortress to suffer a mishap was AN521 on 8 January 1942. Frank Sturmey took 'K-King' aloft for a fuel consumption test but, at 20,000 ft and about six miles northwest of Shallufa oil pressure was lost in the No. 3 engine. Tony Barwood was flying this day with a German oxygen regulator salvaged from a Junkers. He had this Draeger device connected to a single 750-litre oxygen cylinder and had slightly modified his mask to be compatible with the regulator function. After some time at 20,000 ft he saw that the oil pressure on No 3 was zero and immediately informed the captain. No 3 could not be feathered as there was no oil left in the engine sump, due to a broken oil pipe, so it ran away and eventually caught fire. He went aft to warn the rest of the crew who he

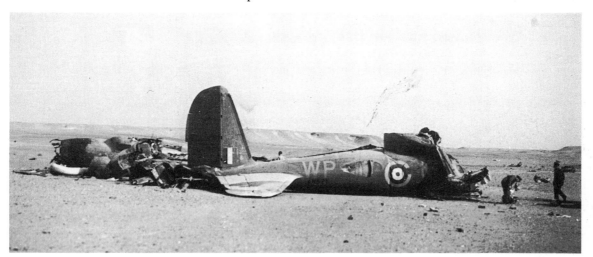

found playing cards, blissfully unaware of their predicament! Barwood had no sooner said 'We have a problem' when he saw two parachutes floating behind them. He had assumed they were going to land but a look up the catwalk to the cockpit revealed that Sturmey, Franks and Mulligan had bailed out.

By now the Fortress was dangerously low. Barwood recalls, 'I picked up a chest parachute and bailed out at 400 ft at 300 kt. My boots flew off and two panels in my 'chute were ripped out but I landed safely. Lt 'Kipper' Baring, a Royal Navy ship recognition expert flying with us on a familiarisation exercise, broke both his ankles on landing. Flt Sgt Mennie bailed out of the astrodome hatch and was killed when he struck the tail and Sgt Tuson died after he bailed out too low.'

On 12 February 1942, No. 90 Squadron was disbanded at Polebrook and the Shallufa detachment became part of No. 220 Squadron serving in that theatre. The two surviving B-17Cs were flown to India complete with ground crews while some of the air crews, including Tom Imrie, embarked on an Imperial Airways Empire flying-boat. 'We boarded Cameronian on the Nile on 10 May and made several two-hour hops totalling 17 hr 15 min flying time across the Middle East and Karachi before landing at Pandeshwar, near Assensol in Bengal on 11 May. We never flew any operations, the two B-17Cs being handed over to the USAAF in December 1942

Left: The crew after bailing out from 'K-King' on 8 January 1942. Back row (left to right) 'Pongo'; Antony Barwood; Tony Mulligan; Tom Franks; Frank Sturmey; Sgt Brown who bailed out last; 'Pongo'; Lt 'Kipper' Baring. (Antony Barwood.)

Below left: Sturmey's crew in 'K-King' (left to right) Flt Sgt Mennie; Brown; Tom Franks; Frank Sturmey; Mulligan; Sgt Tuson; Pawsey. Mennie and Tuson were both killed on 8 January 1942 when 'K-King' was lost. (Antony Barwood.)

Below: Boeing Fortress I parked on the desert airstrip at Shallufa. (Antony Barwood.)

and were used for continuation training.'

So ended an unfortunate period in RAF Bomber Command operations using the Fortress I. It should not be forgotten, however, that many lessons were learned about high altitude flight and these led to improvements in oxygen supply, flying clothing and lubricants while the Fortress design was subsequently improved with the addition of armour plating, self sealing tanks and better armament, all of which were incorporated in the B-17D which followed the 'C' off the production lines.

By this time the Americans themselves had also learned the hard way, in combat in the Pacific, that although it was a dependable, immensely strong fighting machine, the B-17 lacked the necessary turrets and tail guns, firepower and armour plate that were to become a feature of the B-17Fs and Gs used in massed daylight formations of 'Forts' that carried on the offensive from England in the colours of the 8th Air Force during 1942-45. For the time being at least, the RAF Fortress I crews had discovered that high level daylight precision bombing was not the method with which to defeat Nazi Germany.

Left: Boeing Fortress I of No 90 Squadron takes off from Shallufa in December 1941. Note the No 37 and 38 Squadron 'Wimpys' at dispersal. (Antony Barwood.)

Below left: These Boeing B-17Es caused immense interest to members of No 90 Squadron when they passed through the desert airstrip at Shallufa in December 1941. They were particularly interested in the new, additional armament the new type afforded. (Antony Barwood.)

Below: Members of No 90 Squadron make a close inspection of one of the B-17Es which landed at Shallufa in December 1941. (Antony Barwood.)

CHAPTER 2

Pacific War

Shortly before 0800 hrs on Sunday 7 December 1941, 190 carrier-borne aircraft of a Japanese strike force reached the island of Oahu, Hawaii and split into elements. America had broken the Japanese 'Purple Code' and knew that Japan was preparing for war but expected that the first bombs would fall on the Philippines or Malaya.

The trainee radar operators on a rudimentary set north of Pearl Harbor reported the large formation but the Hawaiian base commander assumed the aircraft were some B-17 Flying Fortresses which were expected and the radar operators were told to stand down.

Army personnel watched in awe then dived for

Three B-17Ds of the 11th Bomb Group fly over the main gate at Hickam Field, Hawaii, in May 1941. (Bill Cleveland.)

cover as Zero fighters roared over the island at low level, machine-gunning B-17s, P-40s, Catalinas and other aircraft parked in neat rows at Wheeler Field and Kanaohe. Approximately 15 dive bombers attacked Hickham Field and blew up the Hawaiian Air Depot and Hangar.

Among the units on the ground at Hickham were members of the 11th Bomb Group, which had been formed on 1 February 1940 and comprised the 14th, 26th and 42nd Bomb Squadrons and the 50th Reconnaissance Squadron (later redesignated as the 431st Bomb Squadron). The first bomb hit about 350 ft from the hangar where Ray Storey, the 50th Reconnaissance Squadron armament chief, was working.

'It didn't take long for the fellows on the field to figure out what was happening. Actually, the base was on 50 per cent alert because a Japanese midget submarine had been sunk in the harbour on Saturday. The boys who were really taken by surprise were those still in the barracks. Many of them – particularly the younger recruits – thought the Navy was putting on one of its aerial shows. Some started out of their barracks to take a look and were killed right in the doorways.

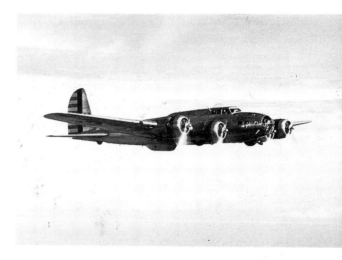

Above: This beautiful air-to-air photograph shows a B-17D of the 50th Reconnaissance Squadron, 11th Bomb Group in flight near Hawaii in the last weeks of peace. (Scevola/Street via Bill Cleveland.)

Below: B-17Ds stand forlornly in the wake of the Japanese attack on Hickam Field, Hawaii, on 7 December 1941. (USAF via Bill Cleveland.)

Japanese Zeros were making strafing runs only 50 ft above ground – so low you could see the pilots' faces.'

Horst Handrow, an aerial gunner in the 50th Squadron, who had emigrated with his family from Germany as a 'kid' in 1932, was in his barracks.

'I was just getting out of bed and looking for my Sunday paper which hadn't come yet. Cursing to myself a little I thought I'd take it out on Lester, my buddy, and so I started to beat him on the head with my pillow. The fight was on when an explosion rocked the barracks. Lester fell and I hit the floor. Now what in the hell could have caused that! Lester was dead. I could see the 3-in hole in his neck. Then another explosion. I ran to the window and with a roar of a dive bomber overhead I saw this plane dive, plane and all, right into H.A.D. The H.A.D. seemed to leave the ground and then settle again in a blast of burning metal and wood. The red circle on the next plane's wing gave out the story. We were at war . . .'

About 12 Japanese Zeros strafed the parking ramp with incendiary fire and set almost all B-18s and B-17s on fire.

'I grabbed a machine gun, rushed out to my airplane No. 81. Ran back for another. When I got back some Jap had shot the tail off. Next time, the plane went up into the air and settled back a burning mass of metal. We lost all our planes the same way . . .'

At Pearl Harbor torpedo bombers and dive bombers attacked the 86 ships of the American Pacific fleet at anchor, inflicting heavy casualties. Eight battleships were reduced to heaps of twisted, blazing metal. The *Arizona* exploded in a pall of smoke and flame and within about 25 min seven other battleships had either been destroyed or reduced to damaged and listing hulks.

Five of the 12 B-17Ds of the 5th Bomb Group, which were lined up in neat rows at Hickham, were destroyed. Four of the 11th Bomb Group's six B-17Ds were also destroyed. Twelve unarmed B-17Ds of the 7th Bomb Group and four B-17Cs and two B-17Es of the 88th Reconnaissance Squadron, all of which were en-route to the island of Mindanao in the Philippines, flew in from Hamilton Field, arriving over

Wrecked B-17Cs and Ds of the 11th Bomb Group lay scattered on the tarmac at Hickam Field after the Japanese attack on 7 December 1941. B-17s of the 50th Reconnaissance Squadron (centre right) appear to have come through the attack unscathed. (USAF via Bill Cleveland.)

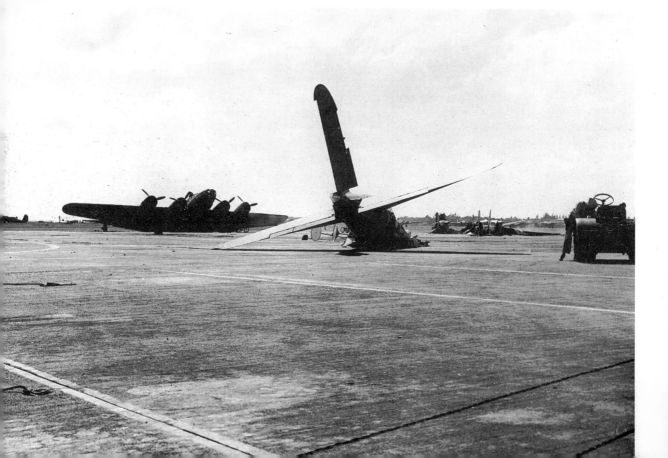

Hawaii during the Japanese attack. Pilots landed wherever they could. Frank Bostrom put down on a golf course while some, like Maj Richard H. Carmichael and Lt Robert Richards, landed on the small fighter strip at Bellows Field. Lt Brandon and his crew, including the navigator, 'Bunky' Snider, jumped from their Fortress before the wheels had finished turning. They sheltered in a drainage ditch as their B-17 was destroyed by strafing Japanese fighters.

Fortunately, not all of the 7th Bomb Group's B-17s were able to fly to Hawaii on this fateful day, as Lt John W. Fields, a co-pilot/navigator in the 22nd Squadron, recalls. 'We were to pick up new B-17Es, the first ones that had come off the production line, from the Sacremento Air Depot. As soon as we got our planes, we were to report to Hamilton Field and were to have left on the night of 6 December. We were picking our planes up one at a time and there were various things wrong with them, minor things, so we didn't all get them on the same day.'

Instead of leaving for Hickam Field on the

night of 6 December Fields flew a 'shake down' flight with Capt Bill Lewis, the squadron operations officer and deputy commander. Lewis was an ex-airline pilot who had been called back into the Air Corps on active duty. The first Fields knew of the attack on Pearl Harbor was when he was awakened on the morning of 7 December at about 11 o'clock by his squadron commander, Maj Kenneth D. Hobson. Fields recalls:

'He said, "Pearl Harbor's been attacked. We've got to get our planes off and take them to Muroc Lake." We all immediately began to get our stuff packed and out to the planes.

'I flew as co-pilot with Maj Hobson, with a crew chief. We didn't have a navigator or any gunners. I was squadron armaments officer and they immediately told us to take our bomb bay tanks out and load the ship with bombs because they were fearful that a Japanese fleet was steaming in to the west coast, that they were going to move in on the west coast and take it. We dropped our bomb bay tanks and loaded up with bombs out and put the bomb bay tanks in. This went on for about seven days. During this time we

Lt Robert Richards B-17C 41-2049 of the 38th Reconnaissance Squadron bellied in at Bellows Field, a fighter strip at Kahuhu, while being attacked during the Japanese strike on the Hawaiian Islands on 7 December 1941. Two crew-members were wounded. (USAF via Bill Cleveland.)

were out chasing imaginary fleets up and down the west coast, flying out of Muroc."

Fields finally left Hamilton Field, California for Hickam Field on 16 December:

'The runways had been cleared off, but many of the buildings had been bombed and there were still burned aircraft visible along the side of the runways. There was still smoke from burning vessels in Pearl Harbor and an oil slick all over the water. It was really a mess. On a visit to Pearl Harbor I wash shocked to see the number of capsized and burned boats in the harbor and in the dry docks. I saw the battleships *Utah*, *California*, *Arizona*, *West Virginia* and the *Oklahoma* as well as several destroyers, either burned or in some other way totally disabled. In some of the ships I learned that many bodies were still unrecovered.

'There was a 20 mm anti-aircraft gun emplacement just outside the officer's barracks at Hickam where I stayed and they told me that it was five days before they got any ammunition for their gun, so they felt pretty low. They were just not equipped for an attack on Pearl Harbor or Hickam Field.

'The Hawaiian Department countermanded our orders, which had been to go to "Plum" which we knew by then to be the island of Mindanao – impounded our equipment, and put us to work flying patrol missions out of Hawaii. Finally, and largely through Maj Hobson's insistence, they decided to let three crews go: Maj Hobson, J. R. Dubose, and Jack Hughes. They departed for Mindanao but they never got there, although they did make it to Java, where they met the 19th Bomb Group, which had evacuated from the Philippines.'

The Japanese had attacked Clark Field, Luzon, in the Philippines 9 hours after the attack on Pearl Harbor. A composite squadron of nine B-17Ds from the 5th and 11th Bomb Groups of the 7th Air Force led by Maj (later Gen) Emmet 'Rosy' O'Donnell, had arrived at Clark Field from Hawaii on 10 September 1941. As the 14th Squadron it had become part of the 19th Bomb Group on 1 November. In October-November, 26 B-17C and D Fortresses, led by Col Eugene L. Eubank, the CO, had also flown in from California via Hawaii, Midway, Wake, Port Moresby and Darwin.

Despite being fully alerted following the attack on Pearl Harbor, 18 Fortresses were destroyed on the ground in the Japanese attack. Only one Fortress at Clark Field, and 19 B-17s of the 14th Bomb Squadron, which had been transferred to Del Monte, a small satellite field on Mindanao, some 600 miles to the south of Clark, escaped.

At the time of the Japanese attacks America had some 13 groups equipped with the B-17 but most were well below group strength of 32 aircraft. Some 150 B-17s, of all models, including 12 YB-17s, were well scattered throughout the Pacific seaboard, Alaska and Newfoundland. Twenty-nine remaining B-17Es on the 7th Bomb Group, which left Salt Lake City, Utah, on 5 December for the Far East, were hurriedly diverted to Muroc to help defend California from possible Japanese attack. Only 19 B-17Bs could be sent to Spokane, Washington to join the five B-17Cs of the 39th Bomb Group while a paltry two B-17Bs were stationed in Alaska. Eight B-17Bs (and 19 B-18s) of the 6th Bomb Group were stationed near the Panama Canal Zone and six B-17Bs (and one B-18) of the 41st Reconnaissance Squadron were based in Newfoundland. During the first week of December eight new B-17Es were delivered to the 6th Bomb Group.

By 9 December the 19th Bomb Group had managed to salvage three or four B-17s from the wreckage strewn around Clark Field and mount a limited reconnaissance mission in search of the Japanese invasion force. Next day five B-17s mounted the first American bomber raid of the war when they attacked a Japanese convoy near Vigan to the north of Clark Field. Hits were claimed and one ship was believed to be sinking when the B-17s left the target area.

Meanwhile, Maj 'Rosie' O'Donnell and a small force of 14th Squadron B-17s had arrived at Clark and they too prepared for a raid on Japanese shipping. O'Donnell made five runs over his targets before the bombs would release while Capt Elmer L. Parsel's crew claimed a hit on a transport. Three other 14th Squadron crews dropped 100 lb bombs on the transports at Vigan or targets of opportunity at Aparri off the coast of Luzon. There had only been time to load one 600 lb bomb aboard G. R. Montgomery's B-17. This was dropped on the Japanese transports and then Montgomery returned to Clark for another bomb load. Armed with 20 100 pounders Montgomery returned to the target area and dropped them before returning alone. He was forced to ditch four miles off Del Monte but all the crew were rescued.

Lt George E. Schaetzel's B-17 was attacked by Japanese Zeros and was badly hit. Schaetzel managed to lose the fighters in cloud and landed the badly damaged Fortress at San Marcelino between Clark and Del Monte with one engine out. The third B-17C piloted by Capt Colin P.

Kelly, only carried a bomb load of three 600 lb bombs. Japanese landing operations were underway at Vigan but Kelly ignored them and carried on to Aparri in search of an enemy aircraft carrier which had been reported. Finding no sign of the carrier Kelly returned to Vigan and proceeded to attack a 'battleship' from 22,000 ft. One of the three bombs hit the aft gun turret and the ship caught fire.

A group of Zeros gave chase and about 50 miles from Clark Field they caught up with the B-17. Successive attacks destroyed parts of the B-17 which then caught fire in the bomb bay area. Kelly and his co-pilot Lt Donald Robins bravely battled to keep the B-17 straight and level while the crew evacuated the stricken aircraft. Six bailed out and landed safely on Clark but the Fortress finally exploded before Kelly and Robins left the aircraft. America badly needed a hero and Kelly made headlines. Officially, he had attacked and 'sunk' the Japanese battleship 'Haruna' but although this story was given out to boost morale at home, Kelly's bravery in attacking a Japanese ship against such overwhelming odds and staying at the controls of his doomed aircraft while his crew escaped, was unquestioned.

Maj David R. Gibbs had assumed command of the 19th Bomb Group from Lt-Col Eugene L. Eubank, who was moved to HQ, 5th Bomber Command in Manilla, on 10 December. Two days later Gibbs took off in a B-18 for Mindanao and was never seen again. He was presumed killed in action. The Japanese successfully established a bridgehead at Legaspi on southern Luzon. Six B-17s from Del Monte tried to intervene on 14 December but only three reached the target area. Lt Jack Adams was attacked by six Zeros and force-landed on the beach on the island of Masbate, just south of Luzon. The crew were fired on as they left the aircraft but they escaped and most eventually returned to Del Monte with the help of Filipino guerilas. Lt Elliott Vandevanter made three runs over Legaspi and returned safely to Del Monte.

The third B-17, piloted by Lt Hewitt T. 'Shorty' Wheless, was attacked by a horde of Japanese Zeros which sprayed the aircraft with gunfire, killing the radio operator and badly wounding three of the crew. Wheless kept the B-17 in the air with a series of violent evasive manoeuvres but the aircraft was badly shot up and losing fuel so he knew Del Monte was out of the question. Wheless headed for a small strip at Cagayan, 20 miles northwest of Del Monte. On the approach Wheless could see that the strip he had to put down on was covered with obstacles. The B-17 smashed its way along the strip until the brakes locked and the bomber stood on its nose before falling back on its tail. Shaken, the wounded crew scrambled out of the bomber safely.

The decision was taken to move the surviving Fortresses of the 19th Bomb Group further south out of range of Japanese aircraft. On 17 December 1941 some of the B-17s began evacuating Del Monte to fly 1,500 miles south to Batchelor Field, Darwin, on the northern tip of Australia. Two days later the Japanese bombed Del Monte but the B-17s remaining escaped damage.

On 22 December a small force of nine B-17s from Batchelor Field bombed Japanese shipping at Davao on Mindanao. They bombed the docks and sank a tanker before landing at Del Monte, which fortunately, was still in American hands, for refuelling. Next day the five serviceable B-17s bombed Japanese transports at Lingayen Gulf on Luzon. With the abandonment of the air in the Philippines on 24 December, Clark Field was evacuated and the ground echelon was re-designated ground forces and trained as infantry. The Group was now dispersed on Bataan, Del Monte, Mindanao; Batchelor Field, Australia and Singsari aerodrome at Malang, Java.

On 30 December 759 officers and men of the 19th Bomb Group were sent by boat from Bataan to Mindanao, where they were made part of the Bisayan-Mindanao Force. On 1 January 1942 Maj Cecil Combs, who was commander of the 93rd Squadron, assumed command of the Air Echelon, which was transferred to Malang, Java. With them went remnants of the 7th Bomb Group, including the 9th Squadron, commanded by Capt Robert 'Pappy' Northcutt, at Madeoin on Java. Personnel who could be evacuated from the Philippines by air and submarine joined the force in Java. On 12 January Maj 'Rosie' O'Donnell, in an old B-18, with auxiliary fuel tanks made from 50-gal drums, flew to Australia with Lt Clyde Box as co-pilot and Lt Edwin S.Green as navigator.

The first mission from Java was led by Maj Combs. Eight B-17s flew to Borneo where they were refuelled, and they went on to bomb Japanese shipping off Luzon. Crews had to fight their way through an equatorial storm, high winds and rain as well a Zeros and anti-aircraft fire. The Fortresses hit a large warship, damaged Japanese submarines and smaller craft. Flying blind through the storm, the crews returned to Borneo, almost out of fuel, and refuelled for another raid.

Through another driving rainstorm and fog, six Fortresses, led by Lt James T. Connally, pushed their way through to a surprise raid on Japanese vessels off the island of Jolo. In dark and rain they landed later at Del Monte, picked up 20 combat pilots who had struggled through from Clark Field. Less than a day later, the 20 men from Clark Field were flying B-17s from Java.

On 24 January a Japanese invasion force landed at Kendari, on the eastern side of Celebes, where in 1940 the Dutch had built the finest airfield in the Dutch East Indies. Ambon, an island to the east of Kendari, was invaded on 30 January and the defenders quickly overrun. On 5 February the Japanese began moving their own aircraft into Ambon to strengthen their air superiority in the area. Nine B-17s from the hard pressed 19th Group were despatched to Kendari.

The formation climbed slowly through heavy clouds. At 15,000 ft they broke out on top and ran straight into a horde of Zero fighters. 'Duke' DuFrane's B-17 was shot down in flames. Another B-17, piloted by Lt W. T. Pritchard, swung around in a wild turn and almost crashed into a Zero. Tracers ripped into the bomber which plunged into the clouds, on fire from nose to tail.

Lt Lindsey made a skidding turn and kicked his B-17 into the cloud top as tracers ripped into his Fortress. Losing speed the half crippled B-17 fell off into a tailspin. At 9,000 ft the bomber was still spinning. The co-pilot and navigator scrambled aft and bailed out through the open bomb bay. The rest of the crew were about to follow when Lindsey miraculously recovered from the spin and pulled the nose up. Circling down carefully, he looked out across the barren Java Sea. There was no sign of the two crews in the water. With his compass and other instruments shot away, Lindsey battled the badly damaged Fortress through a tropical storm and landed back at base.

By the end of January the Japanese had landed at Lae, capital of New Guinea, and at several places on Borneo and Rabaul, where air bases for extending Japanese air operations were constructed. On 3 February Port Moresby was bombed but despite fears of a Japanese invasion,

managed to hold out. The situation on Java, however, was perilous. To save their precious B-17s, pilots and crews took almost any risk. In one raid the Japanese caught one Fortress on the ground and it seemed doomed to destruction but Capt Dean Hovet, a communications expert who had been brought from Bataan to Java in a submarine, dashed to the B-17 and took off with only two engines running. For 20 min he hedge-hopped trees and brush, twisting and banking the bomber like a fighter. He evaded the Japanese fighters until their ammunition was expended.

Practically all the 19th Bomb Group's ground crews were still in the Philippines. The few ground mechanics in Java did heroic work, driving themselves until exhausted. B-17s returning from bombing raids had to make forced landings miles from their base. It wrecked beyond repair, crews tore out badly needed parts and carried them to their base, otherwise salvage crews went out by truck and brought back the priceless parts. 'Wrecker' pilots such at Lt Clare McPherson, risked their lives to fly disabled B-17s out of a clearing where its original pilot had barely been able to land.

When Palembang fell on 16 February, no aerial reinforcements could get through to the beleaguered 19th. At last, each pilot who had a Fortress was on his own. Lt Philip Mathewson was one of a few pilots who made lone attacks on Japanese targets. The Japanese were only 35 miles away and with anti-aircraft fire along the coast, crews had to climb inland to 35,000 ft, if they could get that high, to avoid enemy fire. Lt-Col Eugene L. Eubank realised that resistance was futile. With the Japanese only 20 min away he ordered the few remaining B-17s on Java to Australia on 24 February.

Meanwhile, the 19th Bomb Group received newer and more advanced B-17E models and reinforcements to carry the war to the Japanese. On 11 February 1942 the remnants of the 88th Squadron, some crews out of the 9th and 11th Groups, one pick-up crew and about six crews out of the 22nd Squadron commanded by Maj Richard Carmichael, had left Hawaii for Australia.

Lt John Fields, now assigned as co-pilot on Lt Harry Spieth's crew, recalls.

'The first leg was to tropical Christmas Island. The strips that we landed on were made of crushed coral, rolled and packed by a group of engineers from Hawaii. It was here that I saw my first green coconut

Harry Spieth's crew. Back row (left to right) Golden, asst radio operator and waist gunner; Hall, radio operator; Panosian, asst flight engineer and waist gunner; Ottaviano, tail gunner; Clark, ball turret gunner. Kneeling (left to right) Stashuk, crew chief and top turret gunner; Hulet Hornbeck, navigator; Spieth, pilot; John Wallace Fields, co-pilot. (Ken Fields.)

and learned that in place of a laxative it would do very nicely. We left Christmas Island on the 12th and made an eight-hour flight to Canton Island, a small coral atoll in the Pacific, which only had one tree and one landing strip. This landing strip had numerous goony birds on it. The goony bird can run and flap its wings but cannot become airborne. The personnel on Canton had everything underground.

'We went on to Fiji and spent a weekend waiting for the Free French to chase the Vichy French in New Caledonia up into the hills before we could land at Plindegaig. We got in and refuelled but we had to get off again because we were not particularly safe there.

'We flew on into Townsville, Australia and arrived there around 8 o'clock in the evening. The Australians thought that their great saviours had arrived when we tooled in there in the first B-17Es that they had ever seen. Truthfully, they were afraid that the Japs were going to move in and take Australia and it was a possibility for several months.'

The B-17Es used Garbutt Field at Townsville and were then dispersed to Charter's about 50 miles away, and to Cloncurry, 300 miles from Townsville. There was little to entertain the crews but kangaroo hunting became popular at remote Cloncurry. A number of crews got dengue fever and at times there were parts of 10

crews in the hospital at once. There were other drawbacks as John Fields recalls: 'Mosquitos would nearly carry you off. Additionally, there were kangaroo rats which would come down and check us out at night. They would be likely to jump down on your mosquito netting at any time. You would think a possum had attacked you.'

There were not enough B-17s to quell the all-conquering Japanese tide which had already consumed the entire Netherland East Indies including the Philippines. Gen Douglas MacArthur, the Commander-in-Chief in the Philippines, sought shelter in the Malinta Tunnel on Corregidor. On 22 February MacArthur received a signal from President Roosevelt ordering him to leave his position on Corregidor and proceed to Australia to assume command of all US troops.

The same day a grand total of nine B-17s from the 7th Bomb Group, which was soon to become the famous 435th 'Kangaroo' Squadron of the 19th Bomb Group, left Concurry for Townsville to mount an attack on Rabaul harbour in New Britain. Rabaul was to be the jumping-off point for the Japanese invasion of New Guinea, and further, Australia and New Zealand. Two For-

Above: Boeing B-17E dispersed in a camouflage hangar in Australia. (USAF.)

Below: Gen Douglas McArthur's specially converted B-17E (XC-108) The Bataan *which he used as a flying head-quarters.* (Boeing.)

tresses piloted by Deacon Rawls and Frank Bostrom taxied into each other in the pre-dawn darkness and a third suffered mechanical problems, leaving six airworthy B-17s. These newly minted B-17Es, led by Maj Richard Carmichael, left Townsville on 23 February for an early morning rendezvous over Magnetic Island, and then across the Coral Sea, New Guinea and the Solomon Sea, to Rabaul. A return refuelling stop at Port Moresby, New Guinea, was to cap their hastily planned mission of some 13 hr duration.

Ninety miles out, the formation was broken up by severe weather. Harry Spieth's crew could not get through the weather and had to return after about nine hours. Two of the B-17s, piloted by Capt Bill Lewis, who was leading the second echelon, and Lt Fred Eaton, respectively, were able to locate their target first. Eaton lingered over Rabaul Harbour for half an hour looking for an opening in the clouds through which to commence his bomb run. He was finally able to pick out several large Japanese troop transports and make his bomb run but was unable to get his bombs away and a second run was made. This time the bombs salvoed, though he was unable to observe the result.

While on the bomb run, a Japanese anti-aircraft shell came straight up through the right wing, near the outboard engine, not exploding until it was already through the wing. The concussion knocked the wing down violently but did not otherwise damage the aircraft.

By now, as many as 12 Zeros had reached altitude with the B-17 and they began a series of gunnery passes. At 07.45 hr the first Zero was hit and downed by the tail gunner Sgt J. V. Hall. A second Hinomaru-marked fighter was destroyed by Sgt Russell Crawford at a waist gun position. Sgt Hall hit a third Zero, which was observed to lost altitude but not confirmed to crash. The air battle continued for over 40 min, during which Eaton jockeyed the B-17 from cloud to cloud trying to evade enemy fire. They sustained 20 mm cannon and machine-gun strikes in the vertical stabiliser and the radio operator's compartment.

The long wait over target, dual bomb runs, evasive manoeuvres and battle damage, resulted in Eaton running short of fuel just over the

B-17E 41-2435 in flight over the Owen Stanleys. Note the early remote belly turret. (Ken Fields.)

Lt Eaton's B-17E 41-2446 which crashed in the Agaiambo Swamp, Papua New Guinea on 23 February 1942, photographed in the late 1980s. (Kenneth W. Fields.)

eastern coast of New Guinea. He realized that he would never make Port Moresby on the far coast and across the treacherous Owen Stanley Range, and elected to set the B-17 down in what appeared to be a level and verdant field some eight miles inland. Eaton feathered the two inboard engines and all the crews, except Eaton, co-pilot Henry 'Hotfoot' Harlow and Sgt Clarence Lemieux, the engineer, took up prescribed crash positions in the radio operator's compartment. The B-17 came in neatly and, as it settled in, Eaton was shocked to realize he was

landing in a kunai grass-filled reservoir of water five to six feet deep – the Agaiambo Swamp. The B-17 did a slow 90° turn to the right as it settled in to its resting place where at the time of writing it still remains, more than 40 years later.

The crew – uninjured except for a cut to the head of navigator George Monroe, a pilot pressed into service as a result of a shortage of qualified navigators – removed the Norden bombsight, placed it on the right wing and destroyed it with .45 calibre pistol fire, then tossed it into the swamp. They then set out on a cruel trek out of the swamp, through water five to six feet deep and razor sharp kunai grass. They encountered huge leeches and spiders and heard crocodiles thrashing about. Six weeks later, with the aid of Australian coast watchers they returned to Port Moresby and went back to the war against the Japanese.

The war continued to go badly for the American forces and morale reached a new low. On 27 February 1942 the evacuation of Java began. The next combat mission from Australia was scheduled for the following day but it was called off and crews were sent to Conclurry for dispersal. Six crews immediately went down with dengue fever. On 3 March the Japanese attacked Broome, Australia and wrought havoc.

John Fields recovered from dengue fever and flew his second mission early in March.

'We left on 11 March from Conclurry for Townsville and on the 12th we left for Port Moresby, New Guinea, for a patrol mission on the 13th to Lae where we dropped our bombs. When we flew out of Port Moresby, which was about a 2½ hr flight from Townsville, we lived in grass huts that the natives had built, and flew from a field that was metal stripping placed on swampy ground. We had a grass hut mess hall and had to do our own aircraft servicing. We serviced the aircraft from barrels of gas that were dumped off the ships and floated onto the shore by natives, and we had a little gasoline pump that we used to pump gas out of the barrel into the airplane. We could use the fuel transfer pump from the aircraft itself but we didn't like to do this because we might need that fuel transfer pump in flight and we didn't want to wear it out, because some of these flights involved 2,400 gals of gas.

'We would fly a mission or two or three out of Port Moresby, or occasionally out of Townsville, and then we would come back and go to the bottom of the list, and our turn would come up again later. In truth, it didn't always work out this way, though in principle it was supposed to. We found out early on that if you were married and had a family, well, the tougher the mission the more reasons they had for raising the younger unmarried people up on the list. You would simply move up the list faster if you were single than you did if you were married.

'On 18 March we flew a mission to Rabaul harbour. There were only three aircraft and we flew at an altitude of 31,000 ft. We did not encounter any fighter aircraft. We didn't learn until next day how much damage we had inflicted but we had hit a large Japanese cruiser from 600 ft, blowing the stern off it. Two days later I flew with Morrie Horgan to Lae, a stronghold on the northeastern side of the mountains of New Guinea. We destroyed 17 aircraft on the ground.

'On 24 March I went to the theatre at Charter's Towers. We were called out of the theatre to go back to Townsville and the rumour was that we were going to the Philippines. We got to Townsville on 25 March and sure enough, we had orders to go to the Philippines on an evacuation flight. We left Batchelor Field at Darwin on the 26th for Del Monte on the island of Mindanao. At the time the Mindanao was in Japanese hands with the exception of the airstrip adjacent to the Del Monte pineapple plantation. Our pur-

pose was to bring out Manuel Quezon, president of the Philippines, and Gen Valdez and Romulo, and some of MacArthur's staff.

MacArthur and his family, Adm Rockwell, Gen George and Sutherland and 14 staff members, had been evacuated from Corregidor by four PT boats to Mindanao where, on 12 March, they were flown from Del Monte to Darwin by Frank P. Bostrom. Fields adds:

'MacArthur didn't particularly go for the Air Force. He sent word ahead that he wanted an airliner to meet him at Darwin to take him to Alice Springs. From Alice Springs he got on a train and went on to Melbourne. It took him four days to get there, when we could have had him there in eight hours.

'The flight was long and tiring. We were scheduled to land during the hours of darkness at Del Monte, which we did. They had no lights on the runway, with the exception of smudge pots which they lit for us to line up on, on the grass field in the direction that we were supposed to land. These were old highway markers that looked like a bomb, a black smudge pot that

Wallace Fields' crew. Back row (left to right) Nibley (a former crew member); Skinner, ball turret gunner; Ravenscroft, waist gunner; Rohr, radio operator; Klimpel, crew chief; Stark, waist gunner. Front row (left to right) Mickakaeles, tail gunner; Morton, bombardier; Hulet Hornbeck, navigator; Stanley Casey, co-pilot; John Wallace Fields, pilot. (Ken Fields.)

Lt Gen George C. Kenney presents Wallace Fields with the Distinguished Flying Cross at Townsville for the Philippines rescue mission of 26 March 1942. (Ken Fields.)

burned diesel fuel. The smudge pots were extinguished just as soon as we landed.

'We serviced our 'plane and ate wonderful pineapple and plenty of beef, but they didn't have any bread. They began to assign to us people who were scheduled to go back with us. The people that had priority were Gen MacArthur's staff, of which there were not very many; President Quezon's family and nurse, and his chief of staff, who was Gen Romulo, and one of his advisors, a Gen Valdez. A small staff went with the Philippino generals, and the next priority were the aircraft mechanics. We filled our planes up with people that were placed in these priorities and for whom we had parachutes.

'People were crying, wanting to be smuggled aboard and we told them we couldn't take them; that we didn't have parachutes for them. They would say, "Well, don't worry about a parachute; I don't need one; I won't use one." Anything to get on the plane and get off the island. We flew 32 hr out of the 36 on that flight. We flew back to Darwin, gassed up and

went on to Alice Springs. On the way to Alice Springs Dubose ran out of gas. He had President Quezon's nurse on his ship. Luckily, he was able to land safely out in the middle of the country. We searched for him for five hours before the other 'plane in the flight located him. They landed and pumped some fuel over into his plane.

'We finished up as the Philippine rescue flight in Melbourne. We had engine trouble and we had blown two cylinders, so they told us to stay there and change all four engines before we went back to Townsville. We spent 26 days getting the engines changed out. Del Monte held out for another 10 days after we left.'

By mid-April 1942 the Japanese were well on the way to total domination in the New Guinea–New Britain–Solomons Islands area of the South Pacific. The turning point however, came when the Japanese invasion fleet heading for Port Moresby was defeated in the Battle of the Coral Sea on 7-9 May – the first battle in history in which the two naval forces did not exchange fire but was decided by the two air fleets. John Fields recalls:

'We could tell from the number of surface vessels that were coming into the area and congregating there that there was a big naval battle shaping up. We flew missions out of Townsville on 6, 7, 8 and 11 May. On 6 May we found the Jap fleet. We sighted an aircraft carrier and made a run on it. We were in the same flight as "Hotfoot" Harlow and Harlow bombed a heavy cruiser. Wilbur Beasley was flying with us also. We had heavy anti-aircraft fire but not too many fighter planes, because they were all carrier-based. Their fighters were too busy with the Navy and the low-level stuff.

'On one of our Coral Sea missions there was a bit of confusion. The Navy had told us that everything north of a certain parallel would be friendly. We were north of this line and there was a squadron of B-26s on the mission with us also. We came in at about 18,000 ft and could see some planes flying below and diving at low level. We thought these were the B-26s so we lined up on the battleship that they were bombing and dropped our bombs on it. It turned out to be the Australian flagship *Australia* and the planes we saw diving were Jap bombers. Luckily, we didn't hit the *Australia* and they didn't hit us.'

The next major Pacific battle occurred on 3 June when Japanese forces attacked Midway Island. Nine B-17Es of the 431st Squadron of the 11th Bomb Group led by Lt-Col Walter C. Sweeney had arrived at Midway from Hawaii on 29 May. At 1230 hr on 3 June they took off in search of the Japanese invasion fleet which had been sighted by a PBY an hour earlier only 700 miles from Midway. At 1623 hr the Japanese invasion force was sighted some 570 miles from Midway. Six B-17Es of the 431st with three B-17Es of the 31st Squadron, 5th Bomb Group, attacked in three flights of three B-17s from altitudes of 8,000, 10,000 and 12,000 ft respectively.

Sweeney and his two other B-17s in the first flight picked out a large ship and bombed it. Sweeney wrote, 'At the bomb-release line we encountered very heavy anti-aircraft fire. It contained throughout the attack and, as in the attacks that followed, was plenty heavy. My flight didn't claim any hits on this run. We hit all around the enemy but we didn't see any evidence of damage.'

Capt Clement P. Tokarz led the second element in 'The Spider'. Sgt Horst Handrow, his tail gunner wrote:

'There below was a task force that spread all over the Pacific. We didn't have enough gas to look any farther so we picked out the biggest battlewagon we could find and started to make a run on it with the bomb bay doors open. The anti-aircraft was coming up now and the sky was black with it. Bang we had a hit in No 4 engine. On we went on our run. Bombs away! Two hits were scored with 500-pound bombs. The battleship seemed to blow up in one spot. Black smoke was coming out of her in a cloud. She stopped right there and the cans were coming in to aid the burning ship which couldn't go anywhere under its own power.'

The third element, led by Capt Cecil Faulkner, went after a cruiser and was believed to have hit it at the stern. One pilot in the second flight, Capt Paul Payne in 'Yankee Doodle', had two bombs hang up on the first trip so he made an additional individual run through the ack-ack

Wallace Fields is pictured in front of a B-17 at Townsville astride a motorscooter which he fabricated from scrounged aircraft parts. The motor was provided by a fuel transfer pump and the wheels are P-40 tailwheels taken from wrecked aircraft. Wallace Fields returned to the USA in November 1942. (Ken Fields.)

and scored one direct hit and one near miss on a large transport, setting it afire.

Sgt Handrow continues:

'As we left the area I could see another ship burning and a transport sinking. Not bad for nine Fortresses when it comes to moving targets. The bombing mission was made at 10,000 ft. Home we came again just dog-tired but happy. We had really done some good that day and we all remembered December 7th. We worked all that night loading bombs, gassing the ships and trying to get No. 4 engine in shape because we knew we would really need it the next day.'

That night seven more B-17Es, from the 42nd Squadron, arrived at Midway to reinforce the small Fortresses contingent. At 0415 hr on 4 June 15 B-17Es cleared Midway Island and assembled in the vicinity of Kure Island. Sweeney's crews proceeded out to attack the same main body they had bombed the previous afternoon, but en-route to the target word was received that another enemy task force, complete with carriers, was approaching Midway and was now at a distance of only about 145 miles away. The B-17s turned to intercept and climbed to 20,000 ft. The carriers circled under broken cloud and the Fortress crews had to search for them. Capt Payne spotted the first carrier which was seen to break cloud cover. Payne directed the formation over his radio and the B-17s went into the attack. Colonel Sweeney continues:

'The enemy started firing as soon as we opened our bomb bays. The fire wasn't effective but was a bit disturbing. The fighters came up to attack, manoeuvring beautifully, but they failed to follow through. It appeared that their heart was not in their work and in no case was their attack pressed home.

'We divided our ships into three groups. Each group was instructed to take a carrier and we bombed away. We are fairly certain we hit the first carrier but we didn't claim it. The second group, under the command of Capt Faulkner, hit its carrier amidships. Lt-Col Brooke Allen, commanding the last flight, secured hits on the third carrier. We didn't have time to wait and see them sink but we left knowing they were badly crippled.'

Sergeant Handrow in Capt Tokarz's ship wrote:

'We started our run but couldn't get in. The clouds covered up the target and the anti-aircraft was thick. No 4 engine went out again and we played around at 22,000 ft with the clouds and the anti-aircraft. Then we saw a big 'Kaga' carrier come out from under the clouds. The rising sun on it looked like a big bullseye and we used it as such. Down went the bombs from three ships: the deck got three hits, the water line four; she was sinking and burning at the same time. Zero fighters attacked us on the way home but wouldn't come in close enough so we could get a good shot at them.

'We got a radio report that Midway was being bombed. What a funny feeling we got; what if we couldn't get in there, what the heck were we going to do? We didn't have enough gas to go back to Hawaii. As we drew closer we could see a cloud of black smoke hang over the island. Something was really burning there and our hopes sunk with that sight. In we came and to give us a cheer we saw that the marine ack-ack batteries had kept the runways open even if everything else seemed to be hit.

'We landed and started to gas up and load bombs again for another run on the Japs, who were only 90 miles away now. Up again and this time we picked

out a big cruiser but just as we started on the run, six navy dive bombers drove down on him; at last we were getting help from the navy. So we picked out a nice transport loaded with Japs. Two hits and the Japs were swimming back to Japan. Home we went again, still fooling around with No 4 out, then No 2 started giving us trouble.

'It looked like our little fun picnic was over because we were ordered to go back to Hawaii. Take-off from Midway was made at 0200 hr. It was a tired-out crew that landed at Hickam that night. All the men in the crew got the Silver Star for this battle.'

Other B-17s carried on the attack on 5 June. They scored direct hits on heavy cruisers. One B-17 was lost and another was forced down at sea 15 miles from Midway. All except one of the crew were rescued. By the time the Battle of Midway ended, on 7 June, losses in aircraft and

Left: A remarkable photograph taken by waist gunner McBride of two Japanese 'Rufe' float planes during their attack on Wallace Fields' LB-30, used by the 11th Bomb Group on a mapping mission over Guadalcanal on 10 July 1942. They shot an engine out and Fields had to fly the aircraft 1,000 miles over water back to Moresby on three engines and with the bomb bay tank half in and half protruding out without being able to salvo it. The bombs from the other bomb bay had been dropped on shipping in Guadalcanal. The LB-30 did not have superchargers and was thus unable to fly above 11–12,000 ft. (Ken Fields.)

Below: A captured B-17E in Japanese markings. (USAF.)

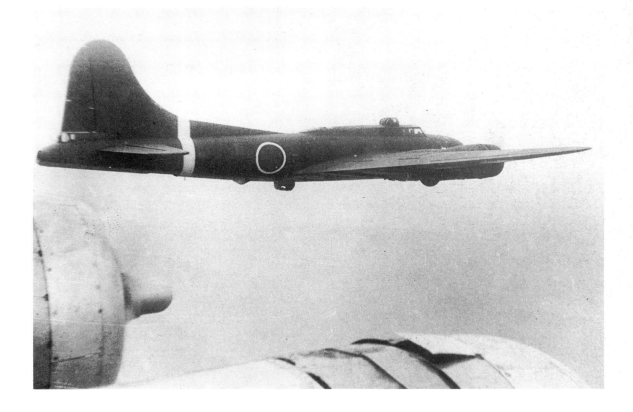

ships were heavy but the Japanese had lost four valuable aircraft carriers.

In the wake of the Battle of Midway a great shake up of commands took place and Maj-Gen George C. Kenney was placed in command of MacArthur's air operations in the Southwest Pacific. One of his first tasks was to clear the skies of Japs over New Guinea and then New Britain and advance on the Admiralties. The 19th Bomb Group (together with the 43rd Bomb Group, which was activated in September 1942) helped considerably in this task. During October several daylight and night raids were made by B-17s on Rabaul, the main Japanese base in the Pacific, on eastern New Britain. Some crews flew as low as 250 ft to hit their targets. When the 19th left Australia for the USA on 1 November 1942 some of the group's B-17Es were transferred to the 43rd Bomb Group.

Raids on Rabaul continued during January and February 1943. During a raid on shipping in the harbour on 5 January, Brig Gen Kenneth Walker, Commanding General of 5th Bomber Command, was killed aboard one of two B-17s shot down. After the Battle of the Bismark Sea in March 1943, in which the Fortresses of the 43rd carried out several decisive actions, Gen Kenney tried to obtain more B-17s but they were needed for Europe. Kenney got Liberators instead and in May the 43rd began converting to the B-24. Some of the surviving B-17Es served as armed transports and troop carriers and were still in action as late as May 1944 during the Pacific island-hopping campaign.

Meanwhile, further east, the Fortresses were also helping to clear the Japanese from Guadalcanal.

CHAPTER 3

Cactus Air Force

On 14 June 1942 the 11th Bomb Group, commanded by Col Laverne G. 'Blondie' Saunders, so-named because of his coal-black hair, had taken off from Hickam Field for a moonlight raid on Wake Island. Horst Handrow wrote: 'We flew from Hawaii to Midway Island, loaded up with bombs and gas and started back for Wake. The moon was bright and everything was perfect for the night raid. Over we roared at 4,000 ft with the bomb bay doors open. We cleaned that place up good. Fires were started all over the island. The anti-aircraft made the night look like the Fourth of July.'

Following the raid the 11th Bomb Group returned to Hawaii and soon speculation was rife that they were to proceed to the South Pacific theatre of operations. Late in July 1942 the 11th Bomb Group left Hawaii and flew via Christmas Island, Canton Island and Fiji to Noumea, capital of New Caledonia, for operations against Guadalcanal, a hilly, tropical, jungle-covered island in the Solomon Islands group where on 4 July the Japanese had started building an airfield on the Lunga Plain.

With Lunga airfield complete the Japanese could send land-based bombers on raids on the New Hebrides for a thrust southward. Guadalcanal is enclosed by the small islands of Tulagi, Gavutu and Tanambogo. As early as April 1942 Tulagi had been deemed the number one American objective in the Solomons. The deep and spacious harbour with air cover from Guadalcanal presented the Japanese with an excellent naval base to threaten the lifeline to Australia. The task of preventing this was given to Vice-Adm Robert L. Ghormley, Commander, South Pacific Area (COMSOPAC). His air commander was Rear-Adm John S. McCain, who controlled all land-based aircraft in the South Pacific area, including those of the USAAF. Maj-Gen Millard F. Harmon was charged with the training and administration of all US Army ground and air force units in the South Pacific.

To cut down on overcrowding Saunders decided to leave the eight 431st Squadron B-17s at Nandi on Viti Levu in the Fiji islands and take the remaining 27 B-17s to Plaines des Gaiacs airfield on New Caledonia. (The island already accommodated 38 fighters of the 67th Fighter Squadron and 10 B-26 Marauders.) On arrival at Tontouta near Noumea, Saunders retained the 42nd Squadron but later despatched the 98th Squadron to Koumac on the north side of the

Left to right: Rear-Adm John S. McCain, who commanded all land-based aircraft in the South Pacific area; Col (later Brig-Gen) Laverne G. 'Blondie' Saunders, CO 11th Bomb Group; and Maj-Gen Millard F. Harmon, Commanding General US Army Forces in the South Pacific area. (Sam Moses via Bill Cleveland.)

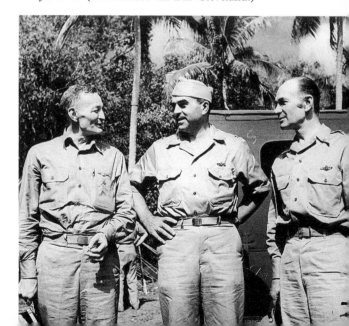

B-17E 41-9122 rests on PSP (Pierced Steel Planking) at the improvised airstrip at Guadalcanal. (USAF.)

island and sent the 26th to Roses Field at Port Vila on Efate in the New Hebrides. The 11th Bomb Group had to be ready for a week of intensive bombing operations against 'Cactus' (the codename for Guadalcanal) as a prelude to the invasion of the island on 7 August by US Marines.

Although an advanced strip on the island of Espiritu Santo about 150 miles north of Efate was ready, Saunders decided to open his attack from Efate, which possessed better servicing facilities. (The 11th Bomb Group's ground echelons did not arrive be sea until early September.) The first 900-mile round trip mission to Tulagi Harbour began on schedule on 30 July. The two 431st Squadron B-17s despatched were badly shot up by Zeros but returned safely with claims of two Zeros shot down. The following day it was the turn of two 98th Squadron B-17s to bomb Lunga airfield. Col Saunders flying with Lt Buie's crew and Lt Waskowitz's crew in *Blue Goose* achieved almost total surprise and only light and inaccurate flak met the Fortresses.

On 1 August the 431st Squadron moved up from Nandi Field to Efate and then to Espiritu Santo but crews were left kicking their heels at Button Field, Bomber 1 as they awaited orders. On 3 August Horst Handrow, tail gunner in Capt Sullivan's crews, and his fellow crew members, were told to get ready for their first crack at the 'Canal' with a raid on the airfield. Handrow wrote:

'After 4½hr of flight we saw our target. We were at

12,000 ft. We made our run and eight 500-pounders hit across the runway and two fires were burning very nicely when we left. The anti-aircraft wasn't very heavy because most of the ack-ack batteries had already been put out for keeps.

'Two Zeros hung over our formation but wouldn't come in to attack. They were sending our speed and altitude to the ack-ack guns below. We soon left them behind and headed back to our base at Santo. More planes were taking off for the "Canal" when we landed. We loaded up again with 20 100-pounders but no orders came through that day so we waited for the next day. Rain set in that night and us with planes out. What rotten luck. Death was in the air because the only landing lights we had were two trucks parked at the end of the runway. We stood there with cold sweat running down our faces. Who wasn't going to make it? We saw a plane light going toward the jungle "That wasn't the runway," I almost shouted. Too late, with explosion of gas tanks and falling of trees the B-17 went down and started to burn. Five men lost their lives; four got out okay. That was the beginning of our bad luck. We watched out there in the rain until they all landed. We had our fingers crossed.

'We took off again for the "Canal" on 4 August and this time did our bombing at 3,000 ft, hitting trucks and supplies. We were so low that you could see the stuff fly up in the air. Seven Zeros were around that day and they would come in every once in a while and make a pass at you!.

The Japanese Zeros came in too close and four were shot down. One of the crashing fighters plunged into a 26th Squadron Fortress flown by Lt R. E. McDonald and brought it down. All the crew were lost.

Raids continued on 5 and 6 August and then

the US Marines landed on 7 August as scheduled. They met no opposition while the Fortresses conducted unproductive searches at sea for the Japanese fleet to the north of the Solomons. Lt Robert B. Loder of the 98th Squadron, who was thought to have crashed in mountains on New Caledonia, and Maj Marion N. Pharr, the 431st Squadron CO, both failed to return. Maj James V. Edmundson of the 26th Squadron assumed command and took the crew previously assigned to Capt Sullivan, who was sent to Fiji to pick up another crew.

On 8 August the US Marines reached the Japanese airfield and discovered that the enemy had fled. The airstrip was named Henderson Field after the commander of the US Marines' dive bombers at Midway. Meanwhile, the Forts continued their search at sea. They saw part of the Japanese Navy turning for home with two ships in the task force burning as a result of action in the Solomons area.

On 11 August the Fortresses of the 11th Bomb Group went on a hair-raising low-level photo mission over a Japanese-held island. Horst Handrow wrote:

'We came in at 40 ft with guns going to keep the ground men away from the ack-ack batteries. It was real fun. We laid it on the two freighters and one can which was unloading the stuff. We were so close I could see the glass coming down. The second time through there they opened up on us. We put it right back, having all the pictures we wanted. We tailed it for home. Happy day that was.

'Next day we were called out of bed at 3.00 am and we knew right away that something was up. Our crew jumped into the plane and in 15 min we were on our way to Guadalcanal which was being shelled by three Jap cruisers. "Get a cruiser" – those were our orders and we were out there to fill them. All alone too. As we came in sight of the island we saw one cruiser which looked like a light one so we passed it up and started looking for the heavy cruiser which was also in there. We saw it five minutes later while we were flying at 9,000 ft. We started to circle it. It slowly circled us so we couldn't made a good run on it. Anti-aircraft was coming up; then with the sun at our backs, down we came with bomb bay doors open. Down until we were at 5,000 ft. Mighty low to be fooling with anything but big. Out went the bombs. Two hits and one close miss. Not bad for four bombs.

'She was burning now and all she could do was go around in a circle. Down we came until we could use our guns on her and that we did. The cruiser threw everything at us but the boat. We watched for an hour and she was still burning and getting worse. She sank

B-17F-10-BO 41-24457 The Aztec's Curse of the 26th Bomb Squadron over the Rendova Islands in the Solomons. (US Navy via Bill Cleveland.)

late that afternoon, so the Marines said. It was a job well done even if we got grounded for three days for getting down that close. I still remember December 7th.'

On 20 August Henderson Field was repopulated with Wildcats and Dauntlesses. The Fortresses' daily action in support of the hard-pressed Marines took its toll. By now the 11th Bomb Group had lost 11 B-17s, although only one was a result of combat. Some crews were sent to Fiji for a well-earned rest.

On 23 August the US Navy received warning that the Japanese were moving on the Solomons from the north. US carrier task forces were despatched to meet them and at 1215 hrs on 24 August Col 'Blondie' Saunders was advised of a contact with the enemy task force 720 miles from Santo. Adm McCain, aware that a B-17 strike would involve hazardous night landings, left the attack decision to Saunders. He accepted the risk and two flights of Fortresses were despatched separately.

Three B-17s of the 42nd Squadron, led by Maj Ernest R. Manierre, and four under Maj Sewart set out over the Pacific to the northwest of Santo. Manierre's flight made contact with the task force in the late afternoon, observing a crippled carrier being towed by a cruiser or large destroyer. On the first run the bombs overshot and the B-17s went around for another try. This time four direct hits were observed on the carrier.

Sixty miles eastward Maj Sewart's four B-17s surprised a second Japanese armada at twilight. Two or more hits were claimed on one large battlewagon. Large numbers of Zeros pressed home attacks and five were claimed shot down by the American gunners with two probables. Two of the B-17s were damaged and all were dangerously low on fuel but the flight returned to Efate safely. Manierre's B-17s were not so fortunate. They returned to Santo after dark and during the landing the Fortress piloted by Lt Robert E. Guenther crashed after his No. 4 engine failed. The pilot and four of the crew were killed.

On 2 September Horst Handrow and the rest of his crew returned from leave on Fiji. The tail gunner was re-assigned to Capt White's crew. The following day Capt Buie of the 98th Squadron, who was on a special photo mission in the Buka Passage, put *Hellzapoppin* down on Henderson Field after encountering heavy but inaccurate flak at Kieta. *Hellzapoppin* was ditched off

Plaines de Galacs, New Caledonia, nine days' later on 12 September, but Maj Rasmussen and his crew survived the water landing after the fuel supply ran out.

Missions continued daily from Santo while the airstrip at Henderson Field was made longer for upcoming B-17 missions. On 12 September Japanese bombers attacked the Field and the following day enemy ground forces launched heavy attacks. The Marines fought back and the Japanese were forced to retreat with heavy losses.

This day the 11th Bomb Group lost two B-17s from the 431st Squadron. Lt Van Haur's *The Spider* and Lt Woodbury's Fortress were forced to ditch in the sea. The latter B-17 was hit by anti-aircraft fire over New Guinea. One engine was knocked out and the left wing was badly damaged. Just after midnight the B-17 hit the water. T/Sgt Ray Storey suffered a badly broken leg in the crash. The crew was picked up the following day and Van Haur's crew were rescued on 19 September, but not before two men had died of exposure.

By 23 September 1942 the 'Cactus Air Force' took shape with the arrival at Espiritu Santo of B-17Es of the 5th Bomb Group's 72nd Squadron, commanded by Maj Don Ridings. At around this time the squadron on Santo also began receiving replacement crews and new B17F models with extra guns. These surprised the Japanese fighter pilots, who had been used to making head-on passes against the B-17Es and 'Ds'. (In mid-October two additional squadrons from the 5th Bomb Group, commanded by Col Brooke E. Allen also arrived. All three squadrons were placed under the command of 'Blondie' Saunders). Also on 23 September Lt Durbin and the crew of *Skipper* in the 98th Squadron, bombed the Rekata Bay seaplane base with incendiaries. They were attacked by five 'Dave' reconnaissance aircraft. One was shot down and the others damaged.

The following day the 98th Squadron was out again tusselling with Japanese reconnaissance aircraft, *Gallopin Gus* flown by Capt Walter Y. Lucas and *Goonie*, piloted by Lt Durbin, dropped their 500-lb demolition bombs on cargo vessels in Tonoleui Harbour on Fauro Island off the southeastern end of Bougainville. The *Blue Goose*, flown by Lt Frank 'Fritz' Waskowitz, a former University of Washington football star, who had been badly burned in the attack on Pearl Harbor, successfully dropped his bombs

Maj Rasmussen, the 98th's CO, stands beside B-17E The Skipper *which was flown by Lt Durbin on the 23 September 1942 mission to the seaplane base at Rekata Bay when it tussled with five Japanese 'Daves'. (USAF via Bill Cleveland.)*

also. A direct hit was scored on one cargo vessel and near misses damaged another.

Ten 'Rufes' and 10 'Daves' attacked while the Fortresses made their bombing runs. One 'Rufe' was shot down in flames, a 'Dave' shot down streaming smoke and several other enemy aircraft were hit. Lucas returned to Santo while the damaged *Goonie* and *Blue Goose* were put down on Henderson Field. None of the crews was

injured. The 42nd Squadron did not fare as well. Charles E. Norton's crew in *Bessie the Jap Basher* failed to return from a search mission.

On 28 September the Fortresses of the 11th Bomb Group headed for Shortland Island Harbour at the southern end of Bougainville Island. Horst Handrow wrote:

'I had a funny feeling already when we got into the plane, "Today we are coming back with holes and lots

Above left: B-17E Galloping Gus *of the 98th Bomb Squadron pictured at Santo in 1942. On 24 September Capt Walter Y. Lucas flew this aircraft on a bombing mission to Tonolei Harbour and returned safely to Santo. (Bill Cleveland.)*

Left: B-17E Goonie *of the 98th Bomb Squadron which was damaged by Japanese fighters on the 24 September 1942 mission to Tonolei Harbour, but Lt Durbin, the pilot, managed to land safely at Henderson Field, Guadalcanal.* Goonie *was badly damaged again on 28 September returning from a raid on Bougainville when 15 Nagoya land-type Zeros attacked. S/Sgt Eber J. Nealy, the navigator, was wounded in the head and right thigh by 20 mm cannon and 7.7 machine-gun shells. (USAF via Bill Cleveland.)*

Above: B-17E Madame-X *of the 98th Bomb Squadron being repaired in the Solomons, 1942.* Madame-X, *flown by Lt Cope, was one of four 98th Squadron aircraft which participated in the mission to Bougainville on 29 September 1942 when* The Blue Goose *failed to return. (USAF via Bill Cleveland.)*

of them,'' I said to the mechanics. We got up to Short-land Harbour and it was closed in by a big storm cloud. There were three planes in our formation. Then out of the clouds the Zeros started coming. I counted 30 in all. Boy, we really were in for it and I didn't mean maybe. The sky was full of the little son of a guns and they started hitting us. One went past the tail and I gave him both barrels and down he went in flames. Good shooting Handrow.

'Then they started to work my position over. A 20 mm shell hit my section and pieces of steel went all over my position, through the seat I was sitting on, over my shoulder, just buzzing past my leg. It burned it more than anything else. "That was close," I thought. Once more the little son of a guns sent bullets through my section and this time a 7.7 went right through the oxygen line two inches from my heel. Little later again the stuff came through the tail. This time they went through the door about three fet from me.

'Another Zero went out past the tail and I gave him the works. That made two that day. Jim Orr and Pepe got one each too. Four in one day; not bad shooting. After a 20 min air battle they went home but not all 30 of them. Thirteen were shot down that day. We'll teach them to fool with our Flying Fortresses.

'We got a breather when we spotted a Jap cruiser; a nice heavy one. We started our run on it but couldn't get our bombs away, so we pulled out of formation to let another ship take our place.'

The *Blue Goose*, flown by Handrow's old co-pilot Capt Frank T. 'Fritz' Waskowitz, pulled in to take their place. On the first run Capt Waslowitz's bombs failed to release. As the B-17 came in on the second run it was attacked by Japanese Zeros. Fire in the cockpit of one Zero forced the pilot to rear back, pulling the stick with him, and turning his fighter straight up and into the underbelly of the B-17. Still loaded with bombs, it exploded in mid-air. Handrow observed, 'Nobody got out. It left me with a cold sweat and I have feared anti-aircraft fire since.'

Fifteen Nagoya land-type Zeros carrying belly tanks attacked the returning Fortresses. In the ensuing battle the B-17s shot down eight Zeros, probably destroying two more and damaging others. *Goonie*, flown by Lt Durbin, was hit, and S/Sgt Eber J. Nealy, the navigator, was wounded in the head and right thigh when 20 mm cannon and 7.7 machine-gun fire exploded in the navigator's compartment. Flak was heavy and accurate and only two B-17s escaped damage. Handrow concludes:

We flew back to the "Canal" and landed there on a flat tyre that bullets had hit. Capt White, our pilot, was really on the ball. We looked for more hits and found them all over the airplane: 450 in all. The rudder was all full, 17 holes in my little tail section,

B-17Es of the 431st Bomb Squadron, 11th Bomb Group between Guadalcanal and Santo. (via Bill Cleveland.) Note the open ball turret door.

one big one in the nose, and a couple of hits in No 3 engine. We had a close call and we were really lucky that nobody got hit. The raid was a flop but he who runs away today comes to fight again another day.'

Further Japanese and US Marine reinforcements arrived on Guadalcanal in September and October. On 11/12 October the Battle of Cape Esperance was fought at sea off Guadalcanal. On the 12th Col Saunders, flying with Maj Al Sewart, CO of the 26th Squadron, led a six-ship formation which took off from Henderson Field for a bombing raid on an airfield just north of the Buka Passage. Maj James Edmundson led the second element with two wingmen from the 431st. Edmundson wrote:

'We dropped 1,000-pounders on the runway. We could see fighters taking off as we were on our bombing run and Zeros were soon at our altitude and continued to work us over as we proceeded south to our second target, a collection of ships at anchor in Buin Harbour at the south end of Bougainville Island. Flak was extremely heavy and the Zeros stayed with us until we withdrew out of their range. Six Zeros were confirmed as destroyed. All six B-17s received battle damage, several engines were knocked out throughout the formation, several crewmembers were wounded and Ed Lanigan, Al Sewart's navigator, was killed.

'We arrived back over Henderson Field just as a bombardment was underway by about 15 Japanese 'Bettys' with fighter escort and the Marine fighters were up after them. We were now low on fuel and out of ammunition and by the time the field was clear for us to come in and land we were mighty glad to get on the ground.

'That night – October 12/13 – will forever be known as "The Night of the Big Shelling" to all of us who were there. The Japanese had succeeded in getting a task force down "The Slot", which included several cruisers and a couple of battleships. They proceeded to lob heavy artillery into Henderson Field throughout the night. Several aircraft were hit and fires were started in the ammunition and fuel dumps. The next morning there was only 2,000 ft of usable runway available to take off from, for those B-17s that were still flyable, to return to Espiritu Santo.'

Lieutenant Hyland, a 42nd Squadron pilot in *Yokohama Express* failed to return from another mission on the 12th. Meanwhile, the 431st Squadron had taken off from Button Field for the 'Canal' and changed bomb loads to 500-pounders and then 1,000-pounders for a heavy raid on the 13th. Horst Handrow wrote:

'We took off from the "Canal" and headed up the string of Solomon Islands, the target the airfield at

B-17E 42-261 The Daylight Ltd *crashed at the new end of the runway at Santo.* (via Bill Cleveland.)

Buka. The weather was bad and we got on the bomb run just as a storm was closing in on the place. Perfect bombing day. We made our run, four 1,000-pounders went right down the middle of the runway. The other formation dropped 60 100-pounders through the parked airplanes and a nice couple of fires were started and 14 planes wouldn't be flying any more.

'Anti-aircraft was coming up but it wasn't any too good. Three Zeros started in attacking us and only have two ships in our formation. They went after us. We did okay on them. I got one as he went past the tail. He went down like a spin wheel on the Fourth of July. The other ship's gunner got one. He just blew up above us and the pieces went right past the tail. It looked pretty good. Again we had some more holes. I got two more through my section. Back to Guadalcanal we went and were grounded because of no oxygen system.

'On 14 October we took off for Santo; "peaceful Santo" we called it. That night was hell on Guadalcanal because the Japs came in with half their fleet and shelled the place all night. Five Fortresses were caught on the ground. Our plane was in the five and so was our old ship. The gas works went up too and there

was only 85 gal of gas left for 85 planes. Not enough to send up a couple of dive bombers.

'On 15 October we took off from Santo to bomb the Jap fleet shelling the "Canal". Our orders were to get the two transports unloading men and guns. We'd rather have gone after some bigger bait but orders are orders. Twelve planes were in the formation. We went in, in waves of threes and we were in the second wave. I have never seen ack-ack so thick. No 1 transport was already blown high and she was burning. Down went our bombs and four 500-pounders hit, blew it all to heck. What a sight. The water was full of swimming Japs. The third wave hit a battleship and left it burning.

'Seven Zeros attacked out of the sun. One went past but couldn't get in a very good shot. Then one started in on my tail. Was this guy nuts? They never do it because it's sure death, yet here he was coming and getting closer. I started in firing with all I had. He kept on coming. He was going to ram us? I kept on firing. Two hundred rounds had already gone his way. Boy, I was sweating blood. He was only 25 yds away when he went down. Ten more yards and I would have got out of the tail. He was out to get us and almost got us. What a life I lead. I really stuck my neck out when

War-weary Douglas-built B-17E Oklahoma Gal *which was converted into a transport after many months of combat in the South Pacific. This aircraft flew 203 bombing missions, sinking eight Japanese ships. Its gunners were credited with shooting down six enemy aircraft. (Douglas.)*

I got on combat. Back to Santo we went. I had more holes in the tail. One of these days they'll have more luck?'

Zeros were not the only Japanese air menace in the Solomons. On 16 October Lt Thompson and crew in the 72nd Squadron tussled with a Japanese four-engined flying boat while on a routine search mission east of Santa Isabel Island, about 60 miles from Rekata Bay. The battle lasted 20 min, at the end of which the flying boat was shot down after making a futile attempt at trying to escape into some scattered cloud. Sgt White, the engineer and ball turret operator, was hit in the eye by shattered glass when a 20 mm shell hit the turret.

Next day a flight of six B-17s took off from

Santo around 1430 hr for Guadalcanal to bomb Japanese supplies and installations in the vicinity of the Kokumbona River. The B-17s arrived at the target shortly before dark and bombed in two elements on the target area. Some 12 tons of demolition bombs were laid squarely on some ammunition supplies and crews felt the concussion at their height of 10,000 ft. Crews returned to Santo at around 2230 hr in the middle of a heavy rain storm but all the Fortresses put down safely, although most had to make as many as three attempts.

On 18 October the 42nd Squadron moved up from Plaines des Galacs to Turtle Bay on the southeast corner of Santo. Here the B-17s would be nearer their Japanese targets and by using

B-17E Typhoon McGoon II 41-9211 (the first was lost on 13 September 1942) of the 98th Bomb Squadron which Capt Joham's crew were flying when they spotted a large Japanese task force northwest of Guadalcanal on 14 November 1942. Note the ASV (Air-to-Surface Vessel) radar antenna protruding from the upper nose (two more of which were fitted under the wings) and six Japanese kills – one for each bombing mission. (USAF via Bill Cleveland.)

Henderson Field as a staging post they could save on precious fuel that was sent in by drums and poured into the tanks of the aircraft from buckets and cans. Fuel was consistently short during the entire campaign. *So Solly Please*, flown by Lt Williams, was packed 'from bombsight to tail' with an assortment of provisions, mess components and cooks, medical personnel and luggage so that a mess could be established on Santo.

Crews were soon to discover that Turtle Bay was no paradise on earth. Rain fell daily and dengue fever and malaria were prevalent. Santo was also in ever present danger from seaborne and aerial attack. The 98th Squadron's base was bombed four times, and twice during October it

was shelled by off-shore submarines. The only damage occurred when a 800 lb bomb felled a tree which crushed the wing of a B-17 attached to the 98th Squadron from the 424th Squadron.

Santo soon became overcrowded, with the 98th Squadron, 5th Bomb Group and some New Zealand air and ground units all being stationed on the island. Taking off in formation from the one way take-off and landing strips at the crowded bases was difficult, but operations continued unabated against Japanese positions on Guadalcanal and the neighbouring islands of Tulagi, Gavutu and Tanambogo.

November proved to be the decisive month in the six-month Guadalcanal campaign. The

Japanese made several large-scale attempts during the month to land forces on the island and drive the US marines into the sea. The US Naval forces were hard pressed and the majority of the enemy fleet units were stopped by small numbers of ships and aircraft. By this time the squadrons of the 11th Bomb Group were operating regularly from Henderson Field. Japanese air raids were daily occurrences and Imperial Naval forces shelled the Field frequently. 'Pistol Pete' – which was actually several Japanese gun positions in the hills surrounding the Field – also made life unpleasant for air and ground crews.

The Fortresses also made life equally unpleasant for the Japanese army and naval forces. On 13 November the 11th Bomb Group despatched 17 B-17s to bomb the damaged Japanese battleship *Hiei*, which was limping along northwest of Savo. One direct hit and five prob-

B-17s of the 11th Bomb Group bomb Japanese shipping in Tonolei Harbour from 12,800 ft on 18 November 1942. (H. Miller via Bill Cleveland.)

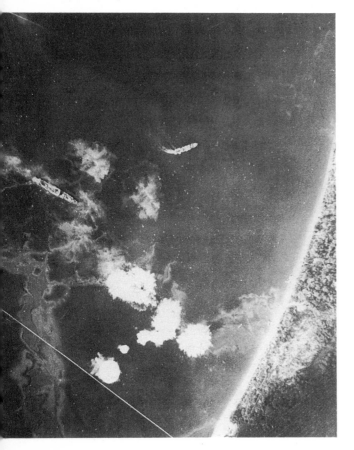

ables were scored and the ship finally sank several days later. During a routine search the following day, Capt Joham and his crew in *Typhoon McGoon* in the 98th Squadron, spotted a large task force including two aircraft carriers northwest of Guadalcanal. Joham's radio operator notified Naval Command while *Typhoon McGoon* maintained a vigil high above the Japanese fleet.

The Japanese ships opened up and six Mitsubishi Zeros and one 'Rufe', soon joined by others, attacked the lone B-17 through the flak. Six enemy fighters were destroyed by the Fortress gunners before the aircraft limped back to Santo at 1600 hr, riddled with 20 mm cannon and 7.7 machine-gun fire. Projectiles had ripped the tail of the B-17 almost to shreds but the tail gunner survived unharmed.

Thanks to Capt Joham and his crew, the 11th Bomb Group, naval surface vessels and aircraft, and the Marine Air Group at Guadalcanal, were enabled to find and attack the task force near Savo Island. The Fortresses, together with SBD Dauntlesses and TBM Avengers from Henderson Field, sank or severely damaged eight of the vessels. Next morning searches revealed many Japanese ships burning and sinking over a wide expanse of sea around Savo Island. Capt Lucas in *Buzz King* led four other 98th Squadron B-17s in attacks which scored direct hits and effective near misses on troop transports. An American force of two battleships finished off the task force, sinking one battleship, two cruisers and several smaller ships.

On 18 November Col "Blondie" Saunders led a 19-plane strike force in a 26th Squadron B-17 piloted by Maj Al Sewart and Lt Jack Lee against Japanese shipping at Tonolei Harbour. Capt Darby's B-17 from the 72nd Squadron became stuck in a shell hole on Henderson Field but took off later. Darby's crew were to account for one Zero destroyed. The other Fortresses, each loaded with cargoes of 1,000 lb armour piercing bombs, went after their targets with a vengeance.

Capt Lucas in *Buzz King*, Lt Durbin in *Omar Khayam* and Lt Morgan in *Gallopin Gus* – all 98th Squadron pilots – scored direct hits on a cargo vessel and several misses. A 20 mm shell shattered the glass and damaged the interior of the ball turret in Morgan's B-17 but no injuries were reported. Maj Whitaker and Lt Classen – both 72nd Squadron pilots – were attacked by Zeros, probably based at nearby Buin airfield. Classen's crew claimed two Zeros destroyed.

After the bombing run was made, about 20 Zeros made head-on attacks on the formation. One fired a burst which raked Saunders' command ship, nicking Maj Sewart's arm and hitting Lt Lee in the ankle. Saunders went back to get a first aid kit and returned to the flightdeck just as a Zero fired a second burst into the control cabin, sending a 7.7 through Sewart's heart, killing him instantly. Jack Lee was hit in the stomach.

The pilot fell back and Saunders lifted Lee from the co-pilot's seat so he could take over the controls of the badly damaged B-17, which by now was flying with one engine out and another damaged. The left wing was blazing from escaping fuel from the wing tank. The only instrument still working was the clock and Saunders told another B-17 to take over the lead. Col Saunders wrote:

'From the co-pilot's seat, I couldn't trim the tabs and handle the plane with those two dead engines on the left, so I got the pilot's body out and moved into the pilot's seat. I decided to make for some overcast and so we dived down. The left wing was red hot. The bank and turn indicator showed we were in a spin.

'We came out of the overcast at about 500 ft and I saw I'd have to put her down. This was about 20 min after the pilot and co-pilot had been hit. Other planes stayed around to protect us but the Zeros didn't follow us that far. I told the other planes to take our position and then headed for a little island in order to come down as close to land as possible.'

Saunders successfully ditched the faltering bomber one-and-a-half miles offshore at Vella Lavella on Ballale Island, although he cut his head when he banged into the windshield whilst putting the B-17 down on the water at 95 mph. The wings hit and the bomber came to an abrupt stop. Saunders and Lt Donald G. O'Brien, the navigator, slid through the cockpit window. The tail broke off and the rest of the crew went out through the break.

Lt Nelson Levi, the bombardier – who had been badly wounded in the thigh – and Lt Lee, were carefully extricated from the wrecked bomber and placed in two life rafts. Lee died as they paddled ashore. Natives found the airmen and took them to a village where the following afternoon a PBY Catalina escorted by P-38 Lightning fighters picked up the men and returned them to Santo.

November witnessed the beginning of the end

of Japanese attempts to retake Guadalcanal and they withdrew to the islands in the north. Three major battles at sea took place off Guadalcanal, culminating in the Battle of Tassafaronga on 30 November. The B-17s were put on stand-by. Horst Handrow relates: 'We got word that Japs were out again so every plane was on double alert. Lt Jacobs got shot down over the New Georgia islands. A Zero rammed them and only one man got out. It was their first flight after Auckland [leave]. Hamalainen, my old radio man, went down in that ship.'

Although many of the decisive battles for the control of Guadalcanal took place at sea, the Fortresses of the 11th and 5th Bomb Groups flew support missions throughout, bombing Japanese ground forces and shipping. One of the B-17s' frequent missions was against the 'Tokyo Express', the Japanese transport and combat ship task force that plied the 'slot' (the channel between New Georgia and Santa Isabel Islands northwest of Guadalcanal) almost nightly to reinforce their hard pressed ground troops on the embattled island.

In December the Fortresses went principally after land targets. On 1 December Capt Jake Jacobs of the 431st Squadron failed to return from a search mission when his B-17 was brought down by an enemy aircraft which crashed into it in the vicinity of Vella Lavella. Corp Hartman, the tail gunner, managed to bail out and was rescued later. He confirmed that the crew had shot down three enemy fighters.

Meanwhile, the Japanese had built a new airfield in a coconut grove on the New Georgia Islands at Munda, leaving the coconut trees standing until the last minute, then felling them and filling in the holes so that the field was ready for Zeros the next morning. On 10 December the first escorts ever used in the area accompanied the bombers to Munda Point. The twin-engined P-38 Lightnings were a welcome addition since as many as 40 Japanese fighters rose to meet the bomber formations. The fighters shot down five attacking Zeros while gunners aboard the B-17s claimed two more. Some of the Zeros flew between 1,500 – 4,000 ft above the B-17s and dropped bombs with timed fuses on the Fortresses. Crews reported approximately 20 bursts from these bombs.

Maj Whitaker, the 72nd Squadron CO, returned alone to Guadalcanal and was attacked by Zeros. Four 20 mm shells hit one wing and

one exploded in the other. Whitaker landed safely but the main spar was damaged to such an extent that the B-17 had to be sent to the depot for major repairs. Another B-17, piloted by Maj Glober and Capt Carl Coleman, on routine search in the Bougainville sector, returned to base with one engine out and another badly damaged. Coleman lay dead in his seat, killed by a 7.7 bullet which entered the control cabin just below the windshield.

For three days running – 19-21 December – the B-17s attacked Munda again. Large craters littered the airstrip and prevented the Zeros from taking off. Meanwhile, pressure was applied to Kahili airfield on Bougainville's southeast tip. On the morning of the raid on the 19th Capt Charters and his crew in the 98th loaded their B-17 *Skipper* with 20 100 lb and several 20 lb

fragmentation bombs, and two baskets of 'secret weapons' – in actuality, beer bottles. For two hours in the dark early morning *Skipper* remained over Kahili, dropping bombs every 15 min. Japanese searchlights probed the skies during the first bomb runs but were suddenly and completely extinguished when the crew hurled out two of their 'secret weapons'!

On Christmas Eve the 11th Bomb Group took off from Guadalcanal between 2100 and 2300 hr for a strike against an enemy shipping concentration at Rabaul. Capt Durbin of the 98th Squadron in *Buzz King* was forced to return early after heavy fuel consumption and a B-17 in the 431st Squadron also had to return early. Horst Handrow, recalls:

'We took off in No 59, the worst ship in the 98th Bomb Squadron. We had 20 min gas to spare if we

Left: B-17E Buzz King *41-2531 of the 98th Bomb Squadron on Santo, 1942. Heavy fuel consumption on the Christmas Eve 1942 strike against enemy shipping off Rabaul, forced Capt Durbin, the pilot, to return to Guadalcanal early. (USAF via Bill Cleveland.)*

Right: B-17E Ole Shasta *(with the Midway Star) of the 98th Bomb Squadron on Santo in 1942, had its nose guns installed locally after a few head-on passes by Japanese fighters. This aircraft was lost in January 1943. (USAF via Bill Cleveland.)*

Below right: B-17E Alley Oop *41-9216, named for Lt Alley, pictured at Santo in 1943. (USAF via Bill Cleveland.)*

made it up and back. It was a sweat mission. Fifteen minutes out of Rabaul No 4 engine went out, so we turned around and started back. Thirty minutes later No 2 engine went out and that left two. We dropped our bombs in the Pacific to make the load lighter. No 1 started to act up and it really looked like we were going to sit the plane down in the Pacific with Japs all around us. But luck was with us and we made it okay. We came in with 10 min gas left. It was No 59's last flight'.

The other B-17s dropped their 500 lb armour piercing bombs on 50 large ships in Rabaul harbour. Maj Lucas in *Typhoon McGoon* and Capt Crane in *Goonie* both 98th Squadron pilots – made bombing runs together, scoring three direct hits on a large troop transport and damaging two other transports. The strike force returned to base and killed the tail gunner of a Japanese four-engined flying boat who 'was demonstrating a machine-gun the Emperor had given him for Christmas'.

On 28 December Lt James Harp and his crew in the 42nd Squadron were lost when their B-17 was shot down. Capt Donald M. Hyland was also shot down but he and his crew were rescued later by US Navy PBY *Dumbo*. Two days later Col Saunders handed over command of the 11th Bomb Group to Col Frank F. Everest. 'Blondie' was well respected by his men and had led them through many difficult air battles. He was promoted to Brig-Gen and was later Chief-of-Staff, B-29 operations, commanding the 58th Wing before sadly having to retire after losing a leg in an aircraft accident.

On 4 January 1943 the Japanese Imperial Staff finally issued orders for the evacuations of Guadalcanal to begin. January was occupied mainly by search missions, with a few bombing

strikes on Bougainville and the Russell Islands, north of Gaudalcanal. On 1 February the depleted 42nd Squadron, which was now down to just four B-17s, suffered a severe blow when three crews failed to return from a strike on Bougainville. Capt Houx' B-17 was hit in the bomb bay by flak and disintegrated in the air. Shortly afterwards the other two B-17s, flown by Capt Hall and Capt Harold P. Hensley, were jumped by Zeros and shot down.

By 9 February the last remnants of the Imperial Army had been evacuated from the 'Canal' by sea. Two days earlier the official orders relieving the 11th Bomb Group from duty was signed. In March 1943 the group returned to the Hawaiian Islands and re-assigned to the 7th Air Force. From May to November the group re-equipped with B-24 Liberators and returned to the Pacific in the autumn to continue the war which ended in victory in August 1945.

CHAPTER 4

The Big League

European Theatre of Operations, 1942 – October 1943

Although the United States could not prevent the Japanese attack on Pearl Harbor on 7 December 1941, far-reaching decisions had been made in the event that America should become involved in the conflict with the Axis powers. Between 27 January and 27 March 1941 agreements between the United States and Great Britain were made for the provision of naval, ground and air support for the campaign against Germany. As a result, a special US Army Observer Group, headed by Maj-Gen James E. Chaney, was activated in London on 19 May 1941.

One of Chaney's first tasks was to reconnoitre areas regarded as potential sites for Army Air Force installations. During late 1941 several tentative sites were explored, including Prestwick near Ayr in Scotland and Warton near Liverpool, the proposed site for a repair depot. Others, like Polebrook, Grafton Underwood, Kimbolton, Molesworth, Chelveston, Podington and Thurleigh, all in the Huntingdon area, would soon become familiar homes of B-17 Flying Fortress groups of the US 8th Air Force.

On 2 January 1942 the order activating the 8th Air Force was signed by Maj-Gen Henry 'Hap' Arnold, the Commanding General, Army Air Forces, and the HQ was formed at Savannah, Georgia, 26 days later. On 8 January it was announced that a bomber command was to be established in England. Arnold designated Brig-Gen Ira C. Eaker as Commanding General of VIII Bomber Command and his duties were to help prepare airfields and installations and understudy the methods of RAF Bomber Command.

Initially, Eaker's HQ was established at RAF Bomber Command HQ, High Wycombe, Buckinghamshire. It was here, on 22 February, that VIII Bomber Command was formerly activated.

Almost six months were to elapse before the 8th mounted its first all-American bombing mission on German-held territory. Between 31 March and 3 April 1942 Eaker and his staff officers made a more detailed reconnaissance of the Huntingdon area and the seeds of the future American presence were thus sown. Meanwhile, in America, B-17 and B-24 heavy bombardment groups were activated for deployment to Britain.

The first of the B-17 groups activated was the 34th, at Langley Field, Virginia, on 15 January 1942, but the group was used to train other groups and remained in America until late March 1944. On 3 February 1942 three more B-17 groups, the 97th, 301st and 303rd, were formally activated. It fell to these three groups together with the 92nd, activated on 1 March 1942, and two Liberator groups, to establish the nucleus of the 8th's heavy bombardment force in England. First to arrive was the ground echelon of the 97th Bomb Group, which disembarked on 9 June and en-trained for its Polebrook base in Northamptonshire where earlier, RAF Fortress Is had taken off on raids over Germany.

In August 1942 the 92nd and 301st Bomb Groups arrived to join Eaker's rapidly increasing air force. The 92nd was the first heavy bombardment group to successfully make a non-stop flight from Newfoundland to Scotland. It took time to get the new groups ready for combat and training was lacking in many areas. Col Frank A. Armstrong, one of Eaker's original HQ staff, was appointed CO of the 97th Bomb Group at Grafton Underwood at the end of July in place of Lt-Col Cousland and he set about re-shaping the group. By mid-August he had 24 crews ready for combat. Meanwhile, as arguments went on behind the scenes about whether bombing in daylight was possible over heavily defended targets in Europe, or even that the Fortresses and Liberators' bomb-carrying capacity and their armament would be enough, the first Fortress strike of the war was scheduled for 17 August 1942.

Gen Carl 'Tooey' Spaatz, the American air commander in Europe, and members of his staff, attended the briefing at Grafton Underwood. At 1500 hrs six B-17Es took off from Polebrook and flew a diversionary raid on St. Omer. Briefing over at Grafton Underwood, Frank Armstrong boarded *Butcher Shop* which was piloted by Maj Paul Tibbets and led 11 B-17s to the marshalling yards at Rouen-Sotteville in northwestern France. Spaatz had felt confident enough to allow Brig-General Ira C. Eaker to fly on the mission. He joined the crew of *Yankee Doodle*, lead aircraft of the second flight of six. Over the Channel, the Fortresses were joined by their RAF escort of Spitfire Vs.

Visibility over the target was good and bombing was made from 23,000 ft. A few bombs hit a mile short of the target and one burst hit about a mile west in some woods, but the majority landed in the assigned area. Several repair and maintenance workshops were badly damaged which put the railway temporarily out of action.

First of the congratulatory messages to arrive came from Air Marshal Sir Arthur Harris, Commander-in-Chief of RAF Bomber Command: 'Congratulations from all ranks of Bomber Command on the highly successful completion of the first all-American raid by the big fellows on German-occupied territory in Europe. *Yankee Doodle* certainly went to town and can stick yet another well-deserved feather in his cap.'

Unfortunately for Eaker, his ability to wage a bombing offensive was hampered by the more pressing needs of Brig-Gen James H. Doolittle's 12th Air Force which would have to be equipped and trained to support the 'Torch' invasion of Northwest Africa in November 1942. The 8th Air Force was thus denied valuable replacement men and machines while new groups had to be trained for eventual transfer to the 12th. Worse, on 14 September both the 97th and 301st Bomb Groups were assigned to the new air force.

Meanwhile, Eaker sent all he had got on missions to shipyards and airfields on the Continent. On 5 September, 37 B-17s from the 97th and 301st Bomb Groups were despatched and the next day the 92nd helped swell the ranks to 54.

Despite their Spitfire escort two B-17s were shot down, the first US heavy bombers to be lost in the ETO. The 92nd later formed the first combat crew replacement centre.

From September to November four new B-17F bomb groups joined the 8th Air Force. It fell to these four B-17 groups (and two B-24 groups) to prove conclusively that daylight precision bombing could succeed in the deadly skies over Europe. The RAF remained unconvinced and even American instructors doubted their crew's ability to survive against German opposition.

The 305th Bomb Group was commanded by Lt-Col Curtis E. LeMay, a man destined to figure prominently in the shaping of bombing doctrine both in the ETO and later, in the Pacific. On 9 October Eaker was able to despatch an unprecedented 108 bombers (including B-17Fs of the 306th, which was making its bombing debut), to Lille. A strong P-38 and RAF Spitfire escort accompanied the bombers. This first full-scale mission created many problems which, coupled with bad weather, saw only 69 bombers drop their bombs on the target area. Claims by the American gunners far exceeded the number of attacking enemy fighters but in fact the Luftwaffe lost just two.

Allied shipping losses rose dramatically in October, and November was to be even worse. On 20 October Brig-Gen Asa N. Duncan, Chief of Air Staff, issued a revised set of objectives to be carried out by VIII Bomber Command. In part it stated; '. . . until further orders every effort of the VIII Bomber Command will be directed to obtaining the maximum destruction of the submarine bases in the Bay of Biscay . . .' The limited number of Fortresses available prevented VIII Bomber Command hitting submarine yards inside Germany.

Losses throughout the remainder of 1942 during missions to the U-boat pens were high, although the planners still believed that the bombers could fight their way through to their objectives without fighter escort. The theory was given further credence on 20 December when only six B-17s from the attacking force of 101 bombers were lost on the mission to Romilly near Paris, despite widespread Luftwaffe fighter activity in France. Romilly was a turning point in the daylight aerial war: for the first time the Fortresses had penetrated 100 miles into enemy territory and had successfully kept the Luftwaffe interceptors at bay (despite high claims, the American gunners actually shot down three and damaged one more).

One fact alarmed Eaker and his staff: only 72 of the attacking bombers had hit the target and these caused only minimal damage. As improvements – some of them temporary until the new B-17Gs with 'chin turrets' to counter head-on attacks came off the assembly lines – senior officers worked on methods for improving bombing and aerial gunnery. Col Curtis LeMay, CO of the 305th Bomb Group, worked hard to find the best method of defence against fighter interceptions without compromising bombing accuracy and vice-versa. LeMay had faith in tight-knit group formations and trained his men hard in very close formation flying.

At first LeMay experimented with 'stacked-up' formations of 18 aircraft, before he finally adopted staggered three-plane elements within a squadron and staggered squadrons within a group. At the same time LeMay discarded the traditional individual bombing and replaced the technique with 'lead crews' – the most expert bombardiers were placed in the lead crews. When the lead bombardier dropped his bombs so did everyone else. Providing he was on target, all bombs landed near the MPI (Mean Point of Impact) and the target could be successfully destroyed instead of damaged. LeMay's tactics were encouraged by Brig-Gen Larry Kuter and later, Brig-Gen Hayward Hansell. Eventually, lead crews – made up of highly trained pilots, bombardiers and navigators – became Standard Operating Procedure (SOP).

Group bombing was first tried on 3 January 1943 when the 8th Air Force visited Saint Nazaire for the sixth time. A total of 107 bombers, with the 305th Bomb Group in the lead, was despatched but only eight B-24s and 68 B-17s found the target. LeMay's tactics also called for a straight and level bomb run to ensure accuracy but seven bombers were shot down and 47 damaged, two so seriously that they were written off after landing in Wales. Most important of all, the majority of the bombloads had fallen on the pens.

If anyone needed further proof about the new bombing tactics it came on 13 January when VIII Bomber Command completed an effective raid on Lille. The 305th Bomb Group again flew lead and Brig-Gen Hansell, Commander of the 1st Bomb Wing, flew in the lead ship to witness the results for himself. Despite strong fighter opposition only three B-17s were lost and gunners claimed six fighters destroyed and 13 probably destroyed. Despite these successes the future of VIII Bomber Command as a daylight bombing force was still in doubt. Losses had continued to rise and in some quarters (particularly the RAF) senior officers believed that the American bombers should join the RAF night offensive. Gen Arnold, Chief of the American Air Staff, was under pressure from his superiors to mount more missions and, in particular, aim them at German targets.

In January 1943 Gen Ira C. Eaker, who since November 1942 had been acting Commanding-General of the 8th Air Force in the absence of Gen Carl 'Tooey' Spaatz, met Gen 'Hap' Arnold at the Casablanca summit in North Africa attended by President Roosevelt, Prime Minister Winston Churchill and the Combined Chiefs of Staff, to make a case for continued daylight bombing. Churchill had obtained an agreement from Roosevelt for the 8th Air Force to cease daylight bombing and join the RAF in night bombing. Eaker saw Churchill and managed to convince him otherwise. Churchill was most impressed with Eaker's brief memorandum which skilfully summarised the reasons why the US daylight bombing should continue. He particularly like the phrase 'round-the-clock bombing' and although not totally convinced, was persuaded that day and night bombing should be continued for a time.

To demonstrate that daylight precision bombing could triumph over area bombing by night, Eaker decided to bomb the U-boat construction yards at Wilhelmshaven. On 27 January, 91 B-17s and B-24s were despatched to the U-boat yards in the port. Unfortunately, bad weather conditions reduced the attacking force to 53 B-17s, which dropped their bombs on the shipyards from 25,000 ft through a German smoke screen and two others bombed Emden. Despite heavy fighter opposition only three bombers (one B-17 and two B-24s) were shot down. The bombing was described as 'fair' but the Press went wild.

Eaker attempted to pile on the pressure but bad weather fronts restricted operations to only three full-scale missions in February. On the 4th, after a series of cancelled starts, in the deepest penetration into enemy territory thus far, 86 bombers bombed the marshalling yards at

Hamm in the Ruhr Valley. Fighter attacks were intense and five bombers were lost. Four more were lost on a follow-up raid on 4 March. Losses rose sharply on 17 April when 16 B-17s were lost from the attacking force of 106 that attacked the Focke-Wulf plant at Bremen.

The German defences were constantly improving. Although flak (Flieger Abwehr Kannonen) accounted for most of the battle damage sustained by the B-17s and B-24s, the Luftwaffe continued to inflict the heaviest losses despite having only 120 fighters based in France and the Low Countries. The 8th on the other hand increased in strength. In April four new groups equipped with the B-17F (all but one group's aircraft were fitted with long-range 'Tokyo tanks') landed in England. A fifth 'new' B-17 group was added to the force when the 92nd Bomb Group resumed bombing operations.

In the absence of suitable escort fighters the Fortresses continued to defend themselves. On 4 May 1943 six squadrons of P-47s and six RAF fighter squadrons accompanied 79 B-17s to the Ford and General Motors plant at Antwerp. No bombers were lost.

On 12 May the 94th, 95th and 96th Bomb Groups formed a new 4th Bomb Wing in Essex and Suffolk under the command of Brig-Gen Fred L. Anderson. On 14 May Eaker was able to muster in excess of 200 bombers for the first time when 224 B-17s, B-24s and B-26 Marauders, attacked four separate targets. B-17s of the 1st Wing, flying without escort, bombed the shipyards at Kiel. Meanwhile, 50 B-17s belonging to the 96th and 351st Bomb Groups bombed the airfield at Coutrai in France and the 94th and 95th Bomb Groups led by Gen Anderson attacked the Ford and General Motors plant at Antwerp. RAF Spitfires and USAAF Thunderbolts gave excellent fighter cover on the Antwerp and Coutrai raids. Altogether, the four targets cost the Americans 11 aircraft, (six of them Liberators). Not all the bombing was accurate but for the first time Eaker had demonstrated that he could mount several missions on one day.

On 17 May the Marauders made a second attempt to bomb Ijmuiden but with even more disastrous results. All 10 attacking B-26s failed to return (After this débâcle the Marauders were transferred from the 3rd Bomb Wing to VIII Air Support command for future medium level bombing operations in a tactical role. Their Essex bases were taken over by the B-17 groups.)

In June Operation 'Pointblank', an intermediate priority objective aimed at the German fighter strength, was finally published. The first steps had been taken at the Casablanca Conference when the Allied leaders had agreed a combined bomber offensive from England. The primary objectives listed were the 'German submarine yards and bases, the remainder of the German aircraft industry, ball bearings and oil . . .' Secondary objectives were 'synthetic rubber and tyres and military motor transport vehicles'. The objective concluded, 'It is emphasised that the reduction of the German fighter force is of primary importance: any delay in its prosecution will make the task progressively more difficult . . .'

The Combined Bomber Offensive plan called for 2,702 heavy bombers in 51 groups to be in place before the Allied invasion of Northwest Europe, earmarked for mid-1944. One of the first missions in the offensive took place on 13 June when the 1st Wing went to Bremen and the 4th Wing visited U-boat construction yards at Kiel. The mission coincided with the transfer to new bases in Suffolk of three B-17 groups in the 4th Wing while three B-26 Marauder groups which had sustained heavy losses, arrived in their place. This move would give the B-26s longer-range fighter cover. Unfortunately, the 94th, 95th and 96th Bomb Groups' last mission from their old bases was a disaster. The mission to Kiel claimed 22 4th Wing B-17s and four others were lost from the 1st Wing.

The new 4th Wing CO, Col (later Brig-Gen) Curtis E. LeMay, moved into the former 3rd Wing headquarters at Elveden Hall near Thetford and began building up his force. Imminent arrivals of three new groups – the 100th, 385th and 388th – would increase the 4th Wing to six groups. LeMay also replaced the 94th and 95th Bomb Group commanders (the 95th had lost 11 B-17s on the Kiel raid).

Eaker, in pursuit of the 'Pointblank' Directive, sent his bombers on the first really deep penetration of Germany on 22 June, to the synthetic rubber plant at Huls. Huls produced approximately 29 per cent of Germany's synthetic rubber and 18 per cent of its total rubber supply. It was

B-17F-95-BO 42-30248 of the 333rd Bomb Squadron, 94th Bomb Group in formation over the enemy coast. (USAF via Geoff Ward.)

Above left: Two B-17Fs of the 385th Bomb Group en route to their target in 1943. (William Nicholls.)

Left: German officers inspect the wreckage of B-17F-85-BO 42-30037 of the 546th Bomb Squadron, 384th Bomb Group, piloted by Lt Lykes S. Henderson, after it was shot down on 26 June 1943. (Hans Heiri-Stapfer.)

Above: B-17F Double Trouble of the 333rd Bomb Squadron, 94th Bomb Group. The pilot Lt Bill Winnesheik, aborted the mission to Bremen on 25 June 1943 after fighters knocked out two engines and he landed in England despite a full bomb load. On 4 October 1943, during a mission to St Dizier, France, fighters knocked out the No 3 engine and the propeller refused to feather but the crew managed to crashland at Margate. Vance Van Hooser, the asst engineer/waist gunner, who was on his 23rd mission, was hit in the head by 20 mm shell fragments and never flew again. (USAF via Peter Frost.)

also heavily defended. Some 235 B-17s were despatched and most of the route was flown without escort. Unfortunately, one of the three diversionary raids planned to draw enemy fighters away from the Huls force only succeeded in alerting them. Sixteen B-17s were lost and another 170 damaged. Even so, some 183 Fortresses bombed the plant so effectively that full production was not resumed for six months.

Bad weather throughout the rest of June and early July restricted the 8th to short haul missions to France. New groups arrived and on 17 July a record 332 bombers were despatched to Hannover. A lengthy spell of good weather was predicted for late July and Eaker was poised to launch a long-awaited all-out air offensive. It started on 24 July and continued all week – or 'Blitz Week' (after the German word for 'Light-ning') as it became known.

On the 24th, 324 B-17s from the 1st and 4th Wings bombed targets in Norway, with one force flying a 2,000-mile round trip to Bergen and Trondheim, the longest American mission over Europe so far. Some 167 bombers from the 1st Wing bombed Heroya and completely devastated a factory complex while 41 bombers bombed shipping at Trondheim. On 25 July Kiel, Hamburg and Warnemunde were bombed with the loss of 19 Fortresses. There was no respite for the bomber crews and on 26 July more than 300 heavies were despatched to Hannover and Hamburg.

Bomber crews were stood down for a much needed rest on 27 July but the battle was resumed on 28 July when 182 bombers made an attack on the Fieseler Werke aircraft factory at

Left: B-17F-35-BO 42-5086 of the 306th Bomb Group, which was flown on the 24 July 1943 mission to Heroya by Capt David H. Wheeler. After the target enemy fighters attacked and a 20 mm cannon shell shattered the instrument panel. Fragments seriously wounded Duane Bollenbach, the navigator, in the side of the head. Sgt Raymond L. Norris, the tail gunner, was seriously wounded in the legs and was left hanging from the aircraft. Wheeler nursed the B-17 back over the North Sea to Thurleigh and landed without flaps, aileron control and with one wheel only partially extended. Bollenbach survived and Norris later completed his tour. (Richards.)

Below left: B-17s of the 94th Bomb Group over the Norwegian fiords on 24 July 1943. (via Ian McLachlan.)

Above: B-17F-95-BO 42-30325 Miss Carry of the 390th Bomb Group over the Alps on 17 August 1943. (via Ian McLachlan.)

Below: B-17s of the 94th Bomb Group over the Norwegian fiords on 24 July 1943. (via Ian McLachlan.)

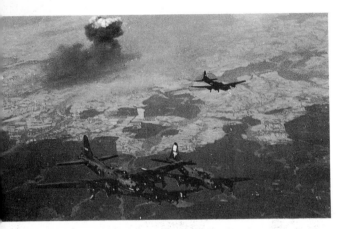

Left: B-17s of the 3rd Bomb Division, 8th Air Force, come off the devastated target at Kassel, Germany, on 30 July 1943. (USAF.)

Below: Ground crews at Thurleigh wait pensively as crews of the 306th Bomb Group, 8th Air Force, circle the airfield prior to landing. (via Gordon & Connie Richards.)

Below right: 385th Bomb Group B-17s cross the target at Regensburg on 17 August 1943. (via Ian McLachlan.)

Kassel, while 120 Fortresses from the 4th Wing bombed the AGO FW190 assembly plant at Oschersleben near Magdeburg. P-47 Thunderbolts of the 56th and 78th Fighter Groups, carrying unpressurized 200-gal ferry tanks below the centre fuselage for the first time, escorted the Kassel force and prevented heavy losses. Fifteen B-17s were lost on the Oschersleben raid but production was halted for a month.

On 29 July the 8th flew its fourth mission in five days. The 1st Wing bombed the shipyards at Kiel again and the 4th Wing dealt FW190 production a heavy blow in its accurate bomb-

ing of the Heinkel assembly plant at Warnemunde. Next day, in a fitting finale, VIII Bomber Command despatched 186 Fortresses to the aircraft factories at Kassel, escorted almost to the target and back again by P-47 Thunderbolts fitted with long-range fuel tanks. Altogether, 12 Fortresses were lost, including some that were so badly damaged that they never flew again.

'Blitz Week' had dealt heavy blows to the German submarine, munitions and aircraft industries but the 8th Air Force had lost about 100 aircraft and 90 combat crews which left under 200 heavies ready for combat. The survivors were exhausted and many had become 'flak happy'. Even so, losses were gradually made good and on 12 August 330 bombers were sent to bomb targets in the Ruhr; 25 bombers failed to return. Three days later VIII Bomber Com-

The green grass of home *A 390th Bomb Group B-17G lands at Framlingham, Suffolk, while others in the landing pattern peel off overhead.* (USAF.)

Forts in Colour

B-17G-95-DL 44-83872 Texas Raiders *pictured in flight over Texas during 1986.* (Author.)

(Above) They flew B-17s *Alvar M. Woodall, gunner in Lt Forrest V. Poore's crew, 385th Bomb Group, poses in the waist hatch of* Pat Pending. *Woodall was killed flying as top turret gunner aboard* Mary Ellen III *on 11 December 1943.* (William Nicholls.)

(Below) *Linn C. Stuckenbruck, bombardier (left), and William Nicholls, navigator, pose in front of the forward hatch of* Pat Pending *painted 'Stuck and Nick's Hotel'. Both men were made PoW after they were shot down in* Mary Ellen III *on 11 December 1943.* (William Nicholls.)

(Right) Preserved Fort: Texas Raiders *prepares to take off at the 1986 Confederate Air Show in the USA.* (Author.)

(Top) The remake of Memphis
Belle: 2 *B-17G-85-VE F-AZDX/44-8846*
Association Fortress Volante *alias* Mother
and Country *at Duxford in 1989.* (Author.)

(Left) The remake of Memphis Belle: 1
*Not a scene from World War Two but B-17s
in formation over England during filming of*
Memphis Belle *in the summer of 1989.*
(Steve Carter.)

(Right) In memoriam *The 3rd Air Division
memorial window in the chapel in the grounds
of Elveden Hall which was used as HQ by
the 3rd Bomb Division, US 8th Air Force,
in World War Two.* (Author.)

(**Left**) *B-17G 42-97976 A Bit O' Lace of the 447th Bomb Group, 8th Air Force, pictured in 1945.* (Charles E. Brown.)

(**Right**) *B-17Gs of the 96th Bomb Group taxi out at Snetterton Heath 1944. Nearest aircraft is 43-37794 AW-T (337th Bomb Squadron) (MIA 19/9/44). Leading B-17 is MZ-L (413th B.S.), following, BX-Y (338th B.S.).* (USAF.)

(**Overleaf**) *B-17G-70-VE 44-8543 Chuckie — owned by 'Doc' Hospers' BC Vintage Flying Machines, Fort Worth, Texas and named after his wife — seen here at the Confederate Air Show, Harlingen, Texas in 1986.* (Author.)

(**Below**) *Lt John H. Pitts' crew pose in front of their B-17E San Antonio Rose of the 98th Bomb Squadron on Koomac, New Caledonia, in August 1942.* (Mrs Pitts via Bill Cleveland.)

mand participated in the 'Starkey' deception plan which was created to make the enemy believe that an invasion of the French coast was imminent. Raids continued on enemy airfields in France and the Low Countries on 16 August. It was a prelude to the Field Order for 17 August, which called for a simultaneous attack by 376 Fortresses on the aircraft plants at Regensburg and the ball bearing plant at Schweinfurt. Regensburg was the second largest aircraft plant of its kind in Europe and its destruction would produce a nine-month delay in production. Regensburg was estimated to produce 200 Bf109s a month, or approximately 25-30 per cent of Germany's single-engined aircraft production.

On 17 August Brig-Gen Robert Williams, commander of the 1st Wing, led his force to Schweinfurt while Col Curtis E. LeMay led the 4th Wing to Regensburg. To minimise attacks from enemy fighters the master plan called for LeMay's force to fly on to North Africa after bombing the target. The 1st Wing, meanwhile, would fly a parallel course to Schweinfurt to further confuse the enemy defences and return to England after the raid. Unfortunately, the 1st Wing was delayed in England by ground mists, leaving the Luftwaffe time to concentrate on the

4th Wing and only one of four P-47 groups assigned to the 4th Wing actually managed to rendevous with B-17s. They could not possibly cover all the seven B-17 groups, which stretched for 15 miles. Enemy fighters ripped the formation apart and shot down 24 B-17s. The 1st Wing force fared worse, losing 36 B-17s to enemy fighters.

Those aircraft that had bombed had been remarkably accurate. Eighty hits were made on the factories at Schweinfurt, and at Regensburg all six main workshops were destroyed or badly damaged. Air Marshal Slessor for the British, called it 'outstandingly successful. Probably the best concentration on target yet seen.'

The official total of 60 B-17s lost was almost three times as high as the previous highest, on 13 June, when 26 bombers were lost. In reality the 8th had lost 147 bombers. Twenty-seven B-17s in the 1st Wing were so badly damaged that they never flew again while 60 Fortresses had to be left in North Africa pending repairs. The almost non-existent maintenance facilities ruled out any further shuttle missions.

VIII Bomber Command flew only shallow penetration missions throughout the remainder of August and early September 1943 while losses were made good. During September the B-17G,

which introduced a 'chin turret' for forward defence, began arriving as combat replacements in the ETO. From November all new B-17 groups arriving in England were similarly equipped. One large raid took place on 6 September when 388 B-17s were despatched to the aircraft components factories at Stuttgart. The raid was a complete disaster. Some 45 aircraft were lost and many crews missed their targets or returned with their bomb loads intact. On 13 September VIII Bomber Command was officially divided into three bombardment divisions. The nine groups of the 1st Bomb Wing formed the 1st Bomb Division and the 4th Bomb Wing

became the 3rd Bomb Division. The B-24 Liberator groups became the 2nd Bomb Division and continued to fly missions separate from the two Fortress divisions.

On 8 October the 1st and 3rd Bomb Divisions were assigned the port at Bremen. The area was noted for its flak defences and much of north-western Germany's fighter strength was concentrated nearby. In order to split the enemy fighter force, plans called for the 1st Division to approach the target from Holland while the 3rd Division crossed the North Sea and approached the target from the northwest. The B-24s of the 2nd Bomb Division – living up to their nickname, the 2nd Bomb Diversion – would fly a long, curving route over the North Sea to attack Vegasack. Unfortunately, after the P-47 escort had withdrawn, low on fuel, the B-17s were met in strength. The unfortunate 381st Bomb Group, flying as low group in the 1st Division formation, lost seven of its 18 bombers, including the lead ship.

To crews in the 3rd Division though, it seemed as if everything was going according to plan. Frank McGlinchey, bombardier aboard Lt Bill MacDonald's B-17 *Salvo Sal*, of the 350th Bomb Squadron, 100th Bomb Group, recalls the mission on 8 October, the crew's tenth:

'Our group had little trouble forming up and it wasn't long before we were out over the Channel. P-47s had given us good support and things seemed rather quiet as we winged our way toward the target. Minutes passed and soon we were over the IP (Initial Point). With bomb bay doors open we turned on the target.

The groups in front of us were enveloped in a huge black cloud as they passed over the target and dropped their payloads.

'It was the most intensive flak I had ever seen. We had a good run on the target and our bombs went away very well. Just after the bomb bay doors closed the ship jumped as we received a very bad hit just to the rear of No 2 engine. All three ships in the lead element were also hit. The two wingmen went down in flames. The leader, apparently partially out of control, fell out of formation. I looked for our two wingmen but saw no-one. Our whole squadron of nine ships had been knocked out. (I learned much later that only one ship made it back to England.)

'Although out of formation and heading back to England by ourselves, we seemed to be doing all right until a flight of German fighters bounced us. Suddenly, the intercom was alive with the actions of fighters bearing in from all directions. All our guns, with the exception of the two nose guns, were knocked out in 15 min. Our waist gunner, Douglas Agee, was killed by

Above left: B-17s of the 96th Bomb Group, 8th Air Force, crossing the Alps after the raid on Regensburg on 17 August 1943. (via Geoff Ward.)

Below left: 339th Bomb Squadron, 96th Bomb Group crew walk from their B-17 42-30359 after arriving safely in Africa after the Regensburg mission on 17 August 1943. This aircraft was lost over Oldenburg on 29 November 1943. (via Geoff Ward.)

Above: B-17F El Lobo of the 551st Bomb Squadron, 385th Bomb Group at Great Ashfield, 28 August 1943. Note the flame dampers on the machine-guns which were installed when this and some of the other Group aircraft were used in night operations with the RAF late in 1943. (via Ian McLachlan.)

Below: B-17F-25-VE 42-5841 of the 423rd Bomb Squadron, 306th Bomb Group, piloted by Lt Martin Andrews, force-landed at Magadino airfield, near Ticino, Switzerland, on 6 September 1943 after flak and fighters had shot out most of its engines over the target area at Stuttgart. The crew was interned. Later, the B-17 was flown to Emmen test and experimental centre. At the end of the war Swiss ground crews performed an engine exchange at Emmen before the aircraft was handed back to the USAF. The shadow belongs to B-17F-105-BO 42-30478. (Hans-Heiri Stapfer.)

Left: B-17F-110-BO 42-30607 Pat Hand *flown by Lt Ken E. Murphy of the 96th Bomb Group, takes a direct flak hit over Paris during a raid on the Hispano-Suisa complex on 15 September 1943. (USAF.)*

Below: B-17F Virgin's Delight *of the 94th Bomb Group comes off the target – the FW190 factory at Marienburg – on 9 October 1943. (USAF.)*

Right: Bombs rain down on Marienburg from the bomb bays of Fortresses on 9 October 1943. (via Ian McLachlan.)

a direct hit from a fighter about 2 min after the fighting started. All our left controls were shattered and we had to put out several fires. Our radio, too, was gone. One engine was "running away" and two more were about to go. We were losing altitude rapidly and it was apparent we would not make it back to England. Suddenly, fire shot out from the rear of No 3 engine. With the Zeider Zee directly in front of us, Bill Mac-Donald gave the order to bale out.'

Incredibly, almost all the crew of *Salvo Sal* had managed to bail out of the doomed aircraft. All

six enlisted men were captured by German patrols shortly after landing. John James, the co-pilot, broke his leg on landing and was captured. Carl Spicer, the navigator, evaded capture and made it home to England via France and Spain. MacDonald and McGlinchey made contact with the Dutch Underground but were caught later while trying to cross the Pyrenees into Spain. They were sent to Stalag Luft I, Barth.

Salvo Sal was one of seven 100th Bomb Group B-17s lost on 8 October including Maj 'Bucky' Cleven, CO of the 350th Bomb Squadron, who was later reported to be a POW. Altogether, the 8th lost 26 bombers, including 14 in the Third Division. If it had not been for the installation of 'Carpet' blinkers aboard some 96th and 388th Bomb Group B-17s, losses might well have been much higher. 'Carpet' was a British invention and used radio signals to interfere with radar-directed flak guns. Over the next few months 'Carpet' devices were fitted to all Fortresses.

On 9 October 115 B-17s were despatched to the Arado aircraft component plant at Anklam near Peenemünde while 263 bombers attacked the port of Gydnia and the Focke-Wulf plant at Marienburg. Gen Robert B. Travis, the 1st Bomb Division commander, led his force to Anklam in *The Eightball*, a 303rd Bomb Group B-17 flown by Capt Claude Campbell. Fighter opposition was heavy and 14 B-17s, all from the 1st Combat Wing, failed to return. The Gydnia force, led by Lt-Col Henry G. MacDonald, 40th Combat Wing Operations Officer, bombed ships and installations. Again, fighter opposition was heavy, as Bill Rose, a pilot in the 92nd Bomb Group, recalls:

'It amazed me how the German pilots could fly through the hail of shells we were firing at them. Every fifth round was a tracer. The fighters came in straight through the formation and knocked down Bill Whelan's plane. Then the fighters left the formation as if knocked down themselves. We realised that this was a game for keeps. They were out to kill us and we were going to kill them.'

The third force of B-17s, which bombed Marienburg, achieved the greatest success of the day. A lack of anti-aircraft defences, thought unnecessary at a target so far from England, meant that the force could bomb from between 11,000 and 13,000 ft. At such heights accuracy was almost guaranteed and 60 per cent of the bombs dropped by the 96 Fortresses exploded within 1,000 ft of the MPI and 83 per cent fell

within 2,000 ft. Before the raid the Marienburg plant had been turning out almost 50 per cent of the Luftwaffe's FW190 production. Results were devastating and Gen Eaker called it, 'A classic example of precision bombing'.

After bombing their targets the three formations of B-17s regrouped and headed for England. The flight back was long (10 hrs and 30 min) and tiring. When they got back to England some groups had to let down by squadrons because of a heavy haze.

Marienburg had been the epitome of precision bombing, but the raid which followed on Sunday 10 October was an all-out area bombing raid on residential areas of Münster to deprive the Germans of its rail workers (practically all of them were based in Münster) and disrupt rail traffic which had to pass through to get to and from the Ruhr. Crews were told at briefing that their MPI would be Münster Cathedral. The news had the impact of a 1,000-pounder going off: some demurred, others cheered. A maximum effort was ordered with 264 B-17s from the 1st and 3rd Bomb Divisions being despatched on a direct route to Münster. Approximately 245 single-engined and 290 twin-engined fighters were expected to oppose the mission so the Fortresses were given a strong Thunderbolt escort while B-24s flew a diversionary sweep over the

North Sea. Aborts reduced the B-17 formations and German fighters wrought havoc among the remaining formations.

Altogether, some 30 B-17s were shot down, including 25 from the unlucky 13th Wing where the 100th lost 12 Fortresses. In all, 88 American bombers were lost on three successive days from October 8-10 1943. It is staggering to note that in the same period the 100th Bomb Group alone had lost 20 B-17s.

Despite the round-the-clock bombing of aircraft factories and component plants, British and American Intelligence sources estimated that the Luftwaffe had a first-line strength of between 1,525 and 1,100 single and twin-engined fighters respectively (actually, the Luftwaffe had 1,646 single and twin-engined fighters). Eaker decided to send 291 B-17s to the ball-bearing plants at Schweinfurt on 14 October in the hope that VIII Bomber Command could deliver a single, decisive blow to the German aircraft industry and stem the flow of fighters to Luftwaffe units.

On 17 August 1943 the 8th had failed to knock out the plants completely and had lost 60 Fortresses in the attempt. It had been a disaster and the lesson was not lost on the young B-17 crews. They knew that despite escorting RAF and 8th Air Force fighter forces, 370 miles of the 923 mile round trip would be without friendly fighter cover.

Brig-Gen Anderson, CO of VIII Bomber Command, and his senior staff officers at High Wycombe, were informed that good weather was expected for the morrow. It was the signal for Anderson to alert his three bomb divisions throughout eastern England and the spark that sent ground crews out to their waiting Liberators and Fortresses to prepare them for Mission 115 – Schweinfurt.

During the evening of 13 October and the early hours of 14 October, all the necessary information for the raid was teletaped to all 8th Air Force bases. At fog-shrouded bases throughout East Anglia, flight crews were awakened early for briefings. At nearly all the briefing rooms the pulling of the curtain covering the wall map shocked the aircrews into silence. Crewmen who had flown only a few missions noticed that even the veteran crews appeared to be in a state of shock. There were few who did not at least have 'butterflies' in their stomachs despite some officers' platitudes that Schweinfurt was going to be a 'milk run'. Briefing Officers spoke of routes

where the flak was minimum, areas where fighters were not expected and spoke in glowing terms of the friendly fighter cover but the majority of crews were not fooled, as 2/Lt Roy G. Davidson at Bury St Edmunds (Rougham), recalls:

'When the covers were drawn on the route map, it showed that the fighter escort only went a short way with us to the target. We would have a long way from France onwards without fighter cover and on the way back too. We knew that we were in for a pretty rough time but we had no idea just how rough it was going to be.

'We had not been on the first Schweinfurt raid and didn't realise how bad Schweinfurt was. Despite this I really looked forward to the mission because I thought the accomplishment would be great. It never crossed the minds of the crew that we would not complete our 25 missions. A telegram was read out telling us that this was one of the most important missions of the war. When we had knocked out the ball-bearing plants the war would come to a halt. We felt we were really going to contribute a lot towards winning the war.'

Roy Davidson's engineer, Fred Krueger, declined the B-17 assigned to the crew (this ship, 42-3453, was flown on the Schweinfurt raid by Lt Silas Nettles' crew in the 96th Bomb Group and a windmilling engine contributed to their demise near the IP) and Davidson was allocated *Wolf Pack* instead. The 333rd Bomb Squadron was used at Rougham as a fill-in squadron. This meant that crews were usually given the tail-end positions as Davidson confirms. 'I was flying in the low squadron as last man – the most vulnerable spot in the entire formation. But we felt safe because even though we were the last 'plane in a string of over 200 bombers, there were going to be a whole lot of Liberators following right behind us. This would really put us right in the middle of the whole string which seemed to be a pretty good spot to be in.'

General Anderson had hoped to send 460 B-17s and B-24s into Germany in three task forces; the Fortress groups of the 1st and 3rd Bomb Division flying 30 miles apart while the 60 Liberators of the 2nd Bomb Division brought up the rear, flying to the south on a parallel course to the B-17s. Unfortunately, the unpredictable weather intervened before take-off and effectively ended the Liberators' participation in the mission.

The 94th Bomb Group, part of the 4th

Combat Wing, also had difficulty in forming. Maj Charles Birdsall led the 24 B-17s of the 94th off from Rougham and soon disappeared into cloud at only 2,000 ft. Crews cursed the weather forecasters who had predicted cloud at 6,500 ft. Birdsall managed to get his B-17s into the correct slot in the wing formation and they headed for the coast.

The 3rd Bomb Division departed the coast of England over the Naze and headed for the Belgian coast. Soon there was an opportunity for the gunners to test-fire their .50 calibre machine-guns. In the waist section aboard Davidson's B-17, Claude Page and Arthur Howell fired off a few rounds. Page had asked Davidson to keep the $600 he had won at a crap game. He was afraid to go to bed with all this money. Page had promised himself 'I'll send it home tomorrow'.

The 3rd Bomb Division crossed the coast of Belgium near Knocke at 1255 hr and proceeded on a converging course with the 1st Bomb Division towards Aachen. The escorting P-47 Thunderbolts departed and the Fortresses carried on alone to Schweinfurt. 'Gus' Mencow, navigator aboard *Betty Boop, the Pistol Packing Mama,* in the 570th Bomb Squadron, 390th Bomb Group, piloted by Lt Jim 'Rally' Geary, recalls:

'We were leading the high squadron, with Bob Brown's crew of the 571st flying group lead. As our fighter escort left us everyone sensed that we were in for a tough mission. The German fighter attacks came sporadically, mostly in waves, and it soon developed into a running battle extending for hundreds of miles across the skies of Europe. Although we were having it tough, it seemed that the 1st Bomb Division was really getting the brunt of the attacks in their formations well ahead of us.'

Most of the 1st Bomb Division groups were torn to shreds in the ensuing battles with the Luftwaffe en-route to the target area, but the 3rd Division groups came through relatively unscathed. The fighter escorts did their best but bomber losses before the target were high. Altogether, some 300 Messerschmitt Bf109 and Focke-Wulf 190s, 40 Pf110s and about 30 Junkers Ju88 night fighters were involved. By the time it entered the target area the 1st Bomb Division had lost 36 bombers and 20 had turned back. The 3rd Division had lost only two bombers. A total combined force of 227 B-17s bombed Schweinfurt. The 1st Division bombed first, followed by the 3rd Division groups.

The 45th Combat Wing of the 3rd Division crossed Schweinfurt and dropped its bombs. The 4th Wing was the second wing to cross Schweinfurt and they headed for the VKF plant. Roy Davidson recalls:

'My position in the group formation as "tail end charlie" really put us in the centre of the whole shooting match. We went into the target amid very heavy flak and fighter attacks. The fighters continued to attack us right through to the target area. They even flew through their own flak with no let up at all. But we were able to fight them off all the way to the target and out. Carl F "Hoot" Gibson, the ball turret gunner, shot down a Bf109 and the boys were really excited about this. But pretty soon the fighters came in thick and fast and everyone was getting to do a lot of shooting. By the time the fight was over I think most of the gunners aboard were out of ammunition. Fred Krueger, in the top turret, ran out and never did get to reload.'

'Gus' Mencow in the 390th formation recalls:

'As we neared the Initial Point the target came in to view and we started to peel off by groups to begin the bomb run. The sky over Schweinfurt was an awesome sight, with the black bursts of flak, and here and there a ball of fire where a B-17 was hit.

' "Mac" McCarthy, the bombardier, looked back at me and from the look in his eyes over the oxygen mask I knew he was experiencing the same feeling of apprehension that I had. Suddenly, the look changed dramatically in his eyes and a twinkle appeared. I knew he was grinning under his mask. He reached for the microphone switch and said, "Bombardier to pilot – Hey Geary, is there any way you can back up this crate? I think that would be our best way out of here!" "Will you shut up, McCarthy and get ready to drop your bombs," said Geary. I could tell from the sound of his voice he was having difficulty to keep from laughing! God bless Mac. I knew then that if anything was going to happen over Schweinfurt at least we would all die in a happy mood.'

(Geary's crew came through unscathed).

It was after the target that the 3rd Bomb Division met its stiffest opposition. Davidson recalls:

'We had gone into the target, dropped our bombs and had started back out, when the fighters made passes through the middle of the formation. They continued to attack the last group *(385th)* until they ran out of fuel and were forced to seek land. Maybe the fighters would make one pass at one group and then keep zigzagging through the formation until they got to the last group where they would continue attacking.

'We outfought the fighters but Richard Mungenast, the tail gunner, shouted that a Bf110 behind us out of range was firing something at us and it was leaving

a black stream of smoke. We didn't know what it was
at the time but we discovered later that it was a rocket.
We had never been told of the existence of such a
device. The first shot burst way behind us. The Bf110
pulled up closer and fired another one. It still burst
short.

'Mungenast cried out, "Here comes another black
stream of smoke!" Right after that the missile exploded
right under our plane. It felt as if we were on an elevator; it lifted us up and did all kinds of damage. The
plane felt as it if was trying to turn a loop. Chochester
and I had to apply full forward pressure with both
hands and our knees on the wheels to keep the plane
straight and level. Right after the explosion there was
an awful lot of excitement on board. All the men in
the back of the plane were wounded and screams of,
"I'm hit, I'm hit!" filled the intercom. I presume the
explosion had also knocked off or damaged the flaps.
The cable must have been broken because I could not
adjust the trim tabs.'

Davidson's crew continued fighting the wheels
but two engines were gone (one refused to
feather and began windmilling) and they were on
fire. Another bomb group was sighted and
Davidson pulled up under them but he was
unable to keep up with them. The oxygen supply
was exhausted and Carl Gibson had a bad bullet
wound in his knee. Louis W. Koth, the radio
operator, had lost an arm. Both the waist gunners and Louis Koth baled out. With no oxygen
for the wounded, Davidson hit the deck and flew
just above a layer of thick haze. Davidson continues:

'It wasn't long before we had a Bf109 off each wing
about 50 yards out. We had no ammunition left and
anyway, three men had baled out and Mungenast was
wounded. The only guns we had left were in the nose.
The 109s were so close we could distinguish the pilots'
facial features. I figured they were talking to each other
to decide who would finish us off. They took it in turns
to shoot at us, turning in directly from 3 o'clock.
Whenever I saw his wings light up with cannon fire
I took evasive action and turned towards him, like I
was trying to ram him. Somehow or other, neither
fighter succeeded in hitting us. I'll never know how
in the world they missed us at such short range. We
really gave it violent evasive action during each of their
two or three passes and the manoeuvring worked.'

Eventually, Davidson's third engine cut out and
he was forced to make a wheels-up landing in
a cow pasture near the village of La Chappele-
sur-Orbais. Guns protruding from the ball turret
caused the B-17 to crack in the centre and bent
the middle and tail sections upwards. Davidson
recalls:

'We hit some cows with a little thud but it did not
slow the plane up. (The French were pleased because
they had more beef on the black market the following
day than since the war started!) We skidded along the
field and we were still going quite fast when we hit
the trees on the other side and came to an abrupt halt.
Everyone was alright because most of the crew had
time to put their seats back and get into their crash
positions.

'We scrambled out and the two Bf109s made a
couple of victory rolls on their passes over us. One of
the German pilots delighted in making a couple of
strafing runs. Fortunately, none of the crew was hit.
We got the wounded out and gave Gibson a shot of
morphine since he couldn't walk.'

The crew scattered in groups of twos and threes
and started walking. Krueger, Mungenast and
Davidson headed in one direction while Charlie
Breuer, the bombardier, and Stan Chochester,
headed in another. Al Faudie took off on his
own. It was the last they all saw of one another.'
(Faudie made contact with the French Underground and lived with them for almost a year
and-a-half until liberation. Louis Koth, Claude
Page, Arthur Howell and Carl Gibson were all
captured and though they spent some time in
German Lazarets [POW hospitals], all survived
the war). Chochester and Breuer made contact
with the French Underground and a few weeks
later were flown back to England aboard an RAF
Lysander. Both men were back in England about
35 days from the time they were shot down.
Davidson and Krueger also made contact with
the French Underground but were later captured
during an unsuccessful attempt to cross the
Channel and were sent to Stalag Luft III.

Meanwhile, the surviving B-17s headed for the
coast. At 1640 hr the 1st Division crossed the
Channel coast and was followed, just 5 minutes
later, by the 3rd Division. To make matters
worse the Fortresses' return to England was hampered by the same soupy weather that had
dodged their departure. In all, the 1st Division
had lost 45 Fortresses on the raid. The 305th
Bomb Group at Chelveston had suffered the
worst casualties, losing 16 of its 18 B-17s which
had taken off that morning. Second highest loss
in the division went to the 306th Bomb Group
with 10. The 92nd Bomb Group had lost six and
a seventh was written off in a crash-landing at
Aldermaston. The 379th and 384th Bomb
Groups had each lost six B-17s in combat and
three crews from the latter group had to abandon their aircraft over England, making nine in

all. The 303rd Bomb Group lost two aircraft, including one which crashlanded after the crew had baled out near Riseley. The 91st, 351st and 381st Bomb Groups each lost one B-17.

The 3rd Division had lost 15 aircraft. The 96th had lost seven, including Lt Silas Nettles' aircraft, which was flying in the 100th Bomb Group formation. His aircraft had been the last B-17 over the target. The 94th lost six Fortresses and the 95th and 390th each lost one B-17. The 100th, 385th and 388th Bomb Groups suffered no losses. Sixty Fortresses (or 19 per cent of its force) and 600 men had been lost. Of the 231 bombers that returned to England 142 were damaged and another five fatal casualties and 43 wounded crewmen were removed from the aircraft. Five B-17s had crashed in England as a result of their battle-damaged condition and 12 more were destroyed in crashlandings, or so

badly damaged that they had to be written off.

The losses were softened by press proclamations that 104 enemy fighters had been shot down. The claims were whittled down to 99 – or 33 per cent loss – but, according to official German records, only 50 fighters were lost. Despite this, the press and the planners alike were carried away on a tidal wave of optimism. Even the British Chief of the Air Staff, Air Marshal Sir Charles Portal said, 'The Schweinfurt raid may well go down in history as one of the decisive air actions of the war and it may prove to have saved countless lives by depriving the enemy of a great part of his means of resistance'. Later, Brig-Gen Orvil Anderson publicly stated, 'The entire works are now inactive. It may be possible for the Germans eventually to restore 25 per cent of normal capacity, but even that will require some time.'

CHAPTER 5

Strategic Air Force

ETO – England and Italy: October 1943 – August 1944

In October 1943 the 9th Air Force was transferred from North Africa to England in order to build up a tactical air force for the invasion of Europe planned for the following spring. Gen Henry H. Arnold, meanwhile, had proposed a plan to split the 12th Air Force in two to create a strategic air force in the Mediterranean, leaving the remaining half of the 12th as a tactical organization. The possibility of a strategic air force based in southern Italy would effectively place Austria, Germany and eastern Europe – previously out of range of the 8th Air Force – within easy reach. Italy also offered potentially better weather conditions than Britain.

Arnold's plan was accepted and on 1 November 1943 the 15th Air Force was officially activated with HQ at Tunis. The 12th Air Force relinquished its two B-24 groups and four groups of B-17s (about 210 aircraft) of the 5th Wing, and these formed the operational element of the 15th Air Force.

Fortress Movements
15th Air Force, Italy: November 1943–April 1944

Date	Group	Remarks
November 1943	2nd Bomb Group	Assigned 15th Air Force
	97th Bomb Group	Assigned 15th Air Force
	99th Bomb Group	Assigned 15th Air Force
	301st Bomb Group	Assigned 15th Air Force
16 March 1943	463rd Bomb Group	Assigned 15th Air Force
12 April 1944	483rd Bomb Group	Assigned 15th Air Force

On 1 November 1943 Fortresses of the 5th Bomb Wing, operating from airfields in Tunisia, attacked the Spezia naval base and the Vezzano railway bridge in Italy. The 97th Bomb Group was among those which participated in this, the first 15th Air Force bombing raid of the war. The Group had also been on the first 8th Air Force mission from England on 17 August 1942 and the 12th's on 16 November 1942.

One of the 97th Bomb Group pilots, who had been with the group since May 1943 and had taken part in the 12th Air Force bombing campaign in North Africa and then raids on Italy, was Ped G. Magness in the 341st Squadron. These raids were far from being 'milk runs' and supplies and munitions were slow to filter through, as Magness recalls:

'Sometimes we have to wait on the ground until the bombs came in because the Germans were sinking our ships.' On one occasion he was shot down. 'On a mission to Bologna the flak was extremely heavy. We had a devil of a battle. The Germans lost about 65 fighters and the USAAF, about 35 fighters. We had two engines out and had to ditch in the Mediterranean.'

A French newspaperman was flying with Magness' crew. After ditching the B-17 the ten-man crew and the reporter had to swim about 400 yds to the coast of Sardinia, which had just been vacated by the Germans. The reporter could not swim and the crew could not get their rubber dinghy out of the aircraft. A British one-man raft floated out of the aircraft and the reporter was put in it. The bombardier dived 30 ft down to destroy the Norden bombsight. Everyone survived, although the crew nearly starved on Sardinia until they were rescued. The 12th Air Force began moving units to Sardinia in October 1943.

Magness had another close shave on 19 October 1943 during a raid on the airfield at Athens when an 88 mm shell from a German anti-aircraft gun had crashed through the nose of his B-17. The shell, which had a time fuse, fortunately went through the nose without exploding but it caused the B-17's ammunition to explode.

'The navigator was badly hit and the bombardier was trying to help him and keep him from falling out of the bottom of the aircraft. The radio operator also was badly injured. He was begging for help but we were at 30,000 ft and couldn't go help him.' After they got out of enemy territory Magness decided to land on Sicily because the injured crew members would have bled to death before they reached Africa. Magness concludes, 'The anti-aircraft fire was so accurate that once we got home the airplane was all to pieces. They junked it.'

On 2 November, 74 B-17s of the 15th Air Force struck at Wiener Neustadt, losing six For-

B-17s of the 94th Bomb Group, 8th Air Force, head for Munster on 11 November 1943. B-17G-15-DL 42-37852 is The Grand Old Lady. *(Cliff Hatcher.)*

tresses. Further raids were made by the 15th Air Force B-17s on targets in Italy and France before bad weather in November-December restricted more raids. On 4 January 1944 B-17s of the 8th Air Force flew their last mission under the auspices of VIII Bomber Command. It was decided to embrace both the 8th and 15th Air Force in Italy in a new HQ called US Strategic Air Forces, Europe (USSTAF – the overall USAAF command organization in Europe) at Bushey Hall, Teddington, Middlesex, previously HQ 8th Air Force. Gen Carl 'Tooey' Spaatz returned to England to command the new organization while Maj-Gen James H. Doolittle took over the 8th Air Force. Maj-Gen Nathan F. Twining took command of the 15th Air Force while Lt-Gen Ira C. Eaker moved to the Mediterranean theatre to take command of the

new MAAF (Mediterranean Allied Air Forces).

Spaatz and Doolittle's plan was to use the US Strategic Air Forces in a series of co-ordinated raids on the German aircraft industry at the earliest possible date, codenamed Operation 'Argument' and supported by RAF night bombing. However, the winter weather caused a series of postponements and the bombers were despatched to V1 rocket sites in northern France. In Italy, meanwhile, the B-17s carried out raids on Luftwaffe bases in southern France and Italy from 21 January onwards, following the Anzio landings south of Rome.

Good weather was predicted for the week 20-25 February and so Operation 'Argument', which quickly became known as 'Big Week', began in earnest. The opening shots were fired by the RAF which bombed Leipzig on the night

B-17F-95-BO 42-30267 Hustlin' Huzzy *of the 341st Bomb Squadron, 97th Bomb Group, 15th Air Force, en route to Sofia, Bulgaria, on 10 January 1944. The old circle, tall 'T' of the 2nd Bomb Group's 49th Squadron, and unit markings, can still be seen.* (USAF.)

of 19/20 February. Next day the 8th put up some 1,028 B-17s and B-24s and 832 fighters while the RAF provided 16 squadrons of Mustangs and Spitfires. In all, 12 aircraft plants were attacked on 20 February, with the B-17s of the 1st going to Leipzig, Bernburg and Oschersleben while the unescorted 3rd Division bombed the FW190 plant at Tutow and the He111 plant at Rostock. The 15th Air Force, which was still committed to supporting the Anzio operation, could only spare 126 B-17s. Bad icing conditions over the Alps forced them to abort en-route to the Messerschmitt assembly plant at Regensburg-Obertraubling.

The raids caused such widespread damage that it led Speer to order the immediate dispersal of the German aircraft industry to safer parts of the Reich. The 8th lost 25 bombers and four fighters. Three Medals of Honor (two posthumously) were awarded to B-17 crewmen – the only time

in the 8th's history that more than one was issued on one day. The first was awarded to Lt William R. Lawley in the 305th Bomb Group which raided Brunswick. A frozen mechanism had prevented the bombs being released. After the target, head-on fighter passes raked the cockpit of the B-17, killing the co-pilot and wounding eight of the crew, including Lawley who was badly hit in the face. An engine was set on fire and the B-17 fell away out of control. Incredibly, Lawley got the dead co-pilot off the controls with his right arm while bringing the aircraft out of its dive with his left.

Two gunners were too badly wounded to bail out so the crew agreed to carry on. The engine fire was extinguished but another fighter attack deprived Lawley of another engine until the fire was put out. In the meantime the bombardier, Harry G. Mason, managed to salvo the bombs. Mason and Lawley took it in turns to fly the

Bombs fall from B-17s of the 452nd BG on the Ju88 plant at Romilly, 6 February 1944. (Sam Young.)

B-17 to England, where one engine died of fuel starvation. As Lawley made his approach to Redhill, the first available airfield, another engine burst into flames but he put down safely on the one remaining engine.

Two other Medals of Honor were won this day. A cannon shell entered the cockpit of *Mizpah*, a B-17 in the 351st Bomb Group, killing the co-pilot and rendering the pilot unconscious. The radio-operator was also wounded and the bomber suffered severe damage. The bombardier decided that *Mizpah* was finished and bailed out. Undeterred, Sgt Archie Mathies left his ball-turret and took over the controls. Mathies elected to fly *Mizpah* back to England. At times the cold became so intense because of a smashed windscreen that Walter Truemper, the navigator, and the others, took it in turns at the controls. When Polebrook was reached the crew bailed out but Mathies and Truemper elected to remain aboard with the badly wounded pilot.

Colonel Romig, the 351st Bomb Group CO, took off in another B-17 and tried to radio landing instructions to Mathies. Unfortunately, he failed to make radio contact and visual directions were impossible because *Mizpah* was flying too erratically to allow Romig to get in closer. Romig told Mathies to fly the bomber towards the sea and bail out. Mathies and Truemper refused to leave their pilot and tried to land. Mathies was too high on his first and second attempts. On the third approach the B-17 stalled and crashed, killing both Mathies and Truemper. The pilot died later. Mathies and Truemper were posthumously awarded the Medal of Honor.

Next day 924 bombers and 679 fighters of the 8th Air Force set out for the two M.I.A.G aircraft factories at Brunswick and other targets. The 15th was grounded by bad weather in the Foggia area. H$_2$X blind bombing equipment was used at Brunswick when heavy cloud prevented visual bombing and some groups bombed targets of opportunity. This time the 8th lost 19 bombers and five fighters but claimed 60 German fighters shot down.

On 22 February it was intended that the 15th Air Force strike at Regensburg while the 8th struck at other targets in the Reich including Gotha and Schweinfurt. The majority of the 8th's bomb groups were forced to abort because of bad weather over England but still lost a staggering 41 bombers. Some 65 B-17s of the 15th Air Force were despatched to the Messerschmitt component plant at Regensburg-Prufening. Five B-17s were shot down.

On 23 February bad weather kept the 8th Air Force heavies on the ground while the 15th bombed Steyr in Austria. Next day the 15th returned to Steyr when its B-17s, led by the 97th Bomb Group, set out again for the Steyr-Daimler-Puch aircraft plant. Despite a heavy escort of P-38s and P-47s, rocket-firing Bf110s and single-engined fighters succeeded in shooting down 10 B-17s in the 2nd Bomb Group, bringing up the rear, before the target was reached. The attacks continued after the target was bombed and a further four 2nd Bomb Group B-17s were shot down. Two more B-17s were also brought down during the onslaught. Another, smaller force, of 27 B-17s, which had become separated from the main force, bombed the oil refinery and torpedo works at Fiume for the loss of only one B-17.

Meanwhile, in England, Doolittle had despatched 867 bombers to a wide range of targets in Germany. The 1st Division attacked Schweinfurt, losing 11 B-17s, while the 3rd Division struck at targets on the Baltic coast without any loss.

Despite the losses, on the 25th the USSTAF despatched some 1,154 bombers and 1,000 fighters to aircraft plants, ball bearing works and components factories throughout the Reich. The 1st Bomb Division heavily damaged the Messerschmitt experimental and assembly plants at Augsburg, and the VFK ball bearing plants at Stuttgart were also hit.

Very considerable damage was caused to the Bf109 plants at Regensburg-Prufening by the 3rd Bomb Division and 149 bombers of the 15th Air Force. Some 46 B-17s were despatched from Italy, led by a valiant 10 Fortresses from the decimated 2nd Bomb Group. However, 10 of the 31 B-17s of the 301st Bomb Group were forced to return shortly after take-off, leaving only 36 B-17s, which were un-escorted, to continue to the target with the Liberators. Attacks by the Luftwaffe began near Fiume and continued to the target. For an hour and-a-half, the Luftwaffe made repeated and incessant attacks on the B-17s, stopping only briefly when heavy flak bracketed the bombers on the bomb run over Regensburg. The 21 B-17s of the 301st bore the brunt of the attacks and lost 11 Fortresses shot down.

The 8th arrived over Regensburg an hour later

and met only token fighter opposition. Bombing by the 8th and 15th Air Forces was highly effective and output was severely reduced for four months following the raids. Despite total losses during 'Big Week' of some 226 bombers, Spaatz and Doolittle believed the USSTAF had dealt the German aircraft industry a really severe blow. However, the destruction was not as great as at first thought.

On 2 March the B-17s of the 5th Wing returned to its support role for the beleaguered troops at Anzio. Next day the Fortresses bombed marshalling yards in Rome while the 8th failed to pierce the bad weather over England and bomb the other Axis capital of Berlin. On 4 March the 8th tried again but only the 95th and 100th Bomb Groups managed to drop the first American bombs on 'Big-B'.

On 6 March the 8th despatched 730 heavies and almost 800 escort fighters to targets in Berlin. A ball-bearing plant at Erkner in the suburbs of Berlin, the Robert Bosch Electrical Equipment factory and the Daimler-Benz engine factory at Genshagen were all bombed. The American gunners claimed over 170 German fighters destroyed but the 8th lost a record 63 bombers with a further 102 seriously damaged, and 11 fighters.

On 8 March all three divisions of the 8th Air Force contributed 600 bombers and 200 escort fighters in the raid on the VKF ball-bearing plant at Erkner. The leading 3rd Division received the worst of the fighter attacks and lost 37 Fortresses. Next day the Luftwaffe was notable for its absence but nine bombers were lost to flak as the 8th attempted to bomb Berlin through thick cloud. Altogether, the 8th Air Force dropped 4,800 tons of high explosive on Berlin during five raids in March 1944.

Meanwhile the 15th Air Force, which had been grounded because of bad weather, took off on 15 March to bomb Monte Cassino which was

Above: T/Sgt Roy Baker, the chief engineer and top turret gunner, and another crewmember (white blobs in the radio room) in C. P. Lombard's crew of the 99th Bomb Group, 15th Air Force, prepare to jump from their stricken B-17 over northern Italy on 18 March 1944. (via Frank Thomas.)

Right: T/Sgt Roy Baker, following his miraculous escape on 18 March. Baker was on his 44th mission and was listed MIA for five months, but eventually rejoined his Bomb Group. (via Frank Thomas.)

Left: Bombs from 452nd Bomb Group, 8th Air Force B-17s are dropped on the Ju88 aircraft factories at Augsburg on 16 March 1944. (USAF.)

Above: B-17s of the 452nd Bomb Group, 8th Air Force, en route to Bordeaux on 22 March 1944. (Sam Young.)

Below: B-17G-70-BO 42-37329 of the 334th Bomb Squadron, 95th Bomb Group, piloted by Lt James Redd, bellied in at Diepoldsau near the Swiss-German border on 16 March 1944. The aircraft was later scrapped. (Hans-Heiri Stapfer.)

proving an obstacle for the ground troops attempting to pierce the Gustav Line. The monastery atop the mountain was reduced to rubble by the B-17s and supporting bombers but the ground troops remained bogged down. Three days later 592 bombers and fighters, the largest 15th Air Force bomber formation hitherto despatched, bombed Luftwaffe airfields in the Undine area of Italy with excellent results. On 30 March 114 B-17s bombed the Sofia marshalling yards. The Fortress ranks were swelled by the addition of the 463rd Bomb Groups based at

Above: B-17G-45-BO 42-97083 of the 782nd Bomb Squadron, 452nd Bomb Group, crash-landed on the shore of the Baltic on the mission to Rostock on 11 April 1944. The crew were made PoWs. (Hans-Heiri Stapfer.)

Right: B-17G-35-BO 42-32073, of the 337th Bomb Squadron, 96th Bomb Group, which William Cooper Potter landed at Dubendorf, Switzerland, on 13 April 1944 after the raid on the Messerschmitt factory at Augsburg. The aircraft was flown back to Burtonwood, England, on 8 September 1945. (Hans-Heiri Stapfer.)

Below: B-17G-45-BO 42-97212 of the 96th Bomb Group piloted by Lt Gillespie, seeks refuge at Malmo, Sweden, shadowed by a Swedish Air Force J9 fighter after the mission to Rostock on 11 April 1944. In all, nine B-17s landed in Sweden this day and Gillespie's was one of 11 lost to the 96th Bomb Group. (USAF.)

Celone near Foggia. On 12 April the sixth and final B-17 group, the 483rd, joined the 5th Bomb Wing in Italy.

By early April The Red Army had overrun German occupied territory in the Crimea and the Ukraine and had made inroads into Rumania. German relief supplies could only be transported to the front lines by using the Hungarian and Rumanian rail network. On 2 April the 15th Air Force carried out the first of 26 attacks on rail and transportation centres in the Balkans. Major marshalling yards at Bucharest, Budapest, Belgrade and Milan and others, were all hit by the 15th Air Force. On 23 April 171 B-17s led by 36 Fortresses of the 99th Bomb Group, attacked the Bf109 plant at Wiener-Neustadt again. Thirty-one of the 99th Bomb Group's B-17s were damaged by flak and fighter attacks. Two 15th Air Force B-17s were shot down. One of them belonged to the 97th Bomb Group.

The bombardier, Albert G. Willing, recalls.

'The outboard right engine caught on fire and that spread to the wing. Then the engine started to run away. The pilot told us we could bail out but he pointed out that we were only two minutes from bombs away. All the crewmen checked in and said they would stay aboard. We got off our bombs but things were still hairy. We fell out of formation and started losing altitude. The fire was going strong and it felt like the engine would shake us to pieces. We were over Yugoslavia when the pilot told us to get out.

'I'd left the bomb bay doors open and went back to get the enlisted men out. After the last one, I jumped too. Just after that the pilot and co-pilot got things more under control and they and the naviga-

tor and flight engineer, flew that bird all the way back to base in Italy.'

Willing and the five others who bailed out were picked up by Yugoslavian partisans and a few weeks later they were flown back to Italy in a C-47.

On 24 April five B-17s in the 301st Bomb Group equipped with Azon remotely guided bombs made the first of two such attacks on the Ancona-Rimini railway line. A second raid was made on the same railway on 29 April.

In April 1944 overall command of the Combined Bomber Offensive had officially passed to Gen Dwight D. Eisenhower, newly appointed Supreme Allied Commander, Allied Expeditionary Forces (SHAEF). Eisenhower immediately ordered all-out attacks on German oil production centres as part of the overall plan for the invasion of Europe, scheduled for the summer of 1944. The 15th Air Force had inadvertently opened the offensive on 5 April when some of the bombs dropped by 135 B-24s and 95 B-17s which were meant for the marshalling yards at Ploesti, cascaded onto the oil refineries nearby causing major damage and disruption. Thus began the oil offensive by the 15th Air Force and with it an all-out attempt to destroy the Ploesti complex, the largest centre in the Reich. Ploesti was bombed again on 15 and 24 April when 'incidental' damage was caused to the refineries. Four more heavy raids followed in May.

Attacks on oil and transportation targets, together with aircraft plants, remained the order of the day in the build up to Operation 'Overlord', the invasion of occupied France which was to take place in June 1944. In England, May Day marked the opening of a series of all-out attacks on the enemy's rail network in France and Belgium, when 1,328 bombers struck at targets in France and Belgium.

Ralph Reese, left waist gunner in Lt Fred Whitlinger's crew of the 731st Bomb Squadron, 452nd Bomb Group, recalls the Group's mission to V1 rocket installations at St. Omer.

'We were on our 11th mission in *Smoky Liz*. Everything was going well until we passed the IP, then another B-17 nearly collided with us. The pilots saw the other ship in time to avoid a collision, by diving the ship sharply for 100 ft. This sudden dive forced the bombs to fall from their shackles onto the bomb bay doors. Everything was thrown out of position and ammunition was thrown out of its cases. I rode as radio man and chaff was all over the radio room.

'We flew back to the Channel and James McLellan, the bombardier, put the pins back in the bombs. One bomb nose fuse was nearly off and a wire had shorted out near it. Everyone clutched at their 'chutes,

ready to jump as the fuse blew. Thank goodness the wire remained quiet. Then the bomb doors would not open electrically or manually. Finally, McLellan worked the doors open so the bombs fell out. Whitlinger said that if the doors had not opened he would have flown near the shore line and we would have bailed out.'

On 7 May, 1,000 8th Air Force heavies were despatched for the first time and two days later 772 bombers attacked transportation targets. On 11 May, 973 bombers bombed marshalling yards in Germany and the Low Countries. On 12 May the 8th Air Force was assigned oil targets at Brux, Bohlen, Leipzig, Merseburg, Lutzhendorf and Zeitz, while a smaller force was to attack the Fw190 repair depot at Zwickau. Some 900 bombers, escorted by over 875 fighters would fly a common course in trail to the Thuringen area where the bomb divisions would peel off and attack five targets: the big Leuna plant at Merseburg, 18 miles west of Leipzig; Lutzkendorf and Bohlen in the same general area; Zeitz, 25 miles southwest of Leipzig; and Brux, 42 miles

Smoke and fire pour from a 15th Air Force B-17 as it goes down over the marshalling yards at Ploesti, Rumania, on 5 May 1944. (USAF.)

northwest of Prague. This was the first time that the 8th had been assigned a target in Czechoslovakia although Brux had been bombed before by the 15th Air Force. Now it was the turn of the Fortress crews of the 3rd Bomb Division.

Ralph J. Munn, the ball turret gunner aboard *Lucky Lady* in the 731st Squadron of the 452nd Bomb Group at Deopham Green recalls:

'Brux was one of the days I happened to be with my original crew (I also flew spares for crews that were short of ball gunners). Dick Noble was our pilot. The briefing at 2 am should have been the message we had been expecting for a week or 10 days. When the map was pulled on the wall there was a hush over the entire room. The condition of our *Lucky Lady* was in no way airworthy or mechanically sound to make a trip of this distance. At best, even with extra fuel, it was the feeling of no return.'

Wilbur Richardson, a ball turret gunner in the 331st Bomb Squadron, 94th Bomb Group, was on his eighth mission. The pilot, John Moser, and the rest of the crew were unaware they would also by flying such a war weary B-17, until they taxied out at Bury St Edmunds.

'061, the "F" we were assigned, had been shot up, repaired, crash-landed and repaired again. This queen had seen her best days. It just didn't fly that well. This all became apparent as we started our roll down the runway. We were at maximum load and 061 just barely got off. John Moser used up all of the runway and I saw green grass as we just lifted off in time. Close? Shades of Lindergh. We were off for what was to prove an historic operation.'

One by one the B-17s took off and completed their complicated group and wing assembly patterns. Manningtree was the final assembly point and crews carried on over the Channel in a bomber stream. The bombers crossed the enemy coast between Dunkirk and Ostend near the French-Belgian border. The 94th Bomb Group missed their rendezvous with the fighter escort. Wilbur Richardson explains the events that followed.

'We weren't long into Belgian airspace when all hell broke loose. The yellow-nosed "Abbeville Kids" and the German Air Force rose to the occasion. Upwards of 400 fighters attacked. In our area there were only six P-51s. Not much help with such odds. I watched

B-17s of the 15th Air Force attack the Schwechat oil refinery at Vienna, Austria, through thick flak. (USAF.)

as a '51 and '109 collided head-on.

'We flew eastwards towards our target area, fighting all the way. The fighters came from all directions – the tail as well as the effective nose-on attacks. In some cases there were 25-30 abreast and even attempts at ramming by using a wing so the pilot could bail out, as we later learned. Attacks were made from 12 o'clock, circled and charged from 6 o'clock level so neither ball or top turret might get a line on them.

'As the upper and lower turrets could fire in all directions Bruton and I were kept busy twisting and turning constantly. The navigator, Les Ulvestad or the bombardier, Frank Sarno, called out "Bandits 10 o'clock low" or "Straight in at 12 o'clock". If I wasn't shooting to the rear, assisting the tail gunner, Gilbert Gabriel or some other direction, I'd swing forward ready to follow through coming from the nose. It was a busy time returning the fire of those fast-moving targets with winking flashes on the wings coming our way.'

While some groups like the 94th were hit hard others, like the 100th, escaped. Richard Wynn, the navigator in Lt Alexander Kinder's crew in the 418th Bomb Squadron, which was on its 14th mission, recalls.

'Our Squadron was at the tail-end of the 13th Combat

Wilbur Richardson.

Wing, which trailed the rest of the 8th. Our ship was the famed *Rosie's Riveters*, made famous by Robert Rosenthal, a legendary figure in the 100th. We inherited the ship from him when his crew finished its first tour. It was really either the second or third *Rosie's*.

'There were fierce fighter attacks on the front end of the formation with heavy counter attacks from our fighter cover. We saw it but were not engaged with fighters the entire way to the target, which was an unusual experience for the 100th Bomb Group.'

Wilbur Richardson continues: 'We were hit in the No. 1 engine. It lost a lot of oil and we had to feather it just prior to the target. It was a struggle to keep up with the group with bombs still aboard. The flak over the target was moderate, which incidentally, I almost welcomed because we had a brief respite from the fighters. We received some flak damage including the loss of some oxygen in my ball turret as well as some on the left side.'

Ralph Munn in the 452nd formation peered out from the close confines of his ball turret below *Lucky Lady* and watched the flak. 'As usual, the enemy was reluctant to attack until our escorts made the turn for home base. We had considerable action, mostly high level attacks down through the squadron, until just short of the target.'

Ralph Reese, who was flying left waist gun in *Smoky Liz* in the 452nd Bomb Group, recalls. 'Everything went smoothly until 15 min from the IP. Then we saw some 'planes on our wing go down in flames. To our delight, they were enemy planes being shot down by our P-47 fighter escorts. We saw one P-47 shoot down three enemy planes.' Ralph Munn continues:

'When we reached the IP the flak was a solid carpet. Up to this point we had not had a casualty outside of small to fist-size holes. I had always made it a practice to turn my turret to 12 o'clock when the bomb bay doors opened. Bruce dropped a salvo and at the same time Dick Noble turned into the downwind leg. We were hardly off the target when we took a direct hit in the bomb bay. I turned around to 6 o'clock to see what was happening. A fraction of a second later there was another very bad jolt. It took out the left inboard engine and knocked out my source of power, my electrical suit, boots and gloves. I was hit in the back and the turret took considerable damage. My guns and intercom were out. It was slippery in the turret. With the engine out we were an open invitation for the remaining fighters to attack.'

Richard Wynn, in the 100th Bomb Group, con-

B-17Gs of the 452nd Bomb Group, 8th Air Force, in formation. (USAF.)

tinues. 'The IP was due south of Brux. Our bomb run was almost due north and we made a hard left at the RP and returned to an intersection with our inboard flight path and followed it home. The weather was ideal, with small cumulus clouds and virtually no wind over the target.'

Ralph Reese in the same 452nd formation describes the flak. 'It was very heavy over the target and beyond. We saw one B-17 shot down and I saw 10 'chutes open and glide towards the ground. The group behind us [100th] was attacked by Bf109s, who stayed out of range and were able to reach our planes. We lost 14 ships out of our group.'

Richard Wynn in *Rosie's Riveters* in the 100th formation, was close behind the 452nd formation.

'Our wing hit the target in three waves. The first wave's target was the centre of the installation and by the time we got there, heavy smoke had risen to well over 10,000 ft. We encountered light flak over the target but observed some rocket-propelled anti-aircraft

fire. We were hit in the No 3 engine and lost oil pressure before the prop could be feathered. Cockpit procedure was complicated by the fact that a faulty flare from the lead ship deposited a heavy film of "guck" over the pilot's half of the windshield, putting the co-pilot in control of the ship. His visibility was also limited to some extent.

'With a windmilling prop and all of the drag it created, we were unable to keep up with the formation and became a single straggler on the way home with heavy fuel consumption on a very deep penetration. It is doubtful whether we could have made Britain. I did a fuel consumption problem after a while and had us running out of fuel about the time we would reach the Channel. It would have been interesting to see whether we could have made it or not. We expected fighter attacks and expected to get knocked down soon because, Holywood not withstanding, a single B-17 is mismatched against a flurry of fighters usually.

'We made it alone without any fighter cover all the way to a point a few miles east of the Rhine before six Me109s hit us from the rear. We got two of them for sure and had a probable, a third that was streaking for the ground with heavy smoke pouring out. The

B-17s of the 390th Bomb Group, 8th Air Force, in formation. (via Ian McLachlan.)

109s plastered us good, knocking out the controls and who knows what else. We bailed out and got out OK, were buzzed, but not fired upon in our 'chutes by the remaining 109s. We were captured immediately a few miles east of St. Goarshausen on the Rhine. Our tail gunner sustained the only serious injury, a bad laceration of his knee and calf; a really nasty and painful wound. Farmers with pitchforks and soldiers were literally waiting beneath for me to land. We spent almost a year in Stalag Luft III and I think almost all of us were picking flak fragments from our hides for weeks to come. My pilot and I managed to escape in April 1945 and make our way to contact with the 45th Division.'

Meanwhile *Lucky Lady* in the 452nd formation had also managed to reach Belgium. Ralph Munn continues:

'I did not see another fighter until we reached eastern Belgium. By this time Moody and Brush had manually cranked me out of my turret. I was bleeding but did not feel pain. About right here two fighters pulled up on our right wing very close. Dick called everyone to hold fire and prepare to jump. I later learned we were out of fuel and too much had been damaged to

make it back to the Channel. To my knowledge, the two fighters were the only ones in the area. One of the men in the waist pulled the emergency lever for the exit. The door was supposed to break away with the slipstream. Two men at a time took turns and had to beat it off with ammunition boxes but the frame did not give. We managed to beat the skin off enough that we could get through the opening with 'chutes on. I had made a fast trip up to the bomb bay to see if we could jump from there. No way; the keel girder was torn in several spots completely in two.

'When I got back to the waist Moody said, "Dick has called and to get ready to bail out". Within a matter of minutes we all evacuated the not so *Lucky Lady*. Surprisingly, it was a very orderly departure; no hesitations either. All of us had had enough for one day.

'The aircraft pancaked in on a hillside at Namur. The fighters stayed with the string of 'chutes. They flew among us. I cannot bring myself to believe that they were trying to spill the 'chutes. A couple of the crew members were down in a lush meadow. They made a couple of passes at them but they did not fire a shot.

'I was picked up immediately by the Underground

B-17F-30-VE 42-5885 Kipling's Error III *of the 96th Bomb Group which was lost over the Baltic on the Rostock mission on 11 April 1944.* (USAF.)

and stayed with them until I was captured. I was taken to Liège prison by the SS and later turned over to the Gestapo, remaining in solitary for 14 weeks. My head was bashed in, all my teeth were knocked out, my toes and fingers were broken and I was beaten to a pulp once, sometimes twice or three times a day. My testicles were the size of baseballs. They kept me naked throughout my stay in a four-by-six solitary cell with a handful of straw and a bucket.'

Munn was eventually sent to Stalag Luft IV at Gross Tychow in Poland where he remained until the end of the war.

Meanwhile, Wilbur Richardson's B-17F was fighting a grim survival battle.

'Soon after bombs away we endured the second half of the German fighter attacks. Twin-engined fighters joined the 109s and 190s. They sat out behind the bomber boxes in groups of 10-20 to fire rockets and cannon just out of effective range of our .50s. With the loss of oxygen we could not remain long in our group formation and we had to lose altitude relatively fast to make it with the oxygen we had left. Stragglers always attracted attention and on our way down 109s

and 190s came at us and we received many hits. Bruton claimed one fighter and the tail and I claimed two apiece.

'As I was in the rear firing at one below, another fighter hit the top turret with cannon fire. I saw the Plexiglass and Jim Bruton's empty special leather flak helmet go over the right horizontal stabiliser. I thought he had had it. I later learned that he lost consciousness for a few moments and came to on the deck before Lt Riley, the co-pilot, could get to him. Jim wasn't hurt. Just highly put out and using four letter words as he couldn't vent his anger by returning their fire. The shells that knocked him out of the turret damaged both .50s and were beyond repair. He was very lucky.

'We also took cannon damage from the rear. One hit the right elevator severely limiting its travel. Moser used the trim tab while Lt Riley exerted pressure on the yoke to maintain a little level flight. Riley locked his left arm around the control column and held on tightly to his left wrist with his right hand while he propped both feet against the instrument panel.

'The shell that damaged the elevator was followed immediately with another that went on through the elevator. The right waist window was hit and the left waist gun on the left side of the case and put the gun out of action. Ken Rasco was uninjured.

'We managed to join another group coming from another target until the fighter attacks let up. We couldn't get in too close because of the difficulty in flying level, but we did get some help in covering the attacks.

'By the time we reached the coast we were some-

Below: B-17Gs of the 96th Bomb Group, 388th Bomb Squadron. Nearest aircraft is B-17G-20-BO 42-31447 Cookie which was lost on 11 April 1944 on the mission to Rostock, and the furthest is B-17G-25-BO 42-31718 which was declared MIA on 12 May 1944 on the mission to Zwickau. (USAF.)

Above right: B-17G-30-BO 42-31889 of the 2nd Bomb Group (previously 'owned' by the 99th Bomb Group) is armed at Poltava by Soviet ground crews during a shuttle mission to Russia. This aircraft landed at Dubendorf, Switzerland, on 18 July 1944 after a raid on Memmingen, Germany. (Hans-Heiri Stapfer.)

Below right: B-17G-35-BO 42-32083 Flatbush Floosie of the 730th Bomb Squadron, 452nd Bomb Group, force-landed in Soviet-occupied territory near Stomniki, 20 miles from Krakow, Poland, in June 1944 during the shuttle flight from Poltava to Italy. (Hans-Heiri Stapfer.)

what behind and below our foster group. We kept losing altitude across the Channel and Moser thought we might need to land at the first opportunity. Riley felt he could hold on a little longer as we seemed to have enough altitude to make just one attempt. Being alone and late we were able to make a straight in approach. This was fortunate because we lost No 3 engine through fuel starvation as the '17 was nosed down and lined up with the runway.

''061 never flew again. It became a hangar queen to keep others in the air. For us, 11.45 hr in the air, according to John Moser. Because we were late and the crews at de-briefing had reported seeing us go down in trouble we were listed as MIA. We returned to our barracks just in time to stop our belongings from being picked up.'

(Altogether, the Luftwaffe shot down 46 bombers and 10 fighters on 12 May for the loss of almost 150 fighters). A week later, on 19 May, Moser's crew returned to combat status when the 8th Air Force went to Berlin. Wilbur Richardson recalls.

'This was our crew's first trip to Berlin although we had to abort twice on our first scheduled run to the "Big City" on 29 April. First, *Luscious Dutchess* had developed turbo problems and then the second ship had a runaway prop at altitude. Lt Chisum's crew that took our place were shot down.

'What made the 19 May trip memorable was that on the bomb run the ship above us just missed us with his bomb load. One of the 1,000-pounders fell behind No 3 engine (I saw this one go by my ball turret). I quickly followed it down only to see it hit the left stabilizer of *Miss Donna Mae* which was out of position below us. Apparently, it jammed the elevator in a down position. It lost altitude rapidly and began a steep dive. I watched in vain for 'chutes. None appeared. Others indicated that the Fort started to break up although I didn't see it.

'The flak was heavy and some fighters were in the area but Brux had been much worse. During some fighter attacks somewhere in the group a P-38 followed by an Me109 followed by a P-51 flew through a formation. A few seconds after this parade went through, some pilot on intercom said, "Look to Lockheed for Leadership". This broke the tension and radio silence with laughter.'

Throughout the rest of May 1944 both the 8th and 15th Air Forces continued making heavy raids on transportation and aircraft production targets: the 8th being used as a tactical weapon to destroy lines of communication in France and the Low Countries preparatory to the invasion of France; the 15th taking part in the bombing of railway networks in southeast Europe in sup-

B-17Gs of the 15th Air Force head for an enemy target on the return trip of their shuttle mission after taking off from Russia. (USAF.)

port of Russian military operations in Rumania. On 2 June the 15th Air Force flew its first 'shuttle' mission, codenamed 'Frantic', in support of Russian operations in the Balkans. Some 130 B-17s and 70 P-51 escorts landed at Poltava and Mirgorod in Russia after raids on marshalling yards in Debreczen, Hungary. The four B-17 groups flew one further mission from Russia before returning to Italy, bombing a Rumanian airfield enroute, on 11 June.

Although both the 8th and 15th Air Forces were heavily committed to pre-invasion attacks on enemy lines of communication, in an attempt to meet both transportation and oil objectives they continued to bomb both types of target right up until D-Day. Even the 15th Air Force was called upon in the campaign to render the French railway system useless. For three days, starting on 25 May, the B-17s and B-24s of the 15th Air Force bombed marshalling yards at Lyon, St. Etienne, Avignon, Nîmes and Marseilles.

By the time the Allies stepped ashore in Normandy on 6 June 1944, the German rail and road systems in France and the Low Countries were in a chaotic state and the sky overhead was clear of German fighters. Ralph Reese of the

452nd Bomb Group at Deopham Green recalls the events of D-Day.

'At briefing at 10.30 on 5 June we were told "this is it". There would be wave after wave of planes hitting the coast. Our target was coastal defences at Le Havre. We could not drop any bombs after 07.30 hr, the time the invasion was to start, for the danger of hitting our own troops. Every airfield in England had its lights on at 02.00 hr – the first time since England had been at war. We carried 38 100 lb demolition bombs but there was a solid overcast so we had to bomb using PFF. Bombs were away at 06.59 hr. We landed back at our base at 10.30 and our *Smoky Liz* was then loaded with 500 lb bombs for another mission within 24 hr.'

Altogether, the 8th flew 2,362 bomber sorties on D-Day, for the loss of only three bombers. The following day further missions were flown in support of the beach-head. Ralph Reese explains.

'We headed for a railway bridge at Nantes. As we crossed the Channel at the beach-head we saw many landing barges up on the beach. I had never seen so many boats before in my life. There were many gliders on the ground near the beach. Our target was well hit and there were few bursts of flak. After the bomb run, we started across the Channel and were flying at 1,000 ft. We passed over 13 ships in a convoy on their return to England for more troops and supplies. We passed over a harbour in southern England which was crowded with boats of every type.'

Post D-Day missions were flown to enemy airfields and troop concentrations in France and the Low Countries before the B-17s returned to oil targets again. On 20 June the Fortresses bombed the oil refinery at Magdeburg. Ralph Reese in the 452nd observed, 'The target was really flaming and smoking as we dropped our bombs and closed the bomb bay doors. Smoke reached as high as 5,000 ft. On the way back to the coast we saw many targets which had been bombed. They were burning and smoking and smoke reached as high as 10,000 ft.'

On 21 June the 8th flew its first of four 'Frantic' shuttle missions during June-September 1944. The 4th Combat Wing and a composite from the 3rd Division led the 8th to Berlin with the 1st and 2nd Divisions behind. After the target 163 Fortresses of the 13th and 45th Combat Wings flew on to landing fields at Poltava and Mirgorod in Russia while the rest of the force returned to East Anglia.

Wilbur Richardson was in the ball turret of *Kismet* in the 94th Bomb Group formation in the leading 4th Wing. He recalls:

'The flak was extremely heavy at the target and we were bounced around by the flak bursts. Holes were appearing everywhere. Just before bomb release John Moser, who was concerned about damage, asked all of us to assess the situation. At that moment I saw fuel in a large stream coming from No 2 turbo. "Feather No 2 quick," I yelled anxiously. My heart was pounding. It was done. Moser then asked why because his instruments had given no hint of danger. *Kismet* made it back to Bury St. Edmunds but was out of action for two days for repairs. One of the spars had received a direct hit. As we left the ship on the taxi-way with a flat tyre, I picked up my 'chute and found it riddled with holes.'

Meanwhile, the 'Frantic' force landed in Russia as scheduled but following the mission, 43 B-17s and several P-51s were destroyed in an audacious attack carried out by the Luftwaffe.

On 23 June the 15th Air Force returned to the Ploesti oilfields which they had last bombed on 6 June before switching to a string of raids on marshalling yards and oil targets in the Balkans. Some 139 bombers arrived over the refineries and dropped over 280 tons of bombs on the target. One of the six aircraft lost this day belonged to the 97th Bomb Group whose bombardier, 2/Lt David R. Kingsley, was posthumously awarded the Medal of Honor for his heroism after the B-17 was badly damaged by flak on the bomb run. Bf109s attacked and damaged the B-17 further, badly wounding the tail gunner. Kingsley gave aid to the tail gunner during which eight more 109s attacked and badly wounded the ball gunner, who was hit by 20 mm shell fragments.

When the order was given to bail out Kingsley immediately assisted the wounded gunners and gave the tail gunner his parachute harness when the gunner's could not be found. Kingsley aided the wounded men in bailing out of the doomed B-17 and stayed with the aircraft until

A B-17G of the 15th Air Force opens its bomb doors over an enemy target. (USAF.)

Above: HM Queen Elizabeth stops to ask Gen Jimmy Doolittle a question with the ground crew of Four of a Kind *present during a royal inspection at Kimbolton on 6 July 1944. (USAF.)*

Above right: B-17G-70-BO 43-37716 Five Grand – *the 5,000th B-17 built at Boeing-Seattle since Pearl Harbor – which flew 78 missions in the 96th Bomb Group. (USAF.)*

Right: A B-17G of the 99th Bomb Group flies over a column of smoke which rose to a height of 23,000 ft during a heavy raid on the Ploesti oilfields on 15 July 1944. (USAF.)

it crashed and burned. His body was later discovered in the wreckage.

Throughout the remainder of June and during July, oil refineries continued to be attacked by B-17s of the 8th and 15th Air Forces. On 9 July the 15th bombed Ploesti for the ninth time before returning to attacks on marshalling yards and then airfields and aircraft factories in Austria and Germany. On 13 July the 8th struck at Munich. For Wilbur Richardson and the rest of the crew of *Kismet* in the 94th, it was their 30th and final mission of their tour. Wilbur Richardson remembers the mission well.

'No. 30 would be remembered for just that, no matter what. Mine, again just a bit different. I was seriously wounded over the target by 155 mm flak. There was one very small hole in the wing and a very large one in my turret and me. Just the two. *Kismet* – fate.

'I stayed in the turret to count the bombs away. I thought I could stick it out longer but I was losing too much blood. I reported to the pilot and he said to get out and the waist gunner could take my place as bandits were reported in the area. The radio oper-

ator, Bernard Jeffers and the right waist, Milo Johnson, stripped off my flight clothes and new pants and shirt I had just purchased. I was treated and placed in a survival electric blanket bag. A short time later we were hit by fighters. I jumped up at the sound of shooting and grabbed the radio gun.

'I didn't have any intercom so I wasn't sure what the action was. I saw only one that I could shoot at from that position. After a bit I realized I had nothing but a T-shirt and shorts on and I was getting awfully cold so I hit the blanket to get warm.

'It was three and-a-half hours back to the base and I was still losing precious blood. We left the formation to get back to base as soon as possible. Another ship joined us as a waist gunner had an arm wound. Upon landing I was strapped on a stretcher, placed in an ambulance for a ride to an Army hospital. I didn't get back to the base for over five weeks. A nurse tossed away the large piece of flak that hit me.'

The 8th lost nine aircraft on 13 July. On occasion, losses could easily mount up on 15th Air Force operations, too. On 18 July, during a raid on Memmingen, Germany, the 483rd Bomb Group became separated from the rest of the 5th Wing and 14 of its B-17s were shot down in a running fight with 200 enemy fighters.

During the last week of July, Gen Doolittle carried out the first stage of his plan to convert all five Liberator groups of the 3rd Bomb Division (which had arrived in England in April) to the B-17. The 486th Bomb Group at Sudbury and the 487th Bomb Group at Lavenham, which formed the 92nd Wing, were taken off operations for conversion to the B-17. Between the end of August and mid-September the three B-24 groups of the 93rd Combat Wing, the 34th, 490th and 493rd Groups, also changed over to the B-17.

August followed the same operational pattern as July with 8th Air Force bombing raids on airfields in France and strategic targets in Germany. On 1 August, while heavy bomb groups struck at airfields in France, some B-17 groups again parachuted supplies to the French Underground movement. On 5 August the 8th returned to strategic targets with all-out raids on 11 separate centres in central Germany.

It was during a deep penetration raid into Germany that humanity returned for a brief moment and time stood still during a battle. Ped Magness of the 97th Bomb Group recalls.

'A B-17 was hit and on fire. The crew was bailing out. One of the crewmen pulled his ripcord too fast and his parachute caught in the bomb bay. The man was hanging and the wind was whipping him. He was doomed to a horrible death. We didn't want to shoot him. We tried to get away from him because we knew the B-17 was going to blow up. The war kind of hesitated because a 109 flew in the middle of the B-17s. Everybody quit shooting. They were amazed he had the guts enough to fly in the middle of us with all our guns pointed at him. He eased up to that boy in the parachute and shot him. Not another shot was fired. He peeled off and came out of there. They let him go and then the war started again.'

On 6 August B-17s struck at Berlin and oil and manufacturing centres in the Reich. This day, 76 Fortresses in the 95th and 390th Bomb Groups hit the Focke-Wulf plant at Rahmel in Poland. After the bombing the two groups flew on to their shuttle base at Mirgorod in Russia, scene of such devastation two months before. During their stay they flew a mission to the Trzebinia synthetic oil refinery and returned to Russia before flying to Italy on 8 August, bombing two Rumanian airfields en-route. Four days later they flew back to Britain on the last stage of their shuttle. Toulouse-Francaal airfield was bombed on the flight back over France. This third shuttle

Above: B-17G-20-VE 42-97555 of the 413th Bomb Squadron, 96th Bomb Group, which went MIA with the 100th Bomb Group on 28 July 1944. (Geoff Ward.)

Left: Button Nose B-17G of the 94th Bomb Group. (via Cliff Hall.)

Right: Royal Flush of the 100th Bomb Group, 8th Air Force, lies in a French field after being shot down on 11 August 1944 during a raid on the airfield at Villacoublay near Paris. (Charles H. Nekvasil.)

by the 8th Air Force proved more successful than the disastrous shuttle of June 1944 with not a single Fortress being lost.

Meanwhile, on 11 August, the 8th raided airfield targets in France again. Villacoublay airfield near Paris was the target for the B-17s of the 13th Bomb Wing. The air raid sirens sounded over Paris as the 54-ship formation flew overhead, spreading as the pilots jockeyed for bombing position. At 1214 hr a furious anti-aircraft fire broke out as the Germans put up a box barrage of 88 mm shells which filled the airspace nearly 4,000 ft deep. Shortly after bombs away, while the last of the anti-personnel fragmentation bombs left the bomb bays, *Royal Flush* in the 100th Bomb Group formation was hit. The first shell hit the No 3 engine. The second and third shells hit – the second just behind the cockpit, and the third in the bomb bay.

Fire broke out immediately. A massive smoke trail moderated to a steady black, sometimes grey, plume as Alf Aske and his co-pilot, Lt Charles S. 'Chick' Barber, featured the No 3 prop and cut off fuel to the engine. For a few seconds *Flush* held its position. A shudder went through the B-17 as the automatic pilot was put into operation. Then perceptibly, the ship began to lose altitude. As though under full control, *Flush* began a slow turn to the right. Down below 12 year-old Leon Croulebois, who was staying with his grandmother, saw an object fall from the *Flush*. It was the waist door. A second object hurtled down then checked its descent as a white canopy of parachute opened above.

Armanda Consorto was the first to leave the stricken aircraft. Now a second hatch door was seen to fall, followed by a body. Lt Jim Magargee, the bombardier, left the ship. Then followed the tail gunner, Sgt Stuart Allison, Barber and Sgt Chuck Nekvasil, the radio operator. Leon Croulebois did not see Sgt Robert F. Williams

leave the ship. Flak had killed him instantly and he plunged from his upper turret into the flaming bomb bay. He did not see Lt Gordon 'Bud' E. Davis, the navigator. His body was shredded by the first flak hit; lifeless, it rode in *Flush* to the ground. The aircraft crashed at Bois de Clamart, a Paris suburb.

He did see Allison leave the ship, shortly after jettisoning the tail gunner's escape hatch. Leon watched as ground fire danced his body around on the shroud lines of his 'chute, leaving him hanging nearly lifeless. Allison died minutes after reaching the ground. Leon watched as Aske hurtled out the waist door. The ship was now low. The same ground fire tore through his body. He died hanging in his parachute.

A tricky wind caught ball turret gunner Norman Fernaays as he left the ship. It raced

him toward Meudon where, still at speed, he bounced off the tile roof of Madame Braconnier's home, landing heavily in the garden of the home next door. He lived, was sheltered by Madame Braconnier and was the first to return to military service soon after Paris was liberated.

Chick Barber and Chuck Nekvasil crashed down in their 'chutes near the Orphelinat Lazaret (hospital). Nekvasil was captured by the SS and Chick was taken only minutes later. Consorto eluded capture for 24 hr but was captured and he and Magargee were taken to Germany. Barber was marched to a German barracks. Nekvasil, his pelvis and his coccyx fractured in the impact of his parachute landing, and shoeless (the force of his 'chute opening had snapped his flying boots off), was marched to Lazaret. Late in the afternoon he was taken on a stretcher to an ambulance which picked up Barber and took them on a long ride through Paris to the Beaujon hospital at Clichy. After a week and-a-half of minimal care both men made a night escape,

with the aid of the FFI and finally linked up with the French 2nd Armoured Division.

Further south the 15th Air Force 'softened up' targets in southern France when the weather permitted, in preparation for the invasion code-named 'Anvil'. On 13 August 136 B-17s bombed gun positions and bridges in southern France. Next day the B-17s raided gun positions around Toulon. The 'Anvil' landings took place in the early hours of 15 August. Later that day and on the 16th, the bombers attacked railway bridges near the invasion beaches.

Three days later, on 19 August, the 15th Air Force bombed Ploesti for the 20th (including one raid by P-38s) and final time. Ploesti was finally overrun by the Red Army on 30 August. Production at Ploesti had been reduced to just one-fifth of its potential capacity. Almost 13,500 tons of bombs had been dropped on the refinery complex at a cost of 223 aircraft. Beginning on 31 August, three B-17 airlifts took liberated American PoWs to Italy.

CHAPTER 6

The Oil Campaign

European Theatre of Operations, August – November 1944

The 15th Air Force had helped deny Germany the precious oil it needed from Ploesti, but several large and important refining centres – many of them at the very limit of the B-17's range – were scattered throughout the Reich. The fact that they were dispersed throughout Germany made a concentrated and effective offensive extremely difficult. It fell to Fortresses of the 8th Air Force to strike at these targets, from Politz on the Baltic coast, to Brux in Czechoslovakia.

Oil targets were the order of the day in August 1944 for the 8th Air Force in England. At Knettishall crews in the 388th Bomb Group who had been on a long, very tiring mission to Brux, Czechoslovakia on 24 August, awoke in the early hours of the 25th to be confronted with another shock. Richard Bing, the radio operator in Lt Leon Sutton's crew in the 561st Squadron, recalls:

'At 6 am tired crew members assembled at squadron briefing. A white sheet covered the wall at the far end of the room. Behind its cleanness was a map of Europe and our dirty work for the day. Hopefully, we prayed, it was a short run to France. Allied armies were on the outskirts of Paris and, just maybe, they needed some help. After Brux, we needed a break.

'In strode the ever-confident Briefing Officer, an English riding crop tucked under one arm. (That was class.) "Gentlemen", he announced dramatically, "today you have the honour of destroying Germany's last remaining oil refinery."

"But Sir," called a voice from the rear, "we did that *yesterday!*"

(laughter)

"All right, Gentlemen, let's get serious."

The sheet was ripped away. Crews whistled and groans filled the room. A thin red line arched high over the map of Europe. It spanned far out over the Baltic

Sea . . . then dropped abruptly into the heart of the German Fatherland. (Oh my God, another deep strike.)

'With crop in hand the Briefing Officer traced the route. "You'll assemble here." he indicated, "and form here with the 3rd Division over the Channel. On the way in, Holland will be on your right. Your first land contact is Denmark. Enemy flak will be low and to your left. You'll continue over the Baltic [*his short*

A B-17G of the 99th Bomb Group, 15th Air Force, drops its bombs on the Szob railway bridge, north of Budapest. (USAF.)

B-17G-40-VE 42-97991, seen here on a test flight over California, joined the 365th Bomb Squadron, 305th Bomb Group. Lt Roland B. Heusser and his crew failed to return from the mission to Merseberg on 24 August 1944 in this aircraft. Two crew members were killed and the rest made PoWs. (Lockheed.)

riding crop proved only partly utilitarian] then south into Germany. This will be your IP (Initial Point of the bomb run) and *here*, gentlemen, is your target . . . Politz; 15 miles northwest of Stettin. Germany's last remaining oil . . . (*All right, all ready!*).''

' ''The route we've indicated,'' he added, ''offers the least amount of fighter and flak opposition. In the target area itself our intelligence estimates about 90 88 mm flak guns. German fighter planes haven't been seen in weeks. Of course, the Krauts have been known to *move both* fighters and flak. They're quite mobile you know?'' [*Boy doesn't that give you confidence?*] I can give you this assurance. Allied fighters *control* the skies over Europe. The Luftwaffe is almost non-existent.'' [*Why didn't he mention flak I wondered. It was intense and accurate.*]

'He hadn't finished. His next gem came straight out of a war movie. ''Gentlemen, I won't be able to join you today. The CO says I'm needed here on important matters. Of course, you know I'd rather be up there with you guys. I wish you all the best of luck.'' I nearly called out, ''Come join us Mr. Briefing Officer. *We* have important matters over the skies of Europe''. I heard only murmurs. Wasn't anyone with me? How about a resounding *boo* for this clod on stage?

'The General briefing became crucial. Crews hurriedly scribbled notes, target information, bomb load,

estimated time of arrival, enemy resistance, etc.

'Individual briefings followed: pilots and co-pilots; navigators, bombardiers and radio operators; engineers and pilots; engineers, radio operators and gunners; that's why they got us up so early.

'We were assigned *Cutie on Duty*, a fairly new B-17G, for the mission to Politz. She had 18 bombing raids to her credit and a welcome change to the clunkers we had been flying.

'The enlisted men were the last to arrive at the revetment area that housed *Cutie*. The officers were already on board. In the pilot's compartment Sutton was joined by his co-pilot, Lt Harlan Thompson, a 25 year-old happy-go-lucky character from Athol, Massachusetts. Sutton, at 20 years of age, was young for a bomber pilot but I had seen Lt-Cols in the 8th Air Force who were still in their twenties. Sutton was the first member of the crew to fly a mission over Europe. On 4 August he went along as an observer on a raid on Hamburg. He was a changed man after that, becoming quiet and withdrawn.

'Tommy had just recently become the favourite of the enlisted men. At his insistence, we had all been promoted staff sergeants. Until then, I must have been one of the few flying corporals in the ETO. Before joining the crew, Tommy was a B-26 pilot in the States. He had it made but chose to volunteer for combat.

B-17G-95-BO 43-38757 of the 547th Bomb Squadron, 384th Bomb Group, comes to grief on landing.
(via Ian McLachlan.)

'In *Cutie's* nose section Lts Healy, the navigator, and Harold Fisher, the bombardier, got ready for the day's mission. Healy – 24 and the only other married man on the crew – was a serious, no-nonsense type. He was quiet and knew his job. Since we had made our peace over the Atlantic he had brought me more into the navigational side of flying.

'Fisher, 22, was our comic relief from Brooklyn, New York. He constantly reminded the crew of his Jewish heritage. "If we're ever shot down, remember, my name is 'Fishetti!'" "Fish" had washed out of pilot training but was rapidly becoming a good bombardier.

'S/Sgt W. "Midge" Midget joined Sutton and Tommy for *Cutie's* pre-flight check. When airborne, he manned the twin 50, in the top turret.

'In the radio room the "Chicago Gangster" (as I had been dubbed) busily tuned the Liaison and Command radio sets, checked the interphone communications and got the code books in order.

'In the waist, J. J. Camarda, E. Coleman and F. J. Bernjus helped the ground crew load the crates of ammunition aboard. They wouldn't load and check their .50 calibre machine-guns until we were over the English Channel.

'At 0805 hr *Cutie* and her crew waited patiently at the tailend of a long line of B-17s near the edge of the runway. It was still a grey, English morning and the ever-present fog threatened to scrub the mission.

"Skies over the target area are clearing," advised tower control, "you should be taking off shortly." Pilots instinctively revved their engines.

'At 0820 hr the fog lifted briefly and a green flare pierced the murk. The mission was Go.'

One by one 22 Forts of the 388th, which was flying lead and low groups in the 45th Combat Wing, roared down the runway and leapt skyward in search of their rendezvous with the 3rd Division over the Channel. One B-17 aborted for mechanical reasons.

'The sky cleared as we climbed steadily. "Let's tighten up that formation," came a voice from Divisional Command, "you're looking a little ragged." Hundreds of B-17s snuggled closer and got to know each other.

'In the radio room, I tuned into BBC in London. The announcer spoke of an Allied success. "The Paris radio announces that the French capital has been liberated, with the German commander ordering his men to cease fighting immediately. Gen Dietrich Von Cholitz, Chief of the Nazi garrison of about 10,000 men, signed the unconditional surrender order today in the presence of French Brig-Gen, Jacques-Phillippe Le Clerc and a US Corps Commander in the Montparnasse railway station."

'I quickly switched to intercom. "Hey it's official. They took Paris this morning." "Whee" came the reply. From the crew's reaction you'd think the war was over.

'It was now 0830hr. England's fog was far behind. Europe's sun was rising. It was going to be a bombardier's sky. From the radio room I could see the coast of Holland. *Cutie* purred along. Her ground crew would be proud. Overnight, they had patched 32 flak holes in her tender body and replaced a two-foot piece of metal blown away from her tail. "The young recuperate quickly," I thought.

We climbed past the 10,000 ft level. The air was getting thin and the crew donned oxygen masks. Every air-mile the weather improved. It would be a beautiful day. German flak greeted us over Denmark. It was low and to the left (one score for the Briefing Officer). My mind began to wander. I thought of something totally unrelated to the mission. Before take off a rigger had said, "you guys better get back today 'cause Glenn Miller and his orchestra are gonna be here tonight for a concert. And according to one rumour, there would be 300 girls from Norwich and another 500 from London and Cambridge." One officer had said, "confidentially, they have to find their own quarters and absolutely be off the base in *three* days!" Musically, Miller was my favourite but what about the rigger's rumours?

"Hey skipper, we gotta get back today," I said feebly on intercom.

"OK. Let's knock off the idle chatter," came the reply.

'Over the Baltic the 3rd Division swung right. Bomber Command broke radio silence. "10 minutes from IP." Silently, I prayed this was Germany's last remaining oil refinery. Brux was a son-of-a-bitch.

"Waist gunner to pilot. Over."

"Go ahead Joe."

"Take a look to the left about 9 o'clock level."

"Looks like a '17? Probably lost and wants to join us?"

"I don't think so. There's no markings on it."

"Keep an eye on it Joe. Could be a Kraut."

"No use skipper. She's leaving us right now."

'The mystery B-17 peeled off and disappeared into cloud cover. It was a Kraut all right and by now German anti-aircraft was zeroed in on our altitude.

' "We've passed the IP," called the Group Commander. "We're committed to target."

'In the nose, Fisher had the best view. He saw it first.

"Oh my God! Look at that flak, its pattern, and they're right on us!"

'Within minutes we were right in the middle of it. "I've seen three or four go down ahead of us," said a dejected voice.

"We're coming up on target," said Sutton. "Bombardier, you've got control; confirm!"

"Roger, I've got control. Bomb bay doors open."

'Thank God I couldn't see what was up front. Outside the radio window flak shells exploded in harm-less looking black puffs. The rain of metal on *Cutie's* fuselage sounded like hail stones on a tin roof.

'Bang! *Cutie* took a hit in the right wing. She rolled a bit but held her course. Fragments of another shell ripped into the radio. The concussion knocked me down. From a prone position I surveyed the damage. The transmitter was smashed and the rudder cables severed. The cables got priority. Three or four were cut. I scooped them up, matched their thickness and held on for dear life. My hands moved with each rudder manoeuvre by the pilot. Was I helping or not? What did I know about flying a plane?

'I heard, "Bombs Away!" *Cutie* rose as she discharged her cargo of death. She took another hit in the waist. Why didn't somebody say something? Another explosion rocked the ship. We fell out of formation. It was a mortal wound. *Cutie* groaned and plunged earthward out of control. In the cockpit Leon and Tommy fought to right her.

"Let's have an oxygen check," said Tommy, breaking the silence. All the crew members responded. No apparent injuries. Coleman didn't answer. "Get him out of the ball! Coleman, get out of that turret!"

"Okay," said Sutton, "here's the situation. We've got her on automatic pilot and have some manual control. Make preparations to abandon ship." (Hell, I had that in mind back on the runway.)

"Ball turret to pilot. We've got a fire on the underside of the No 2 engine."

"Roger, hit the fire extinguisher. Feather No 2. Pilot to navigator, over."

"Navigator to pilot. Go ahead."

"How far to Sweden?"

"I've been checking that, sir. I calculate about 30 min flying time."

"Let's give it a try."

'*Cutie* swung north. The Baltic was clearly visible. The dark land mass of neutral Sweden loomed in the distance. (Come on girl, it was beautiful war over there!)

' "Waist gunner to pilot. Better keep her over land, skipper. We're trailing gas. Fire's hitting the tail section. Fish? Keep the bomb bay open. We can't get out back here."

'The order is definite: "This is Tommy to crew. Get the hell out of this plane!"

'I took off my flak suit, hooked the chest 'chute to the parachute harness and headed for the open bomb bay. None of us had jumped from a plane before but like the "loose wires and jiggling tubes" of radio school, I remembered my Army training. "If you ever have to jump," said a sergeant, "make sure your harness straps go underneath each testicle. 'Cause if they don't, when the 'chute opens, a baritone can quickly become a tenor."

' "Midge" was the first to jump. I noticed a certain fear in his eyes but he didn't hesitate. Camarda was next. "If my tough guy buddy can do it, so can

I.'' He straddled the bomb bay, dropped his GI shoes, brought his feet together and disappeared into space.

'I was up next. Gulp! I hesitated. I looked towards the pilot's compartment. Tommy was almost running towards the bomb bay. He had popped his 'chute and with his arms full of nylon I could see he wanted out in a hurry. Coleman and Bernjus crowded in behind.

'*Cutie's* wing fire was rapidly becoming *Cutie's* bomb bay fire. For some God-awful reason, the words of the Army Air Corps song came to mind. "You live in fame or go down in flame 'cause nothing can stop the Army Air Corps."

"Bullshit! Geronimo!''

'After the world's fastest 1-to-10 count I pulled the rip-cord. The pilot 'chute rushed past my face. Then, WOMP! I looked up and oh, what a sight. A beautiful white canopy held firm at the 9,000 ft level over one scared Chicago staff sergeant. The descent seemed slow. The silence was eerie. I missed the roar of *Cutie's* engines. I saw her die in a burst of glory as she ploughed into a German farmhouse. It all seemed so unreal. I couldn't believe I had just jumped from a burning airplane. I looked for the 388th but they were long gone. The Baltic was clearly visible. My now elusive Swedish dream faded in the distance.

'I began to relax and even started singing and waving to the other guys. Hell, there was nothing to this bailing out of the plane. With a little more practice I could join the 101st Airborne. "Screamin' Eagle Bing". What was I saying?

Dick Bing landed but could only count seven other parachutes. Two were missing. Bing teamed up with Tommy Thompson and together they evaded capture for two hours. Then two shots range out. Bing continues:

'Instinctively, Tommy drew a .32 calibre pistol from his flight jacket. I didn't know he had it. Enlisted men were told not to carry side-arms. That could get us killed. Maybe the officers had other instructions but I wasn't about to find out.

"Tommy, if you plan to use that,'' I said, "then get away from me. I'm unarmed.''

'Before a decision was made, we both saw the biggest of all Germans grinning and pointing a pistol at us. He was huge and must have been 8 ft 10 in at least. And that pistol he was holding was easily an 88 millimetre flak gun.

'Tommy discretely slipped his .32 back into his flight jacket. "Raus" screamed King Kong. We didn't know what "Raus" meant but we believed his command.

' "Kong" introduced some friends; a more belligerent band of civilians. Their hate was understandable. We had just bombed out their town and here was an enemy they could reach. One, an elderly farmer, charged like an angry bull. He telegraphed a right hand

all the way from Berlin. I sidestepped and the blow grazed my head. This infuriated him. He began pounding on my chest.

' "Luft Gangster! Terror Flieger,'' he shouted. I could see he didn't like me one bit.

'Tommy had walked a few steps ahead. I saw it coming but I couldn't warn him. Another farmer slammed a rifle butt into the back of his head. He fell but got up quickly. The crowd moved in for the kill. BANG! A shot rang out and they stopped. Four Luftwaffe regulars arrived to claim their prisoners.

'As they tied our hands, "Kong" got into a heated argument with one of his friends. He had Tommy's pistol, the friend had the box of shells. I'll never know how it ended but my money was on the big guy.

'The guards led us to Midge's body. He'd caught a bullet in the back of the head, almost execution style. His body was stripped of shoes, watch and wedding ring. A young teenager, waving a pistol, was boasting how he had killed the enemy.

'The guards motioned us to pick up Midge. We carried him to a clearing a couple of hundred yards away. A short time later, a truck drove up carrying Camarda, Fisher and Coleman. Sutton, Healy and Bernjus were missing. Tommy and I climbed on the truck.'

Leon Sutton and Healy never showed up. Sutton had gone down with *Cutie* and Healy's parachute failed to open. Bing and the surviving enlisted men were sent to Stalag I and 17B PoW camps while Tommy Thompson and Fisher were sent to Stalag Luft III, Sagan.

Cutie was the only loss from the 388th although 19 out of the returning 20 aircraft at Knettishall showed marked signs of minor flak damage. The oil campaign had claimed yet another victim while for the victors, the spoils. That night the Glenn Miller Orchestra played to a packed house in a Knettishall hangar.

8th Air Force attacks on oil refinery targets in the ever shrinking Reich continued in earnest. On 28 September the 8th attacked the refineries at Merseberg in Leuna, where the majority of synthetic fuel for Germany's rocket-powered fighters was manufactured. The raid is recounted by Wayne E. Cose, the top turret gunner-engineer on David 'Moon' Mullen's crew in the 486th Bomb Group, 8th Air Force, at Sudbury.

'Our crew only had two missions under our belts and didn't realize what was ahead of us. The first one to Bremen on 26 September only involved a relatively few puffs of flak which didn't seem to be close enough to register. Little did I realise the punch behind those puffs at the time. On the second mission, however, to Mainz on 27 September, I took back my thought, "Is this all there is to it?" when a B-17 disappeared

B-17G-50-DL 44-6405 of the 2nd Bomb Group lands at Tri Duby (Three Oaks) airfield in a pocket of liberated Czech territory in September 1944 to fly out American airmen evaders. The area was completely surrounded by German-occupied territory. (Hans Heiri-Stapfer.)

in front of us with a single direct hit burst of flak. Wow, nine men and a plane gone in one puff – those Germans are out to get us!

'On the Merseberg mission we soon found out that the Germans were really guarding their oil with walls of thick flak. The bursts were getting closer and closer. The thin aluminium skin was really taking a beating. In fact it was beginning to look like a sieve. There were huge holes in the wings where the flak pierced the self-sealing gas tanks. Some of the engines were taking hits and beginning to falter.

'A straggler joined our formation off our right wing during the confusion over the target and through the walls of flak. He was challenged by radio, IFF and colour-of-the-day flare sometime before he joined us but he flunked them all. The fact that the straggler was O.D. coloured wasn't all that unusual either, since this was common on all-out efforts. Reportedly, this was a German-manned captured B-17 sent up for the purpose of relaying the planes' altitude and heading to his anti-aircraft batteries. He had obviously accomplished his mission.

'Our straggling plane was initially suspected by our "little friends", the P-51 Mustangs, of being the German-manned B-17 because our radio equipment was malfunctioning and prevented Verdan "Buzz"

Wiedel, our radio operator, from identifying us as friendly but he flashed the code outside the waist compartment with a light and properly identified us. The P-51 found the straggler and shot him down.

'Nilan "Mac" Mack, the bombardier, called me on intercom so I'd be ready to fire the flare (other planes were to drop their bombs when they saw the flare). I then reached out of my turret toward the flare gun and found I'd have to get out of my top turret to reach it. Here we were at 28,000 ft, 50° below, flak popping all over and I had to get out of the turret. Cussing to myself, I unbuckled my turret straps, unhooked my electrical heating suit cord, unhooked the oxygen line and stepped out to hook up a walk-around oxygen bottle. While I was waiting for Mac to zero in with his bombsight and to call me on the intercom (right after I stepped out), I heard a big "Zing" and saw that about half of my top turret bubble was knocked out where my head would have been. I then got Mac's call and fired the flare.

'Up in the nose of the plane, Mac had his helmet and oxygen mask knocked off by flak and the nose compartment caught fire. Elliot Kolker, the navigator, put the fire out with a carbon tetrachloride fire extinguisher. Little did anyone know at this time but experts later determined that carbon tet' on hot metal creates poisonous phosgene gas. Mac got quite a dose of this while he was without his mask. He is probably the only air crewman to receive a chemical warfare wound.

'Nos. 2 and 3 engines were completely knocked out and No 2 was feathered to cut down wind resistance. Mullen said No 3 ran away so he pulled off power while trying to control the aircraft. Power was then applied slowly and the engine stabilized, but if the throttle was moved it would run away. No 3 was not putting out full power, even though the props were turning, because of a big flak hole in the nacelle. Bob Atkinson, one of the waist gunners, was busy in the waist compartment mending severed control cables with electrical heating suit cords.

'Mullen told us to get ready to bail out. Salvatore "Sal" Muscarella got out of his ball turret OK. We enlisted men in the back grabbed our chest pack parachutes, hooked them to our harnesses and stood by the waist compartment door, awaiting the actual bail-out order. Even though none of us had parachuted before, the possibility didn't look that bad now, considering the condition of the plane.

'We waited for what seemed like quite a while when "Moon" called to say we seemed to be holding altitude pretty well and we might ride it out for a while. He told us to throw out anything that had any weight which we could do without. We proceeded to throw out most of the guns and ammunition, extra flying suits, flak aprons and ripped non-essential radio equip-

ment off the walls. We limped on and on this way. We hoped German fighters wouldn't jump us. Kolker was doing a bang-up job of navigating. "Moon" and his co-pilot, Larry Iverson, coaxed more out of the B-17 than the Boeing engineers ever planned or believed possible. Of course, we gradually lost altitude, but they actually brought our riddled plane over the continent and the English Channel to Sudbury.

'My flight records showed this mission to be 8 hr 15 min long; longer than usual. After we deplaned, Maj Rex, the 833rd Operations Officer, proceeded to chew out Mullen for disobeying his instructions to leave the plane on the taxi-way. Instead, he pulled it into a hardstand to avoid blocking other planes. After looking at the plane it was easy to see Maj Rex's viewpoint. The ground crew later commented there were about 300 holes in the plane.'

On 15 September the 8th Air Force attempted a shuttle operation, named 'Frantic 7', to help relieve Polish freedom fighters in Warsaw. Capt Pete Hardiman, a P-51 pilot in the 354th Squadron, 355th Fighter Group, recalls.

'We were to rendezvous with three bomb groups but after one and-a-half hours flying, we received a recall. On 18 September Field Order 577 "Frantic 7" Dash One was started. The 95th, 100th and 390th Bomb Groups were to be escorted to Warsaw by the 4th, 355th and 361st Fighter Groups. Rendezvous was to

This 15th Air Force B-17 took a direct flak hit over the Debreezen railway yards in Hungary, but flew safely back to its base in Italy. Upon landing the tail wheel gave way, causing the aircraft to bend at the point where it received the hit. The entire crew was unhurt. (USAF.)

B-17G-85-BO 43-38452 of the 401st Bomb Group crash-landed at Bäcks torvmosse, Sweden, on 7 October 1944 after sustaining flak damage on a raid over Germany. (via Frank Thomas.)

be 1145 hr at Koszalin on the Baltic Coast; the actual meet was between Stettin and Torun. Heavy flak damage was received by the B-17s near Stettin but 107 of them made it to Warsaw and dropped food and medical supplies. Unfortunately, most of the supplies fell into German hands. One of the damaged B-17s was escorted to land at Brzese [*and one 390th Bomb Group B-17 was shot down*]. The remaining B-17s made it to Poltava and Mirgorod. Our fighter base was Piryatin, where we were all landed by 1520 hr.

'On 19 September most of the fighters left Piryatin to rendezvous with the B-17s at 1330 hr near Horodenka, Poland, and crossed over Czechoslovakia, Rumania and Hungary and bombed their target near Brod, Yugoslavia. There was much heavy flak but we all made it to Italy, landing at Foggia at 1600 hr. After a short rest we left Foggia at 0959 hr on 22 September to rendezvous with the B-17s near Marseilles at 1325 hr. All 355th aircraft were down at Steeple Morden by 1700 hr. This was the most awe-inspiring mission I ever took part in.'

During September 1944 German oil production plummeted to only 7,000 tons and draconian measures were called for. Reichminister Albert Speer was given 7,000 engineers from the army and an unlimited amount of slave labour, to reconstruct the synthetic oil-producing plants. Hundreds of additional flak guns were erected around the *Hydriesfestungen* – as the plants

became known – and workers, who now came under the direct supervision of the SS, built deep shelters in which to take cover during air raids. Plants quickly demonstrated a remarkable ability to regain full production quotas and between bombing raids were able to produce 19,000 tons during October and in November, 39,000 tons.

The Merseberg refineries were bombed again on 2 November when the B-17s were assigned the vast I.G. Farbenindustrie's synthetic oil refinery at Leuna, three miles to the south of Merseberg. It was rated the number one priority target and was estimated to be producing 10 per cent of all Germany's synthetic oil and a third of all the enemy's ammonia and other chemicals. At briefing, crews were warned that German fuel and replacement pilots were in such short supply that Hermann Goering, the Luftwaffe chief, was massing his forces to strike a telling blow on a single mission. All they needed was an opportunity.

The 35 aircraft in the 457th Bomb Group formation were blown 35 miles off course and away from the target by a 50-kt wind. They flew on alone and sought the secondary target at Bernberg. The 'Fireballs' were out on a limb and at the mercy of more than 400 fighters which were in the vicinity. At 1248 hr the 'Fireballs' had still not joined the rest of the Divisional bomber stream and came under attack from about 40 German fighters.

Attacks were made on the low squadron from 6 to 8 o'clock low. The American gunners opened up on the Bf109s and FW190s and some fighters did go down. But then one by one, the 'Fireballs' fell out of formation and hurtled down. *Lady Margaret* had its fin severed by the wing of a passing FW190 and several other hits sent it down in flames. It exploded shortly afterwards with only two men bailing out in time. *Prop Wash* followed her down and another seven B-17s exploded or crashed with a further nine being badly damaged. Only the timely intervention by Mustangs saved the group from total annihilation.

It was for his actions this day that Lt Robert Feymoyer, a navigator in the 447th Bomb Group, was posthumously awarded the Medal of Honor. Feymoyer's B-17 was rocked by three flak bursts, which showered the aircraft with shrapnel. Feymoyer was hit in the back and the side of his body but he refused all aid despite his terrible wounds so that he might navigate the Fortress back to Rattlesden. He was propped up

in his seat to enable him to read his charts and the crew did what they could for him. It was not until they reached the North Sea that Feymoyer agreed to an injection of morphine. He died shortly after the aircraft landed at Rattlesden.

Losses were so bad on this mission – the 91st Bomb Group lost 12 Fortresses – that groups were stood down for two days following the raid. On 9 November two more Medals of Honor were awarded to 8th Air Force B-17 crewmen. This day the heavies returned to tactical missions in support of Gen George Patton's 3rd Army halted at the fortress city of Metz. The 8th was called in to bomb German lines of communication at Saarbrücken and also enemy gun emplacements to the east and south of Metz to enable the advance through Belgium to continue. The mission was deemed top priority and at bases throughout East Anglia Fortresses taxied out in the mist and bad visibility. The conditions were instrumental in the loss of eight bombers during take-offs and landings and further disasters befell some groups as the mission progressed.

While on the bomb run over Saarbrücken the 452nd Bomb Group encountered an extremely

B-17G-45-VE 44-8039 of the 836th Bomb Squadron, 487th Bomb Group, drops its bombs. (Ian McLachlan.)

Above: Clark Gable, Hollywood film star and 8th Air Force gunnery instructor. (via Connie and Gordon Richards.)

Left: James Cagney, star of the 1942 movie of the same name, poses in front of Yankee Doodle Dandy. *(USAF.)*

Above right: Several B-17s were named after movie stars and famous personalities. Here, British star Anna Neagle poses in front of Lady Anna, *named in her honour by the 379th Bomb Group at Kimbolton. (Gordon Richards.)*

Right: HM King George VI and HRH Princess Elizabeth gather in front of B-17G-55-BO 42-102547 Rose of York *of the 367th Bomb Squadron, 306th Bomb Group, during a Royal visit to christen the aircraft at Thurleigh on 6 July 1944. On 3 February 1945 this aircraft, flown by Lt Vernor F. Daley who with several other crew members was on his final mission, disappeared over the North Sea after losing two engines over Berlin. (Gordon Richards.)*

accurate and intense flak barrage. *Lady Janet*, flown by Lt Donald Gott and Lt William E. Metzger, had three engines badly damaged and the No 1 engine set on fire. It began windmilling and the No 2 engine was failing rapidly. No 4 showered flames back towards the tail assembly. Flares were ignited in the cockpit and the flames were fuelled by hydraulic fluid leaking

from severed cables.

The engineer was wounded in the leg and a shell fragment had severed the radio operator's arm below his elbow. Metzger left his seat and stumbled back to the radio room and applied a tourniquet to stop the bleeding. However, the radio operator was so weak from pain that he fell unconscious. The bombs were still aboard and Gott was faced with the prospect of the aircraft exploding at any moment. He therefore decided to fly the stricken Fortress to Allied territory a few miles distant and attempt a crash landing. The bombs were salvoed over enemy territory and all excess equipment was thrown overboard. Lt Metzger unselfishly gave his parachute to one of the gunners after his had been damaged in the fire. As *Lady Janet* neared friendly territory Metzger went to the rear of the Fortress and told everyone to bail out. He then went back to his seat and the two pilots prepared for a crashlanding with only one engine still functioning and the other three on fire.

An open field was spotted and Gott brought *Lady Janet* in. At about 100 ft the fire took hold of the fuel tanks and the bomber exploded, killing Gott, Metzger and the radio operator instantly. Both pilots were posthumously awarded the Medal of Honor.

On 21 November the 8th returned to Merseberg for the first of three more raids on the refineries in a week. Merseberg had become synonymous with flak and crews hated all missions to the city. On 25 November the bombing was so poor that on 30 November the heavies were once again despatched to the oil plants. The plan called for the leading 1st Division force to attack the synthetic plant at Zeitz while the 3rd Division was to strike at Merseberg itself, 20 miles to the north.

Lt Bob Browne, pilot of *Fearless Fosdick*, in the 487th Bomb Group, sat at the briefing given by Col Robert Taylor III, the C.O., and along with everyone else was startled to see that the target was all the way to Merseberg. 'The veteran pilot seated at my right turned to me and said, "Serves us right, I guess, for goofing that last raid five days ago". He was referring to the 25 November mission to the same target, when one of the poorest displays of 8th Air Force "precision bombing" resulted in such minor damage that Germany's hottest target – the synthetic oil refinery at Merseberg – was in full production again, only 12 hr later!'

Both the 1st and 3rd Bomb Divisions flew the route as briefed to Osnabrück but the leading 1st Division formation flew on instead of turning for Zeitz. The 3rd Division wings were some five to 15 miles south of the briefed route. The error placed the 3rd Bomb Division within range of some 90 flak batteries at Zeitz and the Fortresses were subjected to an intense and accurate barrage. A strong headwind reduced their speed and aided the German defences. Bob Browne continues.

'Our escorts followed us to a point approximately 20 miles northwest of Merseberg. As we turned onto a southeast course at this point, it had become apparent where our target was. It was 18 miles straight ahead. The sky was so full of ugly black explosions that none of the blue sky could be seen through it! We were later informed that this was the largest concentration of artillery ever known in the history of warfare! Also, that the Germans even had women and children pulling lanyards while men aimed and reloaded. As the forward bomber groups 10 miles ahead penetrated the flak area, I could see a veritable curtain of Forts streaming earthward in flames.'

Bob Browne watched the terrible sight ahead of him and knew that he would be in the middle of it in less than 3 min.

'An almost hopeless feeling welled up inside of me. It occurred to me that only God could see me through it safely. In desperation I silently bargained with God, "Lord, if you'll bring me through this alive, I'll serve you for the rest of my life." This hasty communication brought much relief from the almost unbearable anxiety.

'Now, our bomb group was at the IP, the point where the 10-mile run began in meticulous sighting and correcting for target alignment. Flak now was bursting all around us. Several bursts exploded right in front of the nose. More bursts right on top of the right wing. Another group burst straight ahead. Black puffs were everywhere. Forts were going down all around us. The colonel had already lost his right wing man. Didn't even see him go. There were two giant white balls of smoke about a mile ahead, showing where two Forts' gasoline tanks had exploded, probably taking other Forts with them. They were still falling. Even through the oxygen masks you could smell cordite. Enemy fighters were waiting outside the flak corridor, not daring to follow us through the seemingly impenetrable barrier of flying steel.

' "Bombs Away!" There was the usual upsurge of the craft, bringing instinctive reflexes for forward control wheel, as the 6,000 lb of bombs dropped free. What an awesome sight, as thousands of 500 lb bombs fell in train simultaneously! Now the formation was in a steep bank to the right. The colonel's voice could

B-17G-20-DL 42-37940 of the 306th Bomb Group in flight over England in 1944. (Gordon Richards.)

be heard over the airwaves, "Let's get out of here!" The flight back was relatively uneventful. What a relief to park old *Fearless Fosdick*. But I dreaded to inspect the old bird for battle damage. Sgt Haley was always so obviously distressed when the Fort's skin was even scratched. How much more if she looked like the sieve I expected?

'As I left the forward escape door I could hear ambulances as they raced to pick up wounded and dead from other aircraft. Sgt Haley was already at the nose of *Fearless Fosdick*, looking her all over. As I approached him, I could hear him muttering some-

thing. As he turned to me, I finally heard what he was saying. "I can't believe it," he muttered over and over. It was the sergeant's way of expressing the fact that he could not find a single scratch on *Fearless*. The old Fort sat there all shiny and spotless, as though she had never left the pad that day!

'It took about two weeks before the 487th could repair enough aircraft for another mission. The 8th and 9th Air Forces had just lost 29 bombers and 40 fighter planes on this bleak day. But Merseberg had suffered its greatest damage, too. And no doubt this helped considerably to bring the terrible conflict to an end.'

CHAPTER 7

In at the Kill

ETO December 1944 – May 1945

On 16 December, using the appalling weather conditions to his advantage, Field Marshal Gerd von Rundstedt and his panzer formations attacked American positions in the forests of the Ardennes on the Franco-Belgian border and opened up a salient or 'bulge' in the Allied lines. In England the Allied air forces were grounded by fog and it was not until 23 December that the heavies could offer bomber support in what became known as the 'Battle of the Bulge.'

On Christmas Eve a record 2,034 8th Air Force bombers and 500 RAF and 9th Air Force bombers, took part in the largest single strike flown by the Allied Air Forces in World War Two, against German airfields and lines of communication leading to the 'Bulge'. The 1st Division made a direct tactical assault on airfields in the Frankfurt area and on lines of communication immediately behind the German 'bulge'. Crews were told that their route was planned on purpose to go over the ground troops' positions for morale purposes.

Beautiful overhead view of a 96th Bomb Group B-17G over enemy territory. (Geoff Ward.)

B-17G-55-DL 44-6606 of the 2nd Bomb Group, 15th Air Force, landed at Miskolc airfield, Hungary, early in December 1944 after being damaged during a raid on Vienna. Miskolc was in an area liberated by Soviet and Rumanian troops and was the home base of the 8th Rumanian Assault Group equipped with Henschel Hs129 aircraft. The B-17 was repaired by Rumanian ground crews who fixed an Hs129 main wheel to the Fortress to act as a tail wheel. Note the B-17's damaged wingtip. (Hans-Heiri Stapfer.)

Brig-Gen Fred Castle, commander of the 4th Wing, led the 3rd Division on his 30th mission in a 487th Bomb Group Fortress. All went well until over Belgium, about 35 miles from Liège, his right outboard engine burst into flame and the propeller had to be feathered. The deputy lead ship took over and Castle dropped down to 20,000 ft. But at this height the aircraft began vibrating badly and he was forced to take it down another 3,000 ft before levelling out. The Fortress was now down to 180 mph indicated air speed and being pursued by seven Bf109s. They attacked and wounded the tail gunner and left the radar navigator nursing bad wounds in his neck and shoulders. Castle could not carry out an evasive manoeuvres with the full bomb load still aboard and he could not salvo them for fear

of hitting Allied troops on the ground.

Successive attacks by the fighters put another two engines out of action and the B-17 lost altitude. As Castle fought the controls in a vain effort to keep the stricken bomber level he ordered the crew to bail out. Part of the crew bailed out and then the bomber was hit in the fuel tanks and oxygen systems, which set the aircraft on fire. Castle attempted to land the flaming bomber in an open field near the Allied lines bur nearing the ground it went into a spin and exploded on impact. Brig-Gen Castle was posthumously awarded the Medal of Honor – the highest ranking officer in the 8th Air Force to receive the award.

Overall, the Christmas Eve raids were effective and severely hampered von Rundstedt's lines

of communication. The cost in aircraft though, was high. Many crashed during their return over England as drizzle and overcast played havoc with landing patterns. Tired crews put down where they could. Only 150 aircraft were available for another strike on 26 December. Next day the wintry conditions were responsible for a succession of crashes during early morning take-offs. On 30 December the 8th again attacked lines of communication and on the final day of the year the 1st Bomb Division kept up the attacks while 3rd Division crews returned to oil production centres. This time they were assigned Hamburg. Clyde Crowley, a bombardier in the 95th Bomb Group at Horham, was flying his 33rd combat mission.

'There was another toggelier in my squadron, Sgt Bates. It was his turn to fly but he had gotten himself grounded because of a cold. I had a bit of a stuffy head myself but I was told that if I flew the mission my flight officer said he would see if he could get my tour of duty ended and send me home. This sounded like a good deal. When I went to briefing and learned that the target was to be Hamburg my spirits dropped. I snapped on my 'chute before take-off, something I rarely ever did.

'The day was a very cold and clear one. At the target area the flak was heavy. We started our bomb run. I opened the bomb bay doors after arming the bombs. When we reached the target I dropped the bombs. The radio operator, who could see into the bomb bay, called me on interphone and said one bomb was hung in the rack. I tried again to unload the bomb but it wouldn't go so I asked Lt O'Reilly to jettison racks and all. He did this and as soon as the radio operator announced the bay was clear I closed the doors. With a combined sigh of relief everyone seemed to be chatting at the same time. But not for long. The radio operator saw an enemy aircraft approaching. Our gunners fired but he got through and near enough to hit us with at least one 20 mm shell. The ship was on fire. The pilot gave the order to abandon. Since I already had my chest pack on I probably was the first to get out. I kicked out the escape hatch and was gone. Four others managed to get out before the plane disintegrated. The rest of my tour overseas was spent in two Stalag Lufts.'

Hamburg was also the scene of another disaster for the 100th Bomb Group, as William B. Sterret, recalls.

'We were supposed to come in above Heligoland Island but instead we came in below and had to turn directly into the wind to reach our IP. We were all talking over the interphones and wondering what was going to happen next. Heligoland was our secondary target and even though we knew that the two islands were well defended we were wishing we could drop our bombs there.

'We finally got to our IP, turned on our rack switch, opened the bomb bay doors and started down the bomb run. At this point we all usually cut off our heated suits because the nervous energy was enough to keep you warm even though it was 50° below zero. Our turn to get on the bomb run was to the right and we were on the outside. This caused us to lag behind a little but finally we were able to get back into position.

'The target could be seen from our IP even though it took us about 10 min to actually get over it. A group hit an airfield off to our right. We could also see the groups in front of us getting shot at and we knew that we would soon be in the middle of it. No-one was saying a word. We were all just hoping and praying that we would come through without any trouble.

'Finally, we got back into the flak which was really close. We could hear the shells as they burst, which is too close for comfort. On our mission to Frankfurt I had told the boys that I could hear the pieces of shrapnel beating on the side of the ship and they had all said I was getting "flak happy." I knew they would agree with me this time.

'At 11.33 hr the lead ship dropped his smoke bombs, which was a signal for all of the wing ships to drop their bombs. Andy hit the toggle switch and out went our bombs. You always felt better as soon as the bombs were gone because you felt like your job was done.'

One by one all the Fortresses in the 100th Bomb Group formation began dropping their bombs. The B-17 piloted by Lt F. Henderson was struck while on the bomb run and dropped sharply, crashing into the B-17 flown by Lt C. Williams, which was cloven in two. Both aircraft fell to earth in flames. The sky over Hamburg was filled with accurate bursts of flak and Lt Bill Blackman's Fortress was struck on the No 3 engine. Bill Sterret continues:

'We started for our rally point but we had only flown about 2 min when Carson, the ball turret gunner, called Bill and said oil was pouring out of No 3 engine. The oil pressure gauge verified this fact so Bill feathered the engine. As soon as No 3 had stopped running Carson called again and said No 4 engine was also losing oil. Bill feathered this engine too. We were unable to keep up with the formation with only two engines but we could hold our altitude.

'Bill Blackman called us all and said, "Stick with it boys. We'll get this thing home yet." I told him to keep the same heading because it would bring us back out over the North Sea. Bill called for fighter escort but he couldn't contact any because they had been unable to get off the ground in England due to bad weather. He turned back on the interphone and said, "Bandits in the area!" At this instant, Joe Pearl, the engineer, yelled, "They're coming in at 6 o'clock!" I looked up through the astrodome and saw two FW190s coming in on our tail. I turned around and grabbed my gun hoping I would get a shot in. No such luck. We could see tracers as they passed us. 20 mm shells were also flying around. We all realised that our chances of getting through were really slim.

'A 20 mm shell exploded in the cockpit and knocked all the insulation between the pilots' compartment and the nose into the section where I was. The ship was also on fire and it started spinning. I realised it was time to leave. When I got to the escape hatch Bob Fortney, the radio-operator, was lying on his back on the catwalk. I thought he was hurt so I started to help him but he got up and told me to get out so I put one foot on the door and pushed it out. Then I jumped. As soon as I cleared the ship I took off my helmet, pulled my ripcord and looked back to see the ship blow up.

'Bill said that he reached behind his head to fire the Very pistol to call for help and a 20 mm shell exploded and knocked him out. When he came to he rang the bell and then managed to get his 'chute on. When he got down to the nose the ship blew up. He came to falling through the air and pulled his ripcord. The next thing he remembered he was on the ground and Krauts were standing around him. They told him that another boy (Bob Freshour) had been found with his 'chute open but he was dead.'

Basil Numack, one of the waist gunners, and Joe Pearl were killed by fighters. Carson was unable to get out of the ball turret and Fortney did not have his 'chute on. Andy Herbert, the tail gunner, and Tom Pace, survived and were made POW. Tom Pace was blown out of the ship. The last thing he remembered he was lying on the floor in the waist and could not move. When he came to he reached for his ripcord but the concussion had broken his shroud and his parachute was dangling above his head. He finally gathered his senses and pulled the ripcord.

'I landed in the middle of a field which was surrounded by woods. I took off my 'chute and started into the woods but the Krauts were coming from all directions with rifles. This was enough to make me stop. There was also about 6 in of snow on the ground. They searched me and said, "For you the war is over." I did not realise the significance of this statement until later.'

Blackman's crew was one of 12 that the 100th Bomb Group lost on the Hamburg raid; half the total lost by the 3rd Division. January 1945 marked the 8th's third year of operations and it seemed as if the end of the war was in sight. The Ardennes breakthrough was on the verge of failure and Germany had no reserves left. In the east the Red Army prepared for the great winter offensive which would see the capture of Warsaw and Cracow and see the Soviets cross the German border. But there were signs that the Luftwaffe at least, was far from defeated. On 1 January the 1st Air Division (this day the prefix 'Bomb' was officially changed to 'Air') encountered enemy fighters in some strength during raids on the tank factory at Kassel, an oil refinery

B-17G-45-DL 44-6142 The Stork of the 337th Bomb Squadron, 96th Bomb Group. (via Geoff Ward.)

Above: B-17G-90-BO 43-38576 of the 413th Bomb Squadron, 96th Bomb Group, burns after crashing on 6 January 1945. (Geoff Ward.)

Below: B-17G-85-BO 43-38358 Big Noise II of the 452nd Bomb Group, 730th Bomb Squadron, crash-landed at Rinkaby, Sweden, on 3 February 1945. It left Sweden on 27 June 1945 along with three other B-17s. Altogether, some 69 B-17s landed in Sweden during the war. (via Frank Thomas.)

at Magdeburg and marshalling yards at Dillenburg. The Magdeburg force came under heavy fighter attack while the Kassel force was badly hit by flak.

Next day the B-17s once again pounded lines of communication and raids of this nature continued for several days until the position in the Ardennes gradually swung in the Allies' favour. On 5 January the severe wintry winter over England was responsible for several fatal accidents during take-off for a mission to Frankfurt.

A period of fine weather, beginning on 6 January, enabled the heavies to fly missions in support of the ground troops once more. These were mostly against lines of communication, airfields and marshalling yards. Finally, the German advance in the Ardennes came to a halt and ultimately petered out. Hitler's last chance now lay in his so-called 'wonder weapons' – the V1s and V2s. Missions were flown to tactical targets throughout the remaining days of January but when the weather intervened the 8th mounted shallow penetration raids on Noball targets in France. The 8th also attempted several tactical missions, but the weather was so bad morale sagged as mission after mission was scrubbed, often just after take-off.

On 3 February 1945 Maj Robert 'Rosie' Rosenthal, flying his 52nd mission, led the 100th Bomb Group and the 3rd Division, to Berlin. Gen Earle E. Partridge approved the selection of a squadron commander to lead the division. Marshal Zhukov's Red Army was only 35 miles from Berlin and the capital was jammed with refugees fleeing from the advancing Russians. The raid was designed to cause the authorities as much havoc as possible. Just over 1,000 Fortresses were assembled for the raid and although the Luftwaffe was almost on its knees, the flak defences were as strong as ever.

A total of 2,267 tons of bombs reigned down into the 'Mitte' – or central district – of Berlin, killing an estimated 20,000 to 25,000 people. The German Air Ministry sustained considerable damage, the Chancellery was hard hit and the Potsdamer and Anhalter rail yards were badly hit. Reconnaissance photographs revealed that an area one and-a-half miles square, stretching across the southern half of the 'Mitte', had been devastated. The 8th lost 21 bombers over the capital and another six crash-landed inside the Russian lines. Among them was Maj Rosenthal, who put his aircraft down in Soviet territory. He and two others were picked up by the Russians while others were picked up by the Germans; one of whom was lynched by civilians. Of the bombers that returned, 93 had suffered varying forms of major flak damage.

On 6 February the 8th resumed its oil offensive with raids on synthetic oil refineries at Lutzhendorf and Merseberg. Bad weather forced all except one 1st Division Fortress to return to England while over the North Sea. Altogether, 22 bombers were lost in crashlandings in England. The sole B-17 continued to Essen and dumped its load before returning home alone without meeting any opposition. Such an occurrence would have been unthinkable a few months before but now the Luftwaffe had been all but swept from the skies. On 9 February the heavies returned to the oil refineries in the ever diminishing Reich. Bombing was made visually.

Again the 8th turned its attention to missions in support of the Russian armies converging from the east. At the Yalta Conference early in February 1945, Josef Stalin, the Russian leader, and his army chiefs, asked that the RAF and 8th Air Force paralyse Berlin and Leipzig and prevent troops moving from the west to the eastern front. British Prime Minister Winston Churchill and American President, Franklin D. Roosevelt agreed on a policy of massive air attacks on the German capital and other cities such as Dresden and Chemnitz. These cities were not only administrative centres controlling military and civilian movements, but were also the main communication centres through which the bulk of the enemy's war traffic flowed.

Spaatz had set the wheels in motion with a raid on Berlin on 3 February. Magdeburg and Chemnitz were bombed three days later but the most devastating raids of all fell upon the old city of Dresden in eastern Germany, starting with an 800-bomber raid by the RAF on the night of 13 February. Two waves of heavy bombers produced firestorms and horrendous casualties among the civilian population. The following day, 400 bombers of the 8th Air Force ventured to the already devastated city to stoke up the fires created by RAF Bomber Command. 8th Air Force crews were to return to the city of Dresden, famed for its porcelain, again in March and April 1945 on similar raids, but the Allied air forces' top priority remained the oil-producing centres.

On 16 February the heavies hit the Hoesch coking plant at Dortmund, estimated to be producing 1,000 tons of benzol a month. Bombing was completely visually and the Luftwaffe was noticeable by its virtual absence. But bomber losses continued to occur, mainly as a result of the bad weather which often affected forming-up operations over England.

On 22 February the 8th launched 'Clarion', the systematic destruction of the German communications network. More than 6,000 aircraft from seven different commands were airborne this day and they struck at transportation targets throughout western Germany and northern Holland. All targets were selected with the object of preventing troops being transported to the Russian front, now only a few miles from Berlin. Despite the low altitudes flown, only five bombers were lost, including one to an Me262 jet fighter.

Satan's Mate of the 385th Bomb Group, Great Ashfield. Lt James L. Fleisher (right) shakes hands with one of his crew after flying Satan's Mate *back from Rheine, Germany, in February 1945. It had got caught in the slipstream of another B-17 over Karlsruhe, shot up 90°, flopped over on its back and went down in a screaming dive. The airspeed read 380 mph by the time Fleisher and his co-pilot, Lt Paul H. Cowling pulled out. There were no injuries even though radio equipment blew out through the gun hatch and the waist gunners, Sgts Bob Cory and Trevor J. Kevan, were pinned to the top of the aircraft until it pulled out of the dive, when they fell to the floor. The only damage were 74 rivets missing from the stabilizer. (Ian McLachlan.)*

B-17G-40-BO 42-97130 of the 452nd Bomb Group, 8th Air Force, in flight. (USAF.)

Next day only two heavies failed to return from the 1,193 despatched. On 26 February even the normally notorious flak defences in Berlin could shoot down only five bombers. 'Clarion' had ripped the heart out of a crumbling Reich and the following two months would witness its bitter conclusion.

By March 1945 the Third Reich was on the brink of defeat and the systematic destruction of German oil production plants, airfields and communications centres, had virtually driven the Luftwaffe from German skies. Despite fuel and pilot shortages, Me262 jet fighters could still be expected to put in rare attacks and during March almost all enemy fighter interceptions of American heavy bombers were made by the *Jagdverbande*. On 2 March, when the bombers were despatched to synthetic oil refineries at Leipzig,

Me262s attacked near Dresden. On 3 March the largest formation of German jets ever seen made attacks on the 8th Air Force bomber formations heading for Dresden and oil targets at Ruhrland, shooting down three bombers.

On 15 March, 109 B-17s of the 15th Air Force bombed the synthetic oil plant at Ruhrland, just south of Berlin. On 18 March a record 1,327 8th Air Force bombers bombed the German capital. Flak was particularly hazardous and 37 Me262s of the *I* and *II. Jagdverbande 7* shot down 16 bombers and five fighters (another 16 bombers were forced to land inside Russian territory) for the loss of only two jets. The jet menace became such a problem that beginning on 21 March the 8th flew a series of raids on airfields used by the *Jagdverbande*. The raids also coincided with the build-up for the impending crossing of the Rhine by Allied troops. For four days the heavies bombed jet airfields and military installations.

On 22 March the 8th was requested by SHAEF HQ to bomb the Bottrop military barracks and hutted areas directly behind the German lines, while 136 B-17s of the 15th Air Force attacked Ruhrland again and caused extensive damage to the plant. Forty Me262s attacked the formation and shot down three of the Fortresses while P-51s shot down one of the jets and damaged five others.

Next day the 8th struck at rail targets as part of the rail interdiction programme to isolate the Ruhr and cut off coal shipping. Since the loss of the Saar basin the Ruhr was the only remaining source of supply for the German war machine. On 23/24 March, under a 66-mile long smoke screen and aided by 1,747 bombers from the 8th Air Force, Field Marshal Bernard Montgomery's 21st Army Group crossed the Rhine in the north while further south simultaneous crossings were made by Gen Patton's 3rd Army. Groups flew two missions this day, hitting jet aircraft bases in Holland and Germany.

Also on 24 March, B-17s of the 15th Air Force bombed the Daimler-Benz tank engine plant in Berlin. It was the first time the 15th had bombed the German capital. The leading 463rd Bomb Group lost four B-17s to an unexpected flak barrage near Brux on the outward leg of the 1,500-mile round trip, and a fifth was shot down by an Me262. A sixth, belonging to the 483rd Bomb Group, was also shot down by Me262s but further losses were prevented by prompt action from P-51 escort fighters. The 463rd Bomb Group's sixth loss occurred over Berlin when it fell victim to flak.

Bombers crews were now hard pressed to find worthwhile targets and the planners switched attacks from inland targets to coastal areas. Beginning on 5 April the weather over the continent improved dramatically and the B-17s were despatched to bomb U-boat pens on the Baltic coast. Everywhere the Allies were victorious but, while the enemy kept on fighting, missions continued almost daily. Such was the 8th Air Force's superiority that the B-17s assembled over France on 5 April, before flying in formation for an attack on the marshalling yards at Nuremburg.

On 7 April the Luftwaffe employed converted Bf109 fighters called 'Rammjägers', flown by suicide pilots from *Sonderkommando Elbe* in the fight against American bomber streams attacking underground oil refineries in central Germany. During their ramming attacks the suicide commandos were protected by Me262s. The *Rammjägers* dived into the bomber formations from a height of 33,000 ft and destroyed 23 aircraft.

On 8 April, the 8th put up 23 groups of B-17s and 10 groups of Mustangs to bomb targets in Germany and Czechoslovakia. On 9 and 10 April the German jet airfields were again bombed. The biggest 15th Air Force operation of all occurred on 15 April when 1,235 bombers were despatched to Wowser near Bologna. Next day the 98th and 376th Bomb Groups were taken off combat status and preparations began for an immediate return to the USA for retraining on the B-29 for missions against Japan.

On 17 April Dresden was again bombed. The German corridor was shrinking rapidly and the American and Russian bomb lines now crossed at several points on briefing maps. During the week 18 April–25 April, missions were briefed and scrubbed almost simultaneously. Gen Patton's advance was so rapid that on one occasion at least, crews were lining up for take-off when a message was received to say that Gen Patton's forces had captured the target the B-17s were to bomb!

Fortress crews flew three or four mercy missions to Holland until the end of hostilities, carrying food. One of them was before the Germans surrendered. Jim French, a B-17 tail gunner in the 452nd Bomb Group, recalls.

'A truce was arranged. We were ordered to reconstruct and strengthen the huge bomb bay doors in order that each bomber could carry 4,500 lbs of canned "C" rations in 50-lb cases. They were to be dropped in a free-fall from an altitude of 300 ft on a bomb-scarred airstrip west of Amsterdam. Armaments were not to be carried.

'As the B-17s crossed the coast of the Netherlands, the 900 combat veterans were scared. Was it a trick? Was this to be where the propaganda machine of Herr Goebbels would bolster the Third Reich? By the destruction of 100 bombers in one blow? The dykes had been blown a few days before to bog down a possible land invasion by the Allies.'

At dawn this bright sunshiny morning a Flying Fortress named *Not Today-Cleo* lumbered with an unusual cargo – would its bomb bay doors hold the shifting weights of the canned delights? There was to be radio silence. As the B-17s approached the European coast, the planes were

B-17s over Schiphol, Holland, during the mercy mission. (Hans Onderwater.)

low enough that rolls of barbed wire could be seen, strung for miles along the beaches. Uniformed German soldiers were patrolling, but only glanced up at the aluminium birds. The airmen began to rest easier at no sign of the deadly ack-ack guns. All of a sudden the intercoms were alive with laughter and joy.

'Look at three o'clock!' someone hollered. The bombers were flying over thousands of tulips in full bloom. Some Dutchmen, or maybe lots of them, had removed part of the tulips in a huge field. Plainly spelled out so it could be clearly read from the air, but not on the ground, were special words which said, 'Thanks Yanks.' The crews were exultant.

'As the four engines roared at full throttle over the airstrip, hundreds – no thousands – of what looked like little matchboxes tumbled from the planes ahead. They were the boxes of "C" rations. As they hit, broken open, and scattered wildly, cheers could be heard. Thousands of people lined the roads outside the airstrip barriers; they were not to collect the food gifts until the drop was complete.

'A native was riding a bicycle on a dyke. He looked up, the cycle turned, he rode into a canal.

'In Europe, cows were staked on a chain 20–30 ft long to graze. One ran in fright. As she came to the end of the chain, she went tumbling head over heels. In England's eastern counties cows were accustomed to low-flying planes, either landing or taking off. The noise would not have caused a stir.

'As the planes thundered over the city of Amsterdam, again the Germans were noticed, some on foot, some in tanks or other war vehicles. On the roof of a 10-storey building stood people waving and holding the "Stars and Stripes" all unseen by the enemy in the streets.

'What a glorious way for the Dutch to express their gratitude to a handful of Yanks. The planes turned northwards across the Zuider Zee, the North Sea and back to base at Deopham Green in East Anglia. In a few days Churchill announced to the world victory in Europe was at hand.'

The end came on 25 April when the 8th Air Force flew its final full-scale combat mission of the war, to the Skoda armaments plants at Pilsen in Czechoslovakia. To 40 aircraft in the 92nd Bomb Group went the honour of leading the strike force. *Fame's Favoured Few* was the oldest group in the 8th and this was its 310th and final mission. The 303rd Bomb Group at Molesworth chalked up the command record this day, flying its 364th mission while other groups came close to equalling it.

Next day the American and Russian armies met at Torgau. The last major air battle took place on 18 April when 305 B-17s and 906 B-24s of the 8th and 15th Air Forces plus more than 1,200 fighters, attacked Berlin. Forty rocket-firing Me262s tore into the 8th and 15th Air Force formations and shot down 25 bombers. During the week 18–25 April missions were briefed and scrubbed almost simultaneously.

On 25 April the 15th Air Force prevented German troops escaping from Italy by bombing lines of communication in Austria and the Brenner Pass.

The Germans in Italy surrendered on 29 April 1945 and the 15th Air Force heavies then joined the 8th Air Force in dropping supplies and evacuating Allied POWs from all over Europe. During the first week of May 1945 the German armies surrendered one by one to Montgomery at Lüneberg Heath, to Devers at Münich and to Alexander at Casserta and finally to Eisenhower at Reims in the early hours of 7 May 1945. The news of the Germans' final surrender was made known to the men at bases throughout eastern England on V.E. (Victory in Europe) Day, 8 May 1945.

When victory came the B-17 groups were assigned many tasks, such as flying Allied POWs home from their camps in eastern Europe to France, and airlifting displaced persons from Linz in Austria to their homes in France, Hol-

In the summer of 1945 this 388th Bomb Group B-17G was used to ferry German PoWs home to Germany. Gen Adolf Galland can be seen at far right. (Hans-Heiri Stapfer.)

land, Denmark and all other recently occupied countries. The B-17s airlifted troops from the United Kingdom to Casablanca where they continued on to the China–Burma–India theatre and also acted as 'moving vans' for fighter groups going to Germany as part of the occupation forces there. In addition, 'Trolley' or 'Revival' missions were flown to bombed out cities crammed with ground personnel to show them what destruction their aircraft had wrought. The flights ranged from 1,000 to 3,000 ft and the routes took passengers on what they described as a 'Cook's tour' of specially selected towns and cities which had been bombed by the 8th over the past four years.

CHAPTER 8

Bremen to Berlin

Larry Goldstein's Combat Log
September 1943 – March 1944

On 7 September 1943 the following message was received from Gen Ira C. Eaker, the Commanding General of VIII Bomber Command in England: 'The 388th Bombardment Group suffered heavy losses yesterday. The spirit of the Group in bearing those losses and coming back with fighting hearts is a matter of great gratification to me . . .'

The 388th Bomb Group, based at Knettishall, Suffolk, had just lost 11 of the 21 aircraft which

B-17s of the 388th Bomb Group cross Bremen on 8 October 1943. (USAF.)

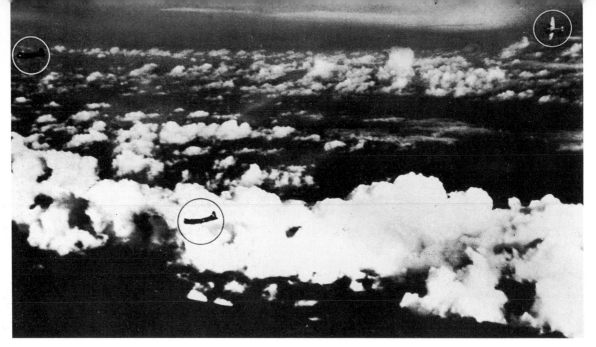

attacked aircraft components factories at Stutt-gart. It was only the Group's 19th mission since entering the air war in Europe. Approximately 150 fighters attacked the 388th formation while its 45th Combat Wing colleagues in the 94th, 96th and 385th Bomb Groups suffered no losses. The attacks centred on the low groups and the low squadron of the 388th, the 563rd, was hit by flak after the IP (Initial Point) and finished off by fighters.

Shedowanna flown by Lt Melville, was set on fire in the nose and one engine. Five of the crew managed to bail out near Strasbourg. The tail gunner was killed when the tail was blown off. Lt Roe's *Silver Dollar*, Lt Cunningham's *In God We Trust* and Lt A. Kramer's *Lone Wolf* were also lost. Flt Off M. Bowen's *Sky Shy* was badly hit by flak. The crew tried unsuccessfully to reach Switzerland and had to bail out near Ulm. The radioman was murdered by German civilians. By the time Spitfires rendezvoused with the forma-tion south of Bernay, France, six of the squa-dron's aircraft had been shot down.

After these heavy losses replacement crews

Left: 388th Bomb Group B-17s under attack from Luftwaffe fighters. (USAF.)

Below left: Crew of the Worry Wart *during training at Pendleton, Oregon. (Larry Goldstein.)*

Right: Larry Goldstein at Wendover air gunnery school July 1943 – the only air gunnery school without aerial gunnery (no flying). (Larry Goldstein.)

Below: Four members of the Worry Wart *crew at Topeka, Kansas, August 1943 (left to right) Sgt Howard Palmer, top turret; S/Sgt Jack Kings, waist gunner; Sgt Robert Miller, tail gunner; S/Sgt Larry Goldstein, radio operator. (Larry Goldstein.)*

were sent quickly to the 388th. One of them, which was sent to the depleted 563rd Squadron, was captained by Lt Belford 'B. J.' Keirsted, a former ballroom dancer from New York City. Larry 'Goldie' Goldstein, the 21-year-old radio-operator and former trainee draughtsman from Brooklyn, recalls:

'The night we arrived at Knettishall it was rainy, dark and cold; a typical English night. When we entered our Quonset hut which held six crews of six enlisted men apiece, there were six men lying around on their bunks. The other 30 beds were vacant with their mattresses all rolled up. The six men were all from Thibodeau's crew who flew a B-17 called *Pegasus*. When we asked "Why the empty beds?" we were told

they were left by the men who had gone down recently. This was rather discouraging.

'We soon fell into routine flying practice, practice and more practice. It seems that the 388th command demanded precision tight formation flying and we flew on many days. Tight formation flying brought more guns to bear and increased our overall protection. Enemy fighters seldom hit good formation flying outfits. Finally, we had the experience which should only come to a man once in his life. To me and all of my crewmates it came some 25 times. That is, the early morning call for a combat flight.'

The rest of Keirsted's crew consisted of co-pilot,

Larry Goldstein at the radio position, Knettishall 1943.
(Larry Goldstein.)

Lt Clifford 'Ace' Conklin, who had been a business student, from New York State. The mid-upper gunner, S/Sgt Howard 'Howie' Palmer, was also an ex-student and hailed from Boston. The bombardier, Lt Kent 'Cap' Keith, was a cowboy from Montana. The rest of the crew came from all parts of the USA. The navigator, Lt Philip 'Bloodhound' Brejensky was from Brooklyn and T/Sgt Jack Kings and S/Sgt E.V. Lewelling, the waist gunners, were from Virginia and Florida while the tail gunner, S/Sgt Robert Miller, was from Chicago. The ball turret gunner, T/Sgt Willie Suggs, came from South Carolina. The crew flew their first mission on Friday 26 November. Larry Goldstein began his combat log:

'It is a cold November morning, the barracks are dark. Each man was in his bed and knows there is a mission today because we had been alerted the night before. At 3:30 am the light is switched on. The CQ reads off the names of the crews for the mission and adds, the briefing is at 0600 hr. We tumble out of a warm bed, dress warmly, shave in cold water and board a GI truck in darkness to the mess halls for a breakfast we are not sure we can eat because of our nervous stomachs. Each man was wondering, "Will we make it back today?"'

'Briefing is cold and matter of fact. The target: Bremen. After the main briefing each man has his special briefing. I went to a communications briefing where radio operators received their special codes for the day. We checked out our parachutes, and the sign over the door "If it doesn't work, bring it back" was intended to lighten the tension. We dressed again in our flying clothes. First some warm underwear, some GI clothes and the famous blue heated suits. We removed all of our personal jewellery, wallets and rings, wearing only our dog tags. Then it was out to the trucks in the cold dawn for the ride to the plane. Nothing is more ominous than a B-17 standing in the early morning light, loaded with bombs, ready for its crew.'

Altogether, 633 bombers, the largest formation ever assembled by the 8th Air Force, were directed against targets in France and Germany. While 128 B-17s were to head in vain for Paris, where predicted clear skies failed to materialize, 505 B-17s prepared to attack the centre of the city of Bremen. Keirsted's crew was one of them. Goldstein wrote:

'Finally, we board the plane for a 0800 hr take-off after each of us has installed our machine-guns in their place. The metal was cold to the touch and at that time of the morning our nerves were tense and our stomachs unsettled. All in all we weren't ready for what was to come.

'The take-off and climb to altitude to get into formation was routine. There was much more flak and fighters always ready to knock the bombers down. The first flak I saw was just after we crossed the enemy coast. Talk about awesome; that was. The burst of black smoke was terrifying. A crewman commented over the intercom, "The ones you see are OK. It's the one's you don't see you have to worry about." A sick joke, but true.

'We saw two mid-air collisions of '17s and to a crew on its first mission it was an awesome sight. To lose an aircraft in non-combat situations seemed to be such a waste.'

Lieutenant W. H. McCown's crew, who were also on their first mission, were lost when a German-manned B-17 weaved around the formation and sliced the tail off their ship *Second*

Chance. Lt G. E. Branham's B-17 was the second 388th B-17 lost on the mission. Larry Goldstein concluded:

'Landed okay and was quite exhausted from being on oxygen for five hours. Although there were no enemy fighters encountered, the flak was heavy over the target. It was very close and I did quite a bit of "sweating it out". Only 24 more to go.

After two days' rest the 8th Air Force returned to Bremen on 29 November for a raid on the centre of the city again. Larry Goldstein wrote:

'Here we go again. Awakened at 3:30 am and was surprised when there were no eggs for the "last meal" as it is sometimes called. Had flap jacks instead.

'Took off okay and was soon headed out over the Channel, straight for Adolf's palace. We had some oxygen trouble and had to restrict our use to a minimal flow rather than 100% flow. The target was a 100% cloud covered and we had to return to Knettishall with our bomb load. This was never a comfortable feeling

to men with 10 500 lb bombs on board. At least I have adopted my mission preparation: the right clothes, the right routine. It was extremely cold today. 50 below zero. I say "God bless the Guy who invented heated flying clothes".

'We had many P-47 escorts today to give us a feeling of comfort also. At least today I knew what to expect. A few more and I will be a combat veteran.'

The mission to Solingen, Germany, on 30 November, resulted in an abort for Keirsted's crew as Larry Goldstein recalls:

'We had a runaway propeller and the engine threatened to catch fire and engulf the fuel cells. We aborted and made an emergency landing. As soon as we braked I heard over the intercom, "Howie, watch the prop". I went out the back with the rest of the crew and we ran across the field thinking our plane was ready to blow at any moment. As I looked over my shoulder I saw B.J. bending on one knee and I saw blood. I assumed he had been hurt but it was Howie Palmer who had been hit as the prop had

Worry Wart *crew in combat, Knettishall, February 1944. Back row (left to right) Lts Phil Brejensky, navigator; B. J. Keirsted, pilot; Cliff Conklin, co-pilot; Kent Keith, bombardier. Front row (left to right) S/Sgt Ed Kozacek, top turret gunner; S/Sgt E. V. Lewelling, waist gunner; T/Sgt Jack C. Kings, waist gunner; T/Sgt Larry Goldstein, radio-operator; S/Sgt Robert Miller, tail gunner. (Larry Goldstein.)*

kicked over on its last turn. Howie was hospitalised
and then returned to the States. He was replaced by
Eddie Kozacek!

Keirsted's crew had to wait until Sunday 5
December for their third mission, to Bordeaux.
Larry Goldstein recalls:

'Getting up early was routine business now. The target
was an airfield near the city. A very long flight, longer
than we were prepared for. While over the Channel
and not yet on oxygen the bombardier usually comes
back to remove the pins from the bombs, arming them.
For the second time in a row the target was cloud
covered and we returned with the bomb load. When
we were at a lower altitude and off oxygen the bombardier again came back to the bomb bay to insert the
safety pins. This was a bit scary because if we dropped
one or lost one we might have an armed bomb aboard
on landing. A few enemy fighters were encountered
but not nearly enough to cause much damage. The
flak, however, was plentiful and again I "sweated it
out". Fighter support was plentiful and there were
P-47s all over the sky. Returned early to dear old
Knettishall. We are now credited with 3 missions!'

On Monday 13 December the 3rd Division was
assigned the docks at Kiel. Larry Goldstein now
had a system of doing things for this type of mission.

'One of my personal hangups was to wear my GI shoes
into the plane, change into my heated slippers and
flying boots, then place the shoes tied together in a
place where I could reach them easily in case of a bale-
out call. Somehow I believed that in an emergency I
could pick them up, tuck them into my jacket and
have a comfortable pair of shoes to wear when I hit
the ground. In retrospect the shoes were to be long
gone once the 'chute jerked open.

'Heavy flak again today, especially from flak bar-
rages off the shore. We returned with a few holes in
the ship. The trip was rather long and it was cold at
altitude. Returned safely to the field but can truthfully
say that I "sweated" a bit today.'

On 16 December, the 8th returned to Bremen
for the first of three raids that month on the
German port. Larry Goldstein wrote:

'This was an all-out effort to blast it off the map.
There were more planes in the air than I have ever
seen before. We were in formation and well on our
way when I looked back from my radio hatch – all
I could see were bombers all over the sky: high, low,
left and right. It always gave a man chills to know that
so many planes were going into the flak after you. We
were told that it took time for the ack-ack gunners to
line up on the first planes. We were somewhat relieved
and luckier to be in the lead group.

'The flak over the target was very heavy and there
were a few ships hit. Just after the target and on our
turn for home we met our first enemy fighters. Our
bombardier said over the intercom "Those guys are
blinking their landing lights at us". Immediately,
"Ace" Conklin, our co-pilot yelled, "Those aren't
lights, they're wing guns". Then, as if by impulse,
every single .50 calibre gun in the formation opened
up. We felt like sitting ducks up there as fighters swept
through our formations. Reluctantly we admired those
enemy pilots making a pass through our formation in
the face of so many guns firing at them. We often dis-
cussed how the German fighter pilots had the guts to
fly through a formation of B-17s with all of our guns
firing at them at the same time. It took some kind of
courage.

'Our group was not hit but those on our right and
left were. We saw six B-17s go down. It's rough to
think that 60 men were involved and we would try
and count the 'chutes as they baled out, or at least
those that could get out.

'This was our Air Medal mission. If you completed
five missions the Air Medal was awarded. These first
five were tough with heavy flak and rough targets. It
was hard to believe that we had to do 20 more to go
home.'

A period of bad weather intervened, but missions
resumed in earnest on Christmas Eve when the
Fortress groups were despatched on a milk run
to the Pas de Calais where mysterious sites code-
named 'Noball' had been erected. Crews specu-
lated what the concrete sites were, but British
Intelligence had discovered that they were
launching sites for pilotless VI flying bombs
packed with explosive and aimed at London and
its environs. At Knettishall Larry Goldstein wrote
cryptically:

'The day before Christmas and all was not quiet in
the ETO. We were called out rather late in the morning indicating that it would be a rather short hop.
Briefed on a very interesting target. It was enemy
installations on the French coast near Abbeville. The
installations are supposed to be "rocket guns".

'At briefing we were told that there would be no
flak. We were also told that three planes would have
two external 500 lb bombs besides the regular 10
500-pounders on board. Those external bombs would
be armed before take-off. When we went out to the
plane we were suddenly aware that we had drawn the
short straw. It gave us a rather uncomfortable feeling
to be aboard that aircraft.

'Flight Control ordered the three aircraft to take off
first. Normally, our ground crews were blasé about the
Group take-offs, but not today. Everybody was on the
flightline to watch this odd occasion. We were number
two plane to take off and as we started our roll down

the runway we kept our fingers crossed. The 17 being the great aircraft it was lifted off okay and the sweat was over for the time being. Now all we had to do was face the flak and fighters.

'The bomb run was made at 12,500 ft which meant no oxygen. The target was hit right on the head and was completely demolished. The lead navigator took a wrong route home and we were almost knocked out of the sky going over the town of Dieppe. The guns opened up on us and were really on the ball as far as tracking us goes. We had quite a few holes but nothing serious. Good fighter cover but no enemy aircraft.'

Christmas came and went and on Thursday 30 December the bombers were assigned Ludwigshaven on the German-Swiss border. At briefing crews looked at the target map and concluded that with the course in and out it looked like a long, rough mission. The 388th's target was the I.G. Farbenindustrie chemical plant. Larry Goldstein recalls:

'This was a very long flight, about 1,100 miles. There was light flak but heavy fighter cover for us. Normally, a better than average mission but I lost a very close friend, T/Sgt D. Letter, this day. I had been with him since Gunnery School at Wendover, Utah, and all through phase training and into combat.'

Letter was the radio operator in 2/Lt A. W. Carlson's crew in *Satan's Sister*. On the bomb run the 388th ran into severe prop-wash from the Group ahead, causing the formation to bounce around. As a result, *Joho's Joker* slid in front of *Satan's Sister*, causing it to go out of control. Larry Goldstein adds:

'As I looked up and out of my radio hatch I saw Letter's plane in the high group swing back and forth several times. Suddenly, it was on a wing and flipped over. It broke in half in the middle of the radio room, fell down and back. *[Four members of the crew managed to bail out and they were later made PoW.]* When my crew realised that this was a crew we had trained closely with we immediately had a weak feeling in our stomachs. I have never lost a close friend before and it is not easy to take.'

'Missions were coming quite fast now,' wrote Larry Goldstein and on Friday 31 December crews were given a dubious New Year's Eve treat with 'milk-runs' to airfields in France. The 388th was assigned an airfield on the outskirts of Paris. 'When we were briefed', recalls Goldstein, 'our CO, Col William B. David, made a point that none of us was to spend New Year's Eve in Paris; it's an order!' A little humour to ease the tension. However, we were told to expect heavy fighter opposition and as heavy flak, as the actual target was an aircraft engine plant and would be heavily defended.

'The flak was not as bad as we had been led to believe. We really hit the plant with everything. From the reports we heard later our bombing was excellent. Pictures showed all bombs on the target and none in the city. The French would be madder than hell if we did. The support was excellent and we returned with no battle damage.'

Fog and rain prevented any further missions until Tuesday 4 January 1944. The briefing was earlier than ever before, with crews at Knettishall being awakened at 2 am. Goldstein wrote 'Most believed it was Berlin and started sweating it out'. However, the 388th was part of a diversionary force attacking Münster while the 1st Division hit Kiel and unescorted groups in the 3rd Division pounded targets in France. By now the crew had nicknamed their faithful 42-30241 *The Worry Wart* but no-one ever got around to painting it on the nose of their B-17.

Goldstein continues:

'The 388th were in the air by 7 am. Flak over the target came very close and Kent Keith, our bombardier, had a rather close call. While Keith was watching for "bombs away" a piece of flak hit the nose of the ship. As the Plexiglas shattered, a small piece hit him just over the left eye. He was extremely lucky.'

On 14 January Keirsted's crew reached double figures with a mission to the Pas de Calais. The crew had been alerted for a ferrying mission in the morning but a briefing at 11.30 changed this to a 1.30 afternoon take-off to France to bomb 'Noball' targets. Bombing was completed from 12,000 ft. With no enemy fighters or flak, Goldstein wrote that it was 'the prefect milk-run'. All of the crew added clusters to their Air Medals.

Seven days later, on Friday 21 January, the 388th returned to the Pas de Calais for another strike at 'Noball' targets. This was Keirsted's crew's 11th mission and it tested their luck as Larry Goldstein wrote:

'This mission was scrubbed two consecutive times and today, the briefing was the same as for the past few days. A rather important day for the crew. Firstly, our ship "241" was taken away from us. Secondly, we took off with the heaviest bomb load that a B-17 has ever carried. These were 12 500-pounders inside and two 1,000-pounders externally. This is 8,000 lbs of bombs. To add to this we had a Lt-Col from the Signal Corps riding with us as an observer. It was a heavy load but B.J. handled the ship okay.

'Unexpected cloud cover crept in and we were forced to make three bomb runs before hearing "bombs away" at 12,000 ft. No enemy fighters or flak so this was another "milk run". At this point 11 missions completed and 14 to go. Never once did we discuss our chances for survival. You could say we lived from day to day, never expecting the worst.

'On our 12th mission on Monday 24 January we had an exceptionally early briefing at 4.00 am. Our target was Frankfurt, a very long flight. Our pilots prided themselves for good formation flying but soon after flying into a cloud bank there were B-17s all over the sky. B.J. decided to abort as there was no formation to join. We were over enemy territory and just the danger of mid-air collision was enough to make that decision. Kent Keith wanted to unload the bombs on an airfield located between two small towns but without a bombsight he did not want to chance hitting the towns.

'To add a little extra excitement we had a new crew-member flying in the ball turret on his first mission. He became airsick and Jack Kings and I managed to get him out of the turret and into the radio room. This was not easy at 20,000 ft. We all returned to Knettishall safely with a full bomb load. The mission was

scrubbed but next day we received credit for a mission.

Mission 13 for the crew of *The Worry Wart* was back to Frankfurt on Saturday 29 January. Larry Goldstein wrote:

'We went all the way this time. Not much flak and no enemy fighters. P-38s and 47s galore. The sky over Europe belongs to the 8th Air Force. I was given the job of throwing chaff out of the radio chute. Our ball gunner got sicker than hell again and Jack, B.J. and I had quite a time with him. Can't go on like this. A fellow gets quite exhausted at 20,000 ft pulling another fellow around.' Mission completed he concluded, 'Over the hump and on the way home'.

Next day, Sunday 30 January, a record 778 bombers raided aircraft factories at Brunswick. Goldstein wrote:

'When the crews heard this at the briefing we remembered the heavy losses the 8th Air Force suffered on

B-17G-45-BO 42-97286 Skipper and The Kids *of the 388th Bomb Group in flight with wing-mounted 1,000 lb bombs. Capt John N. Littlejohn and crew were lost in this aircraft when it crashed on Beinn Nuis on the Isle of Arran during a cross-country navigation flight to Prestwick on 10 December 1944. Keirsted's crew had the unenviable task of flying with underwing bombs, to the Pas de Calais, on 21 January 1944. The safety pins to arm the bombs were removed by the bombardier who made a quick exit and return immediately before the take-off roll. To 'Goldie' Goldstein 'it was like sitting on a keg of dynamite'. (via Larry Goldstein.)*

A dramatic photograph of B-17F-100-BO 42-30362 Wee Bonnie II *of the 561st Bomb Squadron, 388th Bomb Group, flown by Lt Porter, dropping bombs over France on 31 January 1944. (USAF.)*

their last visit. We all tightened up and our stomachs begin to churn. The breakfast does not go down and doubts set in. Surprise, little flak and few fighters but bombing by our group and all the sweat and strain was for nought. We were supposed to bomb from 20,000 ft but we were forced to go to 29,000 ft to get out of cloud cover. Our bomb pattern seemed poor so I expect another visit to this place.'

Keirsted's crew were veterans now and their 15th mission was on Wednesday 3 February when the 388th was assigned Wilhelmshaven. Larry Goldstein recalls:

'The briefing again was early and getting out of a warm bed at 4.45 am and stepping into an English February morning can leave you chilled for the whole day. For some reason this was an easy mission. Picked up a flak hole in the right wing but there was no other damage. The worst part was the extreme cold, which was about 47 below zero.

'We were supposed to bomb from 27,500 ft but bad weather forced us to bomb from 22,000 ft. Because

of a shortage of gunners we had to fly with a nine-man crew, without ball and waist gunners. Operations wanted to cancel us but B.J. was eager to get the mission in. When we went into the combat area we released the turret from a locked position and Jack Kings gave the turret a shove every once in a while to make it appear occupied. Fortunately, the enemy fighters did not take on the 388th today.'

Keirsted's crew sewed on their second cluster and prepared for the 16th. It came the following day, making it their seventh raid in eight days and the target was Frankfurt again. The lead navigator could not locate the target and the 388th bombed the secondary. Goldstein noted:

'We went through the southern part of the Ruhr Valley and it was an awful experience. The "Happy Valley Boys" can really throw up a heavy barrage of flak. It was very heavy today and Jack Kings had a close call. Flak entered just below his gun position but armour plate deflected it. After "bombs away" the pilots used evasive action and really threw the plane around the sky. It was the heaviest flak I have yet to see. Thank God there was no fighter opposition. We sweated this one out. Many planes went down and we settled for quite a few flak holes. Returned to base with a few flak holes, one of which necessitated a wingtip change.'

The crew of *The Worry Wart* only had nine more missions to go. One of the barrack room jokes was '16 mission and no rest home yet.' Crews that had battle fatigue were sent to a rest home for a week or 10 days and then came back to combat flying. Goldstein recalls:

'We reached 17 without anybody suggesting a rest home to us. We went on a two-day pass to London and we arrived in town late in the evening. When we woke up in the morning we read in the papers that American air forces had heavy losses on the raid the day before. It made us relieved that we were safe in London while our friends may have gone down or were PoWs.'

Following the pass, Keirsted's crew flew their 17th mission, to Romilly-sur-Seine, on Sunday 6 February. However, the 388th failed to find the target in the cloudy conditions prevailing and crews brought their bombs back. Despite the failure the mission counted and the crew now had only eight missions to go.

Missions resumed on Tuesday 8 February with a visit to Frankfurt again. Goldstein recalls:

'It was almost a routine combat mission except for the fighter and the extremely heavy flak. The cold was tremendous and my heated gloves and shoes went on the blink. The gloves were plugged in at the wrists and the boots plugged in at the ankles. If one of these shorted out the other three extremities shorted out. This day my left boot shorted out. However, some genius had had the foresight to supply a plug which we carried and when used it closed the circuit for the other three limbs. It took me some time to realise that it was the left boot; the heavy clothes and manning the radio and a gun made this somewhat difficult to accomplish. I did, however, find the right limb and when the plug was inserted I closed the circuit. It was 47 below and I really had to do quite a bit of stomping and clapping all the way to the target and all the way back to keep my limbs warm. I like to think that I walked from France to Frankfurt and back to England.'

Apart from the cold the young American from Brooklyn was also scared at the sight of one of the engines smoking on the way to the target, but the aircraft returned safely to Knettishall. Goldstein noted that he was 'rather tired of visiting Frankfurt' and hoped that 'perhaps it has been finished off by now'.

Another city which was very unpopular with fliers was Brunswick. A mission to the city was scrubbed on 9 February but Keirsted's crew were one of 22 388th crews assigned the target on the 10th. It was their 19th mission and a significant one for Larry Goldstein, whose 22nd birthday it was.

'Today was the roughest mission of all my 18 missions. We hit the French coast and picked up enemy opposition and they continued to attack all the way to the target and back again to the coast. I saw more fighters today then ever before. There were 109s, 190s, 110s and Ju88s. We had good fighter support of 38s, 48s and 51s but I'm afraid that we need more of them. They did a swell job of protecting us but the German fighter pilots were determined to knock down as many Forts as possible. Quite a few planes did go down and even saw our own fighters taking it on the chin.

'The target was hit very hard and I believe that it was a shack job. I really sweated today. The flak at the target was not too heavy, but plenty accurate. It was about 54 below and that's plenty cold. Returned safely with very minor damage. Believe me, I am not ashamed to say that I was scared today and never prayed harder to come through. Nineteen missions completed.'

Three crews in the 388th failed to return. There then came a break in missions. Gen Jimmy Doolittle, Commanding General, 8th Air Force, was biding his time, waiting for a period of relatively good weather in which to carry out a series of strikes on German aircraft production centres. The general was informed that the week 20-25 February would be ideal for such a series of missions. The offensive was to go down in the history of aerial warfare as 'Big Week'.

Like so many mornings in England the sky in the early hours of Sunday 20 February was clear but a few stray clouds drifting in from the North Sea gave warning of an instrument assembly above 10/10ths cloud by take-off time. A force of over 800 heavies was assembled as the anticipated cloud scudded across eastern England, bringing with it snow squalls which threatened to disrupt the mission. The 1st and 2nd Bomb Divisions were briefed to hit the Messerschmitt Bf109 plants at Leipzig, bombed only a few hours earlier by RAF Bomber Command. The 3rd Division, meanwhile, would fly an equally long and arduous route, to Posnan in Poland.

In the 388th Bomb Group briefing room 37 crews viewed the map with a sense of foreboding. The map was covered as always but there was an extension on the righthand side of it. The regular map which reached from England to east of Berlin was too small for this raid! The cover was pulled away and there it was! The red tape ran out from England over the North Sea to Denmark, across it, out over the Baltic Sea, then back in over eastern Germany and into Poland. Poznan, 1,200 miles away, was the target.

'Men', Col William B. David was saying, 'Your bomb load is 5000 lbs, gas load, naturally maximum. Don't start your engines before you have to. You'll need all the gas you have. Altitude is 11,000 feet. Over the Baltic you'll climb to 17,000, which is your bombing altitude. If you lose an engine over or near to the target, check your gas and if you don't think you can make it, head for Sweden. Our wing is bombing Poznan. The 13th Wing will go part of the way but are bombing about where you will hit the German coast, so you'll be alone all the way back. The rest of the 8th will be bombing targets all over central and southern Germany. You'll have no fighter escort so shoot at anything you see in the way of a fighter. Keep on the ball and good luck to all of you.'

Crews at Knettishall began taking off at 0723 hr. Assembly was completed and the formation crossed the North Sea to Denmark. The weather was clear and the Luftwaffe attacked. The German fighters continued attacking until the 388th was well out over the Baltic. The lead ship changed course to the southeast and climbed to 17,000 ft. Clouds began piling up from beneath the formation again and the German coast was blotted from view. By the time the formation was almost into Poland, German fighters were making steady, unrelenting diving attacks on the formation and there was no break in the undercast. Targets in Poland could not be bombed without being identified, so a decision was taken to bomb Rostock instead.

The formation was still at 17,000 ft and using a lot more fuel than it would had the Forts dropped their bombs and gone back down to 11,000. Sixteen of the Group's 21 B-17s were still in formation. One of them was Keirsted's. Larry Goldstein recalls:

'There were quite a few enemy fighters but somehow they were not too eager and did not pester us'.

Bomb doors on the 388th Fortresses swung open and they fell in behind the 96th Bomb Group which had the PFF ship. Suddenly, flak appeared and it became thicker and more accurate as the Group neared the point of bomb release. Two long streams of white from marker bombs dropped by the PFF ship arched downwards.

B-17G of the 388th Bomb Group in flight.
(Ian McLachlan.)

The 388th dropped their bombs, relieved to feel their bombers leap upwards, free of their bombloads. The flak continued for about a minute longer then began to disappear. Keirsted and his fellow pilots, free of the bombloads, were able to cut down on their power settings.

Only a few Ju88s remained and every now and then they lobbed a rocket at the American armada, careful to stay out of range of the B-17s' formidable machine-guns. The rockets sailed into the high squadron, bursting like flak. Fire broke out on the right wing of Lt R. F. Reed's B-17 after it was hit by a 20mm shell. It flew for a minute longer, then rolled up on one wing and started down. Reed and his co-pilot W. E. Osness got the bomber under control and opened the bomb doors for bail-out. Suddenly, there was flash, a huge billowy puff of smoke and jagged pieces of broken, twisted metal fluttered aimlessly earthwards. The co-pilot remained with the aircraft and was killed but the rest of the crew

Above: Loading bombs into a B-17 of the 388th Bomb Group. (Ian McLachlan.)

Right: A B-17 formation leaving contrails. (USAF.)

bailed out and were made Pow. Lt J. B. Payne's B-17 was also hit and all except the tail gunner died when an emergency landing was attempted in enemy territory.

The 388th crossed Denmark and, leaving the coast, let down to 10,000 ft and loosened the formation as the fighters fell away. Needles on the B-17s fuel gauges flickered and many a crew cast an anxious eye at the dials as they flew over the North Sea. The sun was low in the west as the Forts neared England. Every few minutes one of the bombers would drop out of formation to save fuel. Over East Anglia the B-17s dropped through the darkening gloom, still on instruments. Crews were dead tired but alert during the final let-down procedure as they looked eagerly for signs of the ground, or other B-17s which might collide with them.

Finally, at 750 ft the bombers broke out of the cloud. It was raining but visibility was fair. Flares on the runway at Knettishall glowed in the gloom in the distance. Aircraft landed from all directions. It was only after they landed that crews realised how tired they were. Keirsted also had to nurse his bomber back to Knettishall with rapidly diminishing fuel reserves. Goldstein recalls:

'We landed at dear old Knettishall in a heavy late afternoon haze and in almost total darkness. I believe we stretched the B-17 to its maximum and as always it brought us home in one piece. The mission count at this point was 20. We started thinking about it but did not say it out loud: "Can we as a crew make it through 25?" No-one talked about it, but I'm sure we all thought about it.

'No. 21 was another run to Brunswick on 21 February. Our last mission to this city was a nightmare. I'm sure that all my fellow crewmembers felt the same as I did: "Will we survive this one, will we come home to our own beds?" It seemed from past experiences that every time the 8th went to Brunswick it was a bloodbath.

'Our fighter support was plentiful and did a magnificent job protecting us. The rest of the mission wasn't too bad and I recorded this as an "easy" mission. We were very tired flyers. We had been flying many missions, mostly long flights to heavily defended targets and all major aircraft component plants.'

On Thursday 24 February the 3rd Division was assigned Rostock but heavy cloud over the target forced the Fortresses to head for their secondary target at Posnan, missed four days before. Larry Goldstein wrote:

'We ran into some flak along the route and one par-

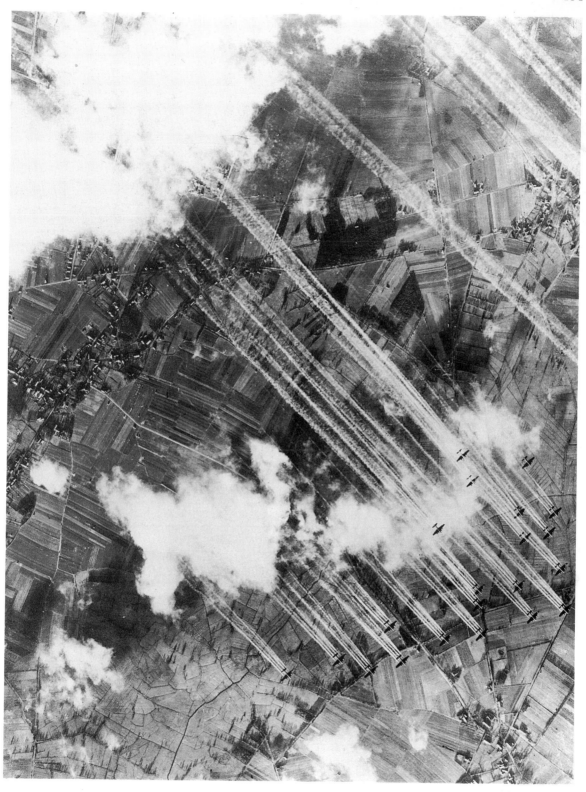

ticular barrage hit us in the right wing. Luckily, it was not in an engine. We were hit by fighters and as we had no support all the way we had a battle on our hands. I did quite a bit of shooting today. A few fighters kept pecking away at us and there were a few 17s that went down.

'Bombs were dropped in a scattered manner. I do not think we did a good job at all. The mission was long and tiresome. We had a heading set for Sweden in case we could not make it back to England. We were airborne for over 11 hrs and the fact that we landed at Knettishall in almost total darkness was in itself a miracle. Our pilots were really great people. They knew how to fly and they knew how to get us home. We were exhausted and could hardly get to the mess hall for the evening meal.

'At this point we as a crew figured that the next three missions to bring us to the magic number of 25, would, by the law of averages, be simple, light missions. How wrong we were.'

Despite the long and dangerous mission to Posnan, tired and weary crews at all 3rd Bomb Division bases were tumbled out of their warm cots at 0300 hr the following morning, Friday 25 February, for an equally arduous mission, to the Messerschmitt plant at Regensburg, while the 1st Bomb Division headed for Augsburg and Stuttgart. The 3rd Division had last visited Regensburg on 17 August 1943 when the B-17s had suffered devastating losses. The Germans had given top priority to the reconstruction of the Regensburg plant and within six months had restored production to something like its previous output. The spectre of Schweinfurt and Regensburg was still uppermost in the minds of all the B-17 crews and this time the 3rd Division would share the bombing of Regensburg with the Italy-based 15th Air Force which would bomb an hour before the England-base force arrived over the city.

Beautiful weather greeted crews as they assembled over England and headed for the continent at 21,000 ft. Flak bracketed the 388th as they crossed the French coast near Le Havre and some ships sustained hits. Soon the B-17s flew out of range and crews peered into the distance in search of their fighter escorts, but they failed to show. For another 30 min the 388th flew on eastwards but still it found itself alone. Suddenly, fighters appeared, but they were Focke-Wulf 190s, Ju88s and Bf109s. They circled in ever increasing numbers, then they pulled up ahead of the B-17s and started their attacks.

It was almost 1200 hr when the 388th sighted a column of smoke rising almost to their altitude from fires at Regensburg left by the 15th Air Force. The Alps could be seen quite clearly to the south. The 388th added its bombs to the conflagration and headed for home through thick flak and heavy fighter attacks. A new tiredness seeped through crews' bodies as the strain of flying several long combat missions during the week began to tell. Larry Goldstein recalls:

'The flak had been mostly scattered and ineffective but at one point over the target it was intensive and very accurate. Some aircraft were hit. Luckily not ours. A few enemy fighters pecked away but fortunately we were not the group to be hit. Our fighter support was supposed to be there but they only showed up when it was too late. This was one of those fouled up missions. The only thing right was our bombing.

'The raid was a great morale booster at a time when it was needed. As it turned out this raid was also important for the invasion which was to come later. My brother was in the US Army tank forces and he later told me that when his unit entered Regensburg the plant was in a shambles.'

The 8th Air Force had exacted a heavy toll on the German aircraft plants for the loss of 31 bombers. The Regensburg raid marked the end of 'Big Week'. Vast cloud banks over the continent prevented follow-up missions so, while the bomb groups licked their wounds, Gen Doolittle and his staff officers spent the time assessing the results and implications of their actions over the past five days. It also allowed crews a long overdue and very welcome respite. Larry Goldstein recalls:

'Between 25 February and 2 March we had bad weather and an abort (on 29 February when the target was Brunswick). We added new crews and new aircraft to our depleted forces. We were veteran fliers and not many crews made it to this point. We had two missions to go; would we make it?'

Unfortunately, a decision taken by Jimmy Doolittle would give Keirstead's crew their sternest test yet. The general concluded that 'Big Week' had dealt the German aircraft industry a really severe blow and he felt confident the 8th could strike at Berlin in the very heart of the Third Reich.

A raid by the 8th Air Force on Berlin had been scheduled for 23 November 1943 but had been postponed because of bad weather. The momentous day arrived on the morning of 3 March. For Keirsted and his crew it was their penultimate mission; one more and they could go home to the USA! Larry Goldstein recalls:

'We were called out to a very early briefing. When we entered the briefing room the chaplains were very visible. This made us uneasy and we thought it must be something big. When the route and the target were explained to us there was not one man in the room who thought he would be sleeping in his own bed that night. At the revetment while we waited to board our aircraft, all of us constantly watched for a flare shot from the control tower scrubbing the mission. It never came.

'As we waited for our chance for take-off I tuned to Radio Bremen which spoke in English. Here we were waiting to take off for a raid over Germany and Radio Bremen was saying "American bombers are on their runways in England now, waiting to attack northwest Germany". How did they know?

'We finally got into our take-off position and rolled down the runway. Take-off was at 0730 hr. Soon after forming, the group was off on its way. I sat at my radio with my headset tight on my ears waiting for the abort signal but it never came. We used a tricky route in to the target and were to bomb and get the hell out quickly. The weather was our friend. It turned bad and the mission was finally scrubbed after our target was socked in.

'I recorded the recall in my log and after many repeats I called to B.J. on intercom. One very sharp operator somewhere in the force acknowledged receipt of the recall even though he was not authorised to do so. Then over the VHF system someone in authority ordered a recall. Non acknowledgement of the recall could have been disastrous. We turned about and headed for home. As we were well over enemy territory and flew in and out of heavy flak we received credit for a mission. We brought our bombs back and returned okay despite a bad engine.

'When we landed and pulled into our revetment, a communications officer drove up in a jeep, confiscated my radio log and ordered me to report to a Group Communications meeting immediately. It seemed that the mission lead and deputy lead radio operators never heard or acknowledged the recall. I was on duty, recorded the recall, and was not one of those reprimanded.'

That night Larry Goldstein wrote in his diary, 'One more to go. God be good to me on the next one!' Crews in the 388th Bomb group were roused from their beds early on Saturday 4 March when 'Big-B' was again the target. Larry Goldstein wrote:

'Extra early briefing attended by all three chaplains: Jewish, Catholic and Protestant, gave added importance to the destination. The briefing was a duplicate of yesterday; back to Berlin for the first daylight raid of "Big B". After briefing we hoped the mission would

be scrubbed and we constantly watched the control tower for a red flare. It never came.

'Take-off and assembly were normal but we were a little bit more on edge. Over France and into Germany we had flak and fighters but no damage or injuries. Just before we reached the target there was a recall of the formation for the second straight day. As a crew we made a decision by vote over the intercom to drop our bomb load on some target. Keith picked out a railroad marshalling yard on the German-French border. We dropped out of formation to make our bomb run despite "Ace" Conklin's warning that the formation was getting father and farther away.

'After "bombs away" we climbed back towards the formation, now many miles ahead. Our bomb bay doors were closing and according to Kent Keith they were closed. My job was to check those doors visually. I did. They were open. Several more attempts to close them were futile so B.J. gave the order for Jack Kings to leave his top turret and hand crank them closed.

'We were at about 25,000 ft. I watched to make sure he did not pass out. Suddenly, there was a loud explosion. An Me109 must have seen a straggling Fort and fired several 20mm shells at us. B.J. and Conklin took evasive action by falling off to the right. Every time we came out of the clouds the German fighter was there with a couple of shots across our nose. We levelled off in the clouds before taking a head count. No-one reported any battle damage or injury. Little did we know that we were severely damaged.

'We finally broke out over France. Our navigator, Lt Brejensky, was unable to plot a course and I was asked to get a heading. Our "G Box" was out of order so I contacted the RAF distress channel for help. God bless them because they answered immediately in the clear with a course for England, but the Germans immediately jammed it. A friend of mine, T/Sgt Wallace Gross, was flying as the alternate radio operator. Normally he was radio man on Hulcher's crew but somehow he was one mission behind his crew and volunteered to fly the ball position. He was not eager to be there for the whole flight and was sitting on the radio room floor. He was a crackerjack radio man and immediately set up another frequency. Again I transmitted and again the receiver message was jammed. We began to panic but Wallace put in a third unit and we received a heading which I gave to the navigator and when we broke out of the cloud we were over the Channel.

'The rest should have been routine – but it wasn't. We were probably the last aircraft to land. Everybody had seen us get hit and figured that we were lost. As we came over Knettishall our landing approach was normal until touchdown . . . no brakes. We went off the end of the runway and did a slow ground loop coming to a halt. The fire trucks all rushed to our aid but they were not needed. The medics wanted to know if the radio operator was hurt. When someone on our

Above: B-17G-5-BO 42-31163 A Good Ship and Happy Ship, *of the 388th Bomb Group which landed at Rinkaby, Sweden, on 6 March 1944 after sustaining flak damage on the Berlin raid.* (via Frank Thomas.)

Left: Larry Goldstein (left) and Wilbur Richardson (see chapter Strategic Air Force) pose in front of B-17G Sentimental Journey *at the National Warplane Heritage show at Geneseo, New York, in August 1989.* (Author.)

plane said I was okay one of the fireman pointed to a tremendous hole in the right side of the radio room. It was then that I realized that we had flown like that for some three hours. I was probably too scared to realise how dangerous it had been. Nevertheless, it was 25 and home. We walked away from the plane and said our own individual prayers of thanks.

'On 5 March there was no raid. On 6 March as we lay comfortably in our beds at four in the morning

there was a call for briefing. It was a great thrill and some satisfaction to all of us to just turn over and go back to sleep.'

The 8th Air Force went to Berlin again. Sixty-nine aircraft, including the aircraft Keirsted's crew had finished on, were lost. The 388th lost seven Fortresses on the mission. Goldstein recalls:

'We were laying on our bunks in the barracks and someone said "Dopko's crew went down today on their first mission". Ft Off Dopko's crew were our room-mates and had flown a B-17 over the African route. Replacement crews always had brand new equipment plus Dopko's had a much cherished item; custom-made leather boots from Africa. There was a made scramble as 25 men reached for the brand new equipment and the leather boots.

'Later that evening after chow one of our barrack members said, "Guess who I saw having late chow – Dopko's crew". They had made it back home [in *Little Willie*] on the deck, had landed at another base and had been trucked over. We were embarrassed. Each of us who had taken some piece of equipment attempted to put it back. Unfortunately, we could not remember where all of the items went so they were just piled on one bed. When Dopko's crew walked into the barracks the quiet was astounding. Although one of Dopko's crew complained to the CO, nothing ever came of it. It seems this was an accepted way of life. (Three days later Dopko's crew did go down. We didn't have the heart to do what we had done once before.)'

On 8 March, five 388th Bomb Group B-17s had failed to return from another raid on the capital. Most came from the 563rd Squadron. Keirsted's decision to fly all possible missions had paid off for the crew of *The Worry Wart*.

CHAPTER 9

Fall of the Forts

One of the seven 388th Fortresses lost on 6 March 1944 was *Shack Rabbits*, flown by Lt A.B. Christiani. This crew was just one of thousands of 8th and 15th Air Force Flying Fortress crews which had to bale out over enemy territory in World War Two. Most were taken prisoner while some were fortunate to evade capture with the help of the resistance armies in Europe and were returned to England and Italy. For those who were 'guests of the Third Reich' though, captivity was often painful, demeaning and uncertain. *Kriegsgefagenen* (prisoners of war) were incarcerated in Stalags throughout Germany and Poland run by the Luftwaffe. Ray Newmark, the bombardier aboard *Shack Rabbits*, recalls the events of the day he would never forget.

'We got to Berlin and could see our checkpoints on the river. We were around 24,000 ft and ready. Suddenly, we were told to circle Berlin again. We had already survived the flak. We almost decided to abort. We made a very sharp turn out of the area and headed for the secondary target. We were scared. We did not want any more flying over Berlin.

'As soon as we relieved ourselves of our bomb load we headed back to base. We dodged some flak and there were no fighters. It seemed we were living under the wings of angels because other groups were getting picked up and strafed. When our lead navigator radioed that up ahead was the Zuider Zee and we could see it, we started a turn and began to relax. Off came our oxygen masks and we started eating our Mars bars. All of a sudden, at about 2 o'clock high, I saw some specks in the distance. "Here come the P-51s. It's about time," I said. A few seconds later someone said, "Hey they're flashing their lights at us". Someone else said, "they're not lights: they're shooting at us!" Sure enough they were the yellow-nosed kids from Abbeville.

'Those German pilots were terrific. They came

through our group and we closed in as tight as we could possibly get. I shot at one that came across our nose from around 3 o'clock. I led him and saw him blow up. Then I ran my guns to another one which was coming in at 2 o'clock but I forgot to release my finger on the trigger and my guns froze. The formation at this time had really spread out and we wound up as tail-end charlie. All of a sudden I got hit in my left forearm by a 30-30, a 20 mm armour piercing incendiary (API) and another 30-30 simultaneously. (We knew they were firings APIs because we could see them going through the airplanes and exploding elsewhere instead of on impact. It was lucky for me because the API went right through my arm and exploded in the No 1 and 2 engines. One of the 30-30s bounced off my flak helmet and the other bounced off my flak suit. The impact of all three knocked me clear all the way back to the hatch underneath the pilot's seat.

'As I lay there looking up I could see that the plane was a blazing inferno. T/Sgt S Ciaccio, the engineer, was screaming in his top turret. He was on fire from head to foot. There was no way of saving that boy. I did not see Christiani the pilot or Farrington, the co-pilot. I yelled to Lt Levy, the navigator, to get me an oxygen mask; I was starting to lose consciousness. Mine was knocked off by the impact and shredded. Luckily, the extra mask was laying near the escape hatch. He slapped it on me, plugged into the oxygen system and revived me. The next thing I know, I said "Get my 'chute". My chest pack was completely shredded. Luckily, the extra 'chute was available to be snapped on. Levy said, "I'm going to pull the hatch door and get you out of here". I said "OK, providing you follow me".

'He pulled the release and shoved me out at around 20,000 ft. As I left the door, suddenly it became quiet. I passed out momentarily. I revived and realised that I had to pull the ripcord on my parachute. I reached over and could not find my left arm, I thought, "Oh my God; my arm's been blown off." I pulled at my flight suit and there was my arm but it was dangling.

I could do nothing with it so I picked it up and put the thumb in between my teeth so that it would remain there if and when I pulled the ripcord the impact wouldn't snap off my arm. I passed out again. The next time I revived I was face down and floating like a falling leaf. I was at about 2,000 ft and the ground was rushing up to me. I just did not have the strength to pull the ripcord. I said, "God, give me the strength" and with one big yank I pulled the ripcord. The 'chute popped open and I bit my thumb so hard I killed all the nerves, permanently.

'I landed in a field that had just been ploughed. It was as soft as a feather bed. I was a young 22 year-old and like most of us, didn't have much religion in those days. But suddenly I believed that there was something or someone looking out for me. I tried to remove the parachute and harness from my body when a farmer and his two children came up to me. They spoke to me in what appeared to be German but I realised it had to be Dutch. I needed to get out of the harness and also get some morphine because I was in a heck of a lot of pain. I unzipped my first aid kit attached to my harness and reached inside for the morphine sachet. I broke it open with my teeth and was about to inject it into my arm when the farmer grabbed it and threw it away. He said, "No, no! Do not commit suicide! We will help you." It seems as though the Germans had indoctrinated those people to believe that American flyers would rather commit suicide rather than be captured; which was wrong. So there I was without anything to kill the pain.

'I looked down to unhook my harness and realised that my right leg parachute harness had not been fastened but I was still alive with nothing wrong with my crotch. It was a miracle because I had always been told if the harness was not tightly fastened it could pull you apart. All these wonderful things were beginning to dawn on me. Who am I to deserve all this? I shouldn't be here; I should be dead.

'The farmer marched me to his house. His daughter was crying because I must have looked like the man from Mars, covered in grease and blood. The farmer sent his 12 year-old son to get a doctor in Zwolle who was helping downed Allied airmen. The farmer's wife made me some porridge and tried to clean and console me. She used my white silk scarf to make a sling for my arm. It eased the pain a little. About four hours later near dusk the boy returned. He was crying bitterly. The doctor had been executed in the town square by the Gestapo.

'The farmer could get me back to England via the Underground but it would take at least a week and probably I would not make it because of my wounds. Alternatively, I could be turned in so I could get immediate medical attention under the terms of the Geneva Convention. It would save my life. I decided I would become a POW.

'I gave him my .45 pistol. He turned it on me as if he had just captured me and marched me up to the road from his house. It wasn't very long before a black car with two men dressed in black with hats on came along. As luck would have it they were the goddamned Gestapo. They thanked the farmer, took the gun and put me into the car to take me to town. I was thrown into jail, interrogated, beaten and my wounded arm kicked time and again. I told them I didn't know anything and cussed them. The more I cussed them the worse it got. Thank God I passed out. The pain was excruciating.

'Next morning the Luftwaffe came to get me and drove me to an airfield where the 109s who shot down were based. A lot of captured Americans were there. So too was Hermann Goering himself! He was up on a stage in front of us and the whole squadron of Luftwaffe pilots. Over the loudspeaker he lauded us. "Only the flyers are heroes in this war" he said, "I salute you." He broke out the champagne and passed round glasses. We all had to drink a toast with him. The irony of it all. He told us that the wounded would be sent to hospital and the others would be sent to a POW camp. Christiani, Levy and the two waist gunners were the only survivors from my crew. They were shipped off to POW camps. I was put in a truck with four other fellers, on top of a bunch of dead bodies.

'We were taken across the Ems River to Lingen in northwestern Germany. An improvised barn was turned into a Lazarett (hospital) where about 10 of us were laid on beds with wooden slats and straw. An 18 year-old gunner, who was wounded in the shoulder, was laid next to me. A badly burned P-51 pilot was in terrific pain. A P-38 pilot who had his ankle

Smoke marker narrowly misses a B-17. (USAF.)

blown off was in another bed. There was another guy with an arm blown off and another with an eye out.

'The place was run by French collaborators; two doctors and a padré. I was becoming a nervous wreck. They decided to amputate my arm but before I went to the operating room one of the German nurses asked me demurely if she could have a piece of my soap from a Red Cross parcel I had been given. I said "Sure," providing she would not let the doctors cut off my arm. I had feeling in my fingers and I wanted my arm saved. She felt my fingers and they were warm. When I woke up back in my bed my arm was still intact. They had improvised a cast and a big wire cage. All that was visible was an artery and there was a hole about 5 in wide right across the whole arm. I did not have a connected arm except for the artery.

'One of the Polish orderlies prepared a solution and cleaned out my arm. The searing hot bullet and freezing cold sealed my arm and miraculously I never got an infection. He spent night after night pulling out the flak from my face and eyes with a pair of tweezers by the light of my Ronson lighter. If he had been caught he would have been shot. After six weeks my wrist was 3 in from my elbow because the artery kept shrinking. I kept begging those bastards to clean the wound of the 18 year-old because I could smell the infection. They ignored him and within two weeks he died of gangrene poisoning.

'In early June four of us left on crutches and were moved on to Dulag Luft and then prison camp.'

Twenty-one year-old Rueben 'Ruby' Fier, a B-17 navigator in the 94th Bomb Group at Bury St.

Edmunds, Suffolk, is another airman who suffered at the hands of the Gestapo. Fier had been shot down on his 10th mission, in *Pacific Steam* on 31 December 1943, over Cognac. His pilot, Edward J. Sullivan, co-pilot Cliff Robinson and Elmer Shue, the flight engineer, were captured on landing by parachute. The remainder of the crew evaded capture and escaped over the Pyrenees into Spain and were subsequently returned to England.

Fier evaded capture for two months by living in various parts of France with Maquis groups and others who risked their lives to hide him. After an unsuccessful attempt to cross the Pyrenees, in which Fier developed frost-bitten toes, he and two others were captured by French gendarmes on a road between Axat and La Pradelle. They were turned over to the Gestapo and taken to Gestapo headquarters in Carcassonne. Fier recalls:

'After questioning, being threatened and being smacked a couple of times because of my responses, I was taken to Paris by train and then by bus to Fresnes Prison on the outskirts of the city.

'During my stay at Fresnes Prison, Levi Collins, a Dutch sergeant and I were caught trying to cut our way out of our fifth-floor cell. The Dutch sergeant was taken from our cell and I never saw him again. Levi Collins and I were removed to individual cells on the first floor of our section of the prison. I was put in a darkened cell with all bedding removed and my

A direct hit. There were no survivors. (USAF.)

hands were handcuffed behind my back.

'After four days' confinement Collins and I were taken to the Kommandant's office and after a "royal chewing" through an intepreter, were told that we would be confined to solitary on half rations for a week as punishment for our attempted escape. Though we were told our punishment would be in solitary, Collins and I were put in a corner cell in the condemned row, without bedding and on a damp, cobblestone floor. After many attempts to obtain bedding by banging on the door and yelling in general, the door opened and the guard threw four blankets into our cell. Two were spread on the damp floor and the other two were used to cover us when we lay down, which is what we did most of the time.

'What really concerned me was that the food was better in the condemned prisoner's cell, in comparison to the rations we received in our fifth-floor cell. Our meals consisted of a "coffee" for breakfast and

Lt Loren E. Jackson, pilot of Crash Wagon III *in the 551st Bomb Squadron, 385th Bomb Group, 8th Air Force, who was shot down on 12 June 1944. (Loren Jackson.)*

supper, while we were given soup or a piece of bread on alternate days for lunch. Our commode in the corner of our cell also served as a sink with a water-spicket about 18 in above the commode. Writings and scratchings on the walls of the cell indicated others condemned to death by German tribunals had been occupants of the cell prior to our incarceration there.

'After a week, Collins and I were taken out of our punishment cell and placed in different cells on the fifth floor of the prison. After spending five weeks in Fresnes Prison, 19 of us Allied fliers were removed to Frankfurt-am-Main by train. At Darmstadt station a group of civilians on the platform looked us over. We were in civilian clothes, surrounded by armed guards and handcuffed. When they found out we were downed fliers their invectives came our way. If the guards hadn't kept the growing crowd back, I believe we would have had been lynched. Bombing results were evident everywhere.

'At the Frankfurt-am-Main jail we were placed in individual top-floor cells for 21 days. During air raids we were left in out cells while other prisoners were removed to shelters. Viewing the raids was exciting but knowing you were in the middle of a raid by your own people was very frightening.'

Fier was sent to Dulag Luft and then on 14 May to Stalag Luft III at Sagan. Shortly thereafter, in June 1944, Lt Loren E. Jackson, aircraft commander of *Crash Wagon III* in the 551st Bomb Squadron, 385th Bomb Group, also arrived at Sagan. Jackson was shot down on his 10th mission on 12 June. This day the 385th, based at Great Ashfield, Suffolk, was part of the 3rd Air Division force which was engaged in bombing lines of communication around the Normandy bridgehead. The B-17s were tasked with bombing the marshalling yards at Montdidier.

The short mission across the channel to the beach-head became even shorter when, approaching the target, flak disabled Jackson's No 2 engine.

'Ross M. Blake, my co-pilot and I, were unable to feather the propeller. It kept windmilling and making a rather unsettling racket. We continued on course but began to lag behind the main formation. Shortly thereafter, a flak hit in our No 4 engine disabled it but we were able to feather the propeller. By now we were considerably behind the formation.

'When fire broke out and enveloped the entire left wing I rang the emergency bell and instructed the crew to bail out. I was eager to get out too, but hit a snag. I was wearing a parachute harness and had stowed my parachute under my seat. I reached over to get the 'chute but it was hooked on something under the seat and I was unable to free it. I wrestled with it and finally got it loose. As I was attaching it to the harness, I looked out the left window and saw that the fire was out. (I suspect that as I leaned forward with my shoulders pressed against the control column, I put the airplane into a shallow dive. Apparently, the increased air speed blew out the fire.)

'I called the crew on interphone to see if anyone was still aboard but I received no answer. I flew along alone for about 10 min, following the formation in the distance. When the fire erupted again and had the No 2 engine and the left wing obscured by flames. I left my position in the left seat and went out the nose hatch.

'The smoking, flaming B-17 circled me twice resembling a huge wounded bird. As I was descending, I plotted my escape route. I was falling into a clear field and could see a thick cluster of trees not far away. I planned to head for the trees and hide until nightfall. I landed in tall grass and lay on my back to disengage my parachute harness. I got up and started walking casually toward the forest. Then I heard a shout, "Halt!" I pretended not to hear it and continued toward the trees. Again the command to halt. I turned around and saw a German soldier on one knee with his rifle pointed at me. I threw up my hands. He came toward me, still holding his rifle on me and said the words I dreaded to hear, "For you the war is over".

Jackson and Joe Haught, his bombardier, were imprisoned in Stalag Luft III from the summer of 1944 until the end of January 1945. Jackson recalls:

'My navigator, Gerald Shaffer was killed when his parachute failed to open. I saw the Germans bury his body near Beauvais. Some French women onlookers tossed flowers on his grave. Fred Martini, my assistant flight engineer-gunner, evaded capture for some time, masquerading as a Catholic priest in France. He was finally betrayed and incarcerated in the concentration camp at Buchenwald for some time until he was able to convince the authorities that he was an American military man. Sam Pennell, one of the waist gunners, also did a stint in Buchenwald with Martini. They evaded together, were captured together and spent time together in that infamous camp. Felipe E. Muzquiz, my Mexican ball turret gunner, Ted Dubenic, the tail gunner, Ervin Pickerel, the radio operator, Blake and Armando Marsilii, my flight engineer, all survived the war.'

Some shot down B-17 crewmen were sent further afield, to Stalag XVIIB, Krems, 85 km southwest of Vienna. During 1944 Krems was bursting at the seams with 4,500 prisoners of all nationalities herded into 12 compounds: five of them holding Americans, the others Italians, Russians, French, Serbs and Poles. The barracks, built to accommodate 240 men, were just like cattle sheds and at least 400 men were crowded into them. Only boards and battens hid the

Orlo Natvig, radio operator in the 91st Bomb Group, 8th Air Force, pictured in May 1943. (Orlo Natvig.)

cracks and the floors were made of wood. The prisoners' straw-filled palliases were a wonderful haven for fleas.

Orlo Natvig, a radio operator in the 91st Bombardment Group, recalls: 'When I first arrived at Stalag XVIIB it was in a deplorable state'. Natvig had been one of the first Americans at Krems, having been captured on 27 September 1943 when his B-17, *Local Girl*, was shot down over Holland after dropping its bombs on Emden.

Local Girl was attacked by Bf109s which made their attacks from below because the ball turret was out of action, the gunner having passed out through lack of oxygen. The No 2 engine was set on fire and a shell exploded in the radio compartment. Splinters missed Natvig by inches. The intercom was knocked out and most of the crew began evacuating the aircraft.

Lt Peagram, the pilot, remained true to his word that in the event of an emergency, he would

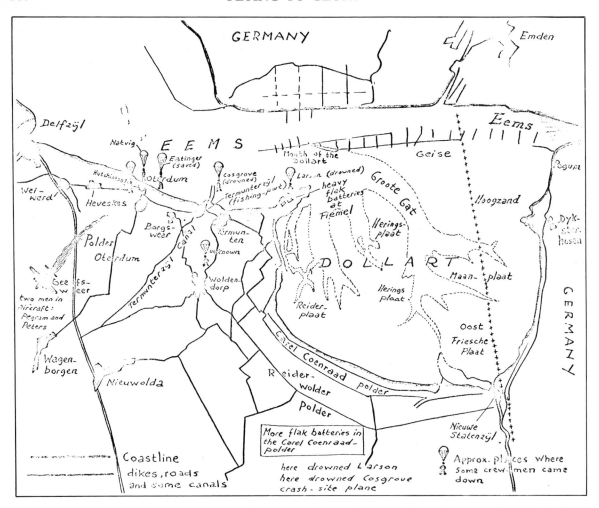

Map showing landing sites of the crew of Local Girl *which was shot down on 27 September 1943.* (Orlo Natvig.)

remain at the controls to allow the rest of the crew to bail out. (The brave pilot was later found dead among the wreckage of the bomber.) Eight men bailed out of the doomed bomber over the coast of Eems. For some it was a close shave, as Natvig recalls:

'The waist gunner, S/Sgt Hutchinson, and I, put a parachute on the ball turret gunner and pushed him through the waist door hatch, pulling his ripcord as he went. I pulled at the coveralls of Melvin Peters, the other waist gunner, to get him to go with us but he made no effort to follow us and we did not have time to force him, as he was still hanging on to his waist gun.' (Peters went down with *Local Girl*, firing his gun to the end.)

'Larson, the engineer, and Cosgrove, the navigator,

drowned when the cords of their parachutes became entangled in the *"botschuttings"* or "flounder fences" – a device of twigs and branches to catch fish – and in their heavy clothing they were powerless. Norman Eatinger, the bombardier, was more fortunate. He was rescued by a Dutch fisherman who at that moment was fishing on the Dollart and rushed to the scene.

'I landed on a *"kwelder"* behind a dyke about 200 yd outside the village of Ouderdom. I had missed landing in the water by only 100 ft. I noticed a group of people coming towards me. I got out of my parachute, gathered it together, and walked over to meet them. One of the group was a policeman so I raised my arms to show I had no weapons. I handed over my parachute to the civilians and gave away my escape and emergency ration kits. One of the Dutch people made a wedding dress from my parachute and another used part of it for a christening set.

'I asked a young Dutch lad about half my age if

Local Dutch citizens pose in front of Local Girl *and a very young German sentry.* (via Natvig.)

there was any chance of escape. He said the area was heavily defended and the Germans would arrive shortly. I was taken to the café of Jan van der Laan and taken prisoner by the Germans who lost no time in getting to the scene. It was quite a shock to have a fully fledged German officer walk up to me brandishing a .38 pistol and cocking it before he reached me. He stuck it in my stomach and my blood turned to water.'

Natvig and five others were transported to Dulag Luft at Frankfurt, stopping off at a German fighter base at Jevers.

'We were placed in an old guard house on the base for three days and then taken to the local train station. While we were on the platform some civilians wanted our skins. We backed up by a concrete wall and our guards stood out in front pointing their rifles

Two elderly guards pose in front of the wreckage of Local Girl. *Two propellers missing on these photos were later recovered by the Dutch and used as a memorial to the crew. Long after the war Orlo Natvig was given the blades and he had them shipped to the USA where they now stand in his front garden!* (via Natvig.)

with bayonets fixed. I did not blame the civilians because I had been told by the truck driver on the way from the airstrip that some of our bombs had fallen in a schoolyard. He also said an aircrew member who had bailed out in the vicinity had been strung up on telegraph poles. He may have been trying to scare us, but judging by the attitude of the civilians I am sure they would have had our hides but for the guards.

'At Dulag Luft we were placed in solitary confinement. I was put in a room about 5 ft wide by about 13 ft long and spent six days there. It was quite surprising to me, talking with my interrogators, to discover they actually knew more about the 91st Bomb Group than I did. It came as a real shock that they could list the history of my 324th Squadron commander who was of Jewish descent. I am sure there was little they could gain from me and pretty soon I was taken to a holding camp. There I met an English-speaking Luftwaffe officer who had been a salesman for an optical firm in Iowa. He had even travelled through New Hampton, my home town. It was quite amusing for him to show me a photo he had of his car parked on the main street. He maintained he had been caught up in the war after he had gone back to Germany to visit his parents.

'During my sojourn in Frankfurt, the 8th Air Force paid us a visit and bombed a propeller works. That night the RAF dropped flares preparatory to their raid on the factory and one of them became entangled in the wire fence surrounding the compound. Apart from quite a bit of fire in the downtown area we came to no harm. Later that night we were put on a train and told that we were on our way to a permanent camp. The train was so overcrowded that we had to take it in turns to occupy the seats. On the outskirts of Nuremburg we ran into more bombing. I swear the Germans backed our train right into the main part of the city in the hope that we would get caught up in it.'

Natvig and the other prisoners survived the raid and were transported to Krems to sit out the rest of the war. To guard against escape attempts, the American prisoners were not allowed out of the camp to join work details. As a consequence they had no opportunity to procure food. Instead, they had to depend on other nationalities who were allowed out and paid them in cigarettes for any goods they brought back.

During the winter of 1944 some escapers were

Lt Francis Shaw's crew, which was shot down on 11 April 1944, at Wendover Field, Utah, in December 1943 before assignment to the 614th Bomb Squadron, 401st Bomb Group, 8th Air Force in February 1944. Back row (left to right): Hansen, navigator; Alfred Autry, bombardier; William Cole, co-pilot; Francis Shaw, pilot. Bottom row: Sgt Howard Kneese, tail gunner; Robert Gorden, waist gunner; Rich Macomber, engineer; Kenneth Terroux, radio operator; John Hurd, ball turret; Carl Geaglen, waist and tail gunner. (John Hurd.)

caught, shot and hung on the wire as a deterrent against future escapes. In the winter of 1944 the prisoners had little coal for heating water. In desperation they cut down the sub-floors in their huts and even their bed slats for fuel. Winter gave way to spring and prisoners poured into Stalag 17B.

John L. Hurd, a B-17 ball turret gunner in the 401st Bomb Group at Deenthorpe, arrived at Krems on 17 April after he was shot down on his 11th mission, to Politz, on 11 April. It was the start of a very degrading routine as Hurd recalls:

'After my picture was taken my hair was cut off and my clothes were put in a gas chamber and deloused. My clothes had a strong odour of gas about them when I put them on again. I was then taken to a barracks where other POWs were already living, and stayed there several days until the Germans opened another compound with four empty barracks. I finally got my own bunk in Barracks 31B.'

Despite the privations and poor food, during the early part of 1944 the prisoners at Krems were in reasonably good physical condition. In June 1944 rumours of an Allied invasion prompted John Hurd to start a diary. On Tuesday June 6 he wrote: 'Rumour going around that the invasion has started. After supper it was confirmed by the news man . . .' The war news generally during 1944 gladdened the heart of every POW incarcerated in the Reich for everywhere the Allies were advancing. German reverses in Italy resulted in thousands of Allied POWs being transferred to Austria and parts of Germany. By October 1944 some camps were housing prisoners in tents.

On 9 October the Kriegies' long-awaited push began with violent battles being waged on the western front. The Russians were moving in the Balkans and the Baltic states, but PoWs had now been on half rations for several weeks. Time was running out for the prisoners at Krems and throughout the Reich. Victory was still not in sight even though on land and in the air, the Allied armies and air forces were enjoying great success.

Lawrence Jenkins, a co-pilot of a B-17 in the 2nd Bomb Group, 15th Air Force, arrived at Stalag 17B in October 1944 after a long and harrowing existence in a German hospital following the loss of his Fortress during a mission to Vienna on 16 July. Already a veteran of 14 missions, including one to the oilfields at Ploesti, two to Budapest and one to Vienna, Jenkins had had every reason to hope that a second trip to the Austrian capital would be without incident.

'It was a beautiful day. You could see for 100 miles in any direction. We could see Vienna one hour away with a heavy black cloud hanging over it. All of us had seen this before and we knew what it was. Several times you could see bright flashes and flames shoot out from the black cloud and then your heart would sink just a little lower 'cause you knew 10 more men had met their fate.

'We turned on to the IP and adjusted our flak suits. By now the first bursts were coming up so I pulled my helmet a little lower to shade my eyes from most of the flak. They were tracking us and each burst seemed to come closer. I watched the bomb release light and counted to see if all 12 500 lb GP bombs were released. The bomb bay doors were closing and we made our turn to the left. I was breathing better now as the flak was beginning to thin out. Then there came a loud crash and a ripping sound. Everything happened in the matter of seconds.

'I knew we had been hit hard but I could not see. The oxygen had burst and my eyes were flash-burned. I could hear the engines whining at a terrific speed and the fire burning like a large blow torch. I ripped my flak suit off, reached under my seat for my 'chute and fastened it, tore my safety belt loose and jumped up. I fell back down in my seat when both legs collapsed. Hard luck, both my legs were broken. I tried walking and pulling myself until I reached the bomb bay. By this time my power was gone and I fell into the bomb bay only to find the doors closed. I was too weak from the loss of blood and oxygen by now so I lay there and said to myself, "It won't take long and everything will be over with".

'In my mind I had drawn a picture of the ship hitting the ground. Luck! I felt a hand reach my shoulder and tried to lift myself up but it was no use. I was too weak to help. I pointed in the direction of the bomb bay emergency release. Soon I started to roll and found myself falling into space. I pulled the rip cord and passed out. I owe my life to Sgt Ray Voss, one of the gunners, who stayed there and got me out, while the ships was burning and tearing itself for the earth.

'I woke up with my 'chute pulling my nose through a ploughed field. I heard voices and felt hands grab me. I knew they were Jerries and passed out again. I woke up hours later in a first aid station and by that time I could see. There were three Germans around me. One spoke a little English and said, "For you the war is over". He also asked me who would win the war. I looked at my legs which were wrapped in paper and drenched with blood. He told me both legs would have to come off but I didn't care for the pain was terrible.

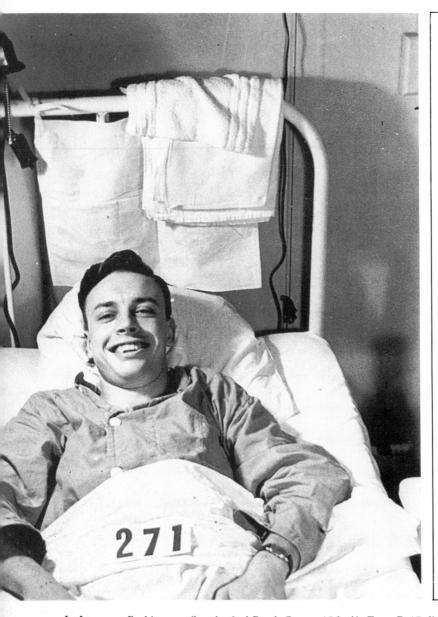

Local B-17 Pilot Lost Over Austria

Lieut. Lawrence L. Jenkins, 20, a B-17 bomber pilot, is believed to be Battle Creek's first casualty of the recently launched Italy-to-Russia bombings. His mother, Mrs. Lewis Smith of route two, Emmett Township, has been notified he has been missing in action over Austria since July 16.

According to the July 16 communique, 500  heavy bombers of the 15th Air Force based in Italy hit Vienna, and it was believed some of the raiders might have shuttle-bombed to Russia. The Allied planes encountered numerous Nazi fighters and heavy ground fire during the attack.

JENKINS

Lieutenant Jenkins, who had been overseas only two months, spent several weeks in North Africa before his assignment to a base in Italy.

He was a graduate of Lakeview high school, where he was a member of the baseball and basketball teams. He started his cadet training in March, 1943, and won his commission and wings at the Columbus army air field, Columbus, Miss., in January. He took his final Flying Fortress combat crew training at Sioux Falls, S. D.

Lt Lawrence Jenkins, co-pilot of a 2nd Bomb Group, 15th Air Force B-17, lies in a hospital bed after capture following the raid on Vienna on 16 July 1944. (Lawrence Jenkins.)

The grim reality: the story in a US newspaper that Lt Jenkins had been shot down. German interrogators gleaned nearly all the information they needed about crews and groups from US newspapers. (Lawrence Jenkins.)

'They came and picked me up in a truck, using a parachute to carry me in. There was great pain as the bones rubbed back and forth. In the main hospital they found one of my arms was also cut bad by flak. I was given a shot and sent to a room with 10 other Americans. The windows were all barred and the door locked with a guard at it all the time. I became unconscious again and didn't wake for three or four weeks. My legs were wrapped in paper with metal trays to support the bones. The swelling was so bad they could not put them in casts.'

Jenkins endured several Allied bombing raids while at the hospital, using a mirror to look out of a window as he lay on his back. German doctors carried out three operations on his legs and in September 1944 he was told he would spend the winter at Krems. However, bombing raids on Vienna put the city in turmoil and he was unable to be moved out immediately. Operations on his legs continued later at the camp hospital. 'One day I reached our door and opened it. The fresh air just about knocked me down. I couldn't believe the room was so stinking from all kinds of infections. SS boys of between 12 and 16 would come around and show off by spitting in our faces or calling us names. They always carried sub-machine guns and potato mashers in their belts.'

On 30 November 1944 Bernal 'Rusty' Lewis, co-pilot of *Sad Shack*, a 527th Bomb Squadron Fortress in the 379th Bomb Group at Kimbolton, was also destined to become a 'guest of the Germans' after concentrated flak brought down his B-17 on the mission to synthetic oil targets at Zeitz, southwest of Leipzig. The mission began badly as 'Rusty' Lewis, who was flying his 22nd mission, recalls.

'In order to maintain visual contact with the ground, our group leader dropped down through thick cloud, putting us in the low squadron at 23,000 ft, Maj Theodore G. Ramsdell, the pilot, and I, attempted to relinquish the lead to the deputy lead, who was my ex-aircraft commander, on my right wing, but he ignored the green light. We were without radio communication so we pulled back and attempted to stall the aircraft so that he would slide ahead of us. Unfortunately, he stalled right with it (I found out later that his co-pilot's control yoke was laying in his lap).

'At last the deputy lead crew realised that we wanted them to take over the lead. We made a turn to the right, making sure we had not passed the target. Maybe we had gone a little bit beyond it when we made a swing to the right and passed near Leipzig where we encountered flak. During the 190° turn onto our secondary target at Merseberg, the deputy lead aircraft finally took over. We completed a 270° turn, taking us right back over the target area where we were again showered by flak. The secondary target was covered by overcast so we headed for the third target at Fulda.

'On the bomb run Maurice M. Gropper, our "Mickey" radar operator, screamed over the interphone that the target was to the left. Then I heard, "No, we're on the bomb run itself". They were checking checkpoints but when we arrived over the target area the target was not there! We heard some explosions off to our left and realised that the Germans had camouflaged the checkpoints to fool our visual men

in the nose. Most crewmen at the time always believed their eyes and instruments and not the "Mickey" sets of which little was known except by the technicians who used them.'

In the resulting confusion the formation broke up and scattered in complete disarray. Bernal Lewis continues:

'We got a fire in the No 4 engine and we had to shut it down. Aircraft from our squadron were going down all around us and we only had three aircraft left in

Bernal 'Rusty' Lewis, pilot of Sad Shack *in the 527th Bomb Squadron, 379th Bomb Group, 8th Air Force, who was shot down on 30 November 1944.* ('Rusty' Lewis.)

the formation. [*Take Me Home*, *Dimples* and Lewis' ship, which were all lost together with *Landa*, *Lucy* and *Miss Lace*, which had already gone down.]

'Our intercom was dead. All electrical supply to the top turret was dead and we lost another engine and the propeller ran away. I looked out across the wing and saw that all the oil tanks appeared to have been riddled by rifle fire, although it was obviously flak. The oil ran low and the engines began overheating. Finally, a third engine went out and we had another runaway propeller. We were now flying around 4,000 ft with lost power. It was time to leave the ship.

'I held the aircraft level, looking down through my knees through the escape hatch below me until the hills came up underneath. John W. McDermott, the navigator, had been hit in the head and was unconscious. It was my intention to take him out with me in my arms with his "D" ring in my hands so that when we jumped out the airspeed would hit him and pull him away. Luckily, he regained consciousness just prior to our jump.

'We were over Heligolandstock, south of Hannover when I went to bail out and I could see right over the town. I noticed it had a high pointed steeple. I had always rehearsed parachute jumping in my mind and had day dreamed about getting hung up on a steeple.

'I thought I might as well enjoy the parachute jump but all of a sudden, I realised I had left the aircraft at only 4,000 ft! I quickly pulled the ripcord. I was wearing a 28-ft back pack 'chute and its opening created a very big impact. The ring fell out of my hand and I thought, "Oh Hell, I won't be able to get into the "Caterpillar Club" without it. Then I noticed that those who had jumped before me were just opening their 'chutes. I thought how smart they were because they would not drift over the town like I was going to thanks to the prevailing wind. (It was only later that I found out that three of the crew had to claw their 'chutes out of their chest packs with their fingernails after the rings had failed).

'I landed right on the edge of Heligolandstock where people were waiting with pistols. I gave my parachute to a pretty girl in the group. There was rapid firing. Did I make it back this close to the front lines? I asked a young German soldier, who was about 16 years old and had a broken arm, if we were in Holland or Germany. A little nine year-old German kid laughed and said, "No, Germany". The rapid firing was only the ammunition exploding in our burning Fortress.'

Lewis was taken to the Burgomeister. He recalls.

'I was asked through an interpreter what target we had bombed but I said I could tell him nothing. He mouthed and slapped me with his bare hands. I figured if he really wanted to hurt me he would have used his fist. I looked him straight in the eyes and said to myself, "Don't look scared". In my mind I called him every dirty name I could think of. He gave up. It was

said that the crowd outside were calling for my blood because I had dived our 'plane into their village.

'About six hours later the Germans started bringing in the rest of my crew, including Maj Theodore G. Ramsdell who had been flying with us. He was quite a soldier and the Germans recognised that they had a prize catch. The next day we were despatched to Oberussel (Frankfurt). We stood on the platform at the packed Bahnhof and I had the urge to escape until I saw a guard with his eyes locked on me waiting for me to attempt to escape. Had I tried to get away I would have been shot.

'At Oberussel we were herded into an overcrowded basement. Most were friends from my squadron, 10 out of the 12 ships having been shot down. Next day we were put in solitary confinement. We had been shown a movie about Dulag Luft in England so we knew what to expect. During my interrogation I refused to give the Germans any information. I said I understood the Germans to be good soldiers and I was one too. I had been ordered to stick to "name, rank and serial number". After about seven days solitary confinement I think I would probably have become mentally ill had I not had the training in mental discipline. I could see where people had tried to scratch some messages on the wall with their finger nails and they had probably gone mad eventually.

'After solitary I was taken before a hauptmann; another shaven-headed type. As I entered his office I saw a complete mock up of a "Mickey" set. He asked me questions but I still stuck to the "name, rank and serial number" routine. On the wall was a board showing the squadrons in the 379th Bomb Group. The hauptman gave me a propaganda lecture and said, "You will win the war but not as soon as you think (unknown to me the "Battle of Bulge" had just started).

'On my 21st day at Dulag Luft I was told that if I did not give more information, I would be left to rot. I said, "OK, I'll give you my birthday, but that's it". The hauptman laughed and said, "OK". I was put on a long train journey across Germany. I was completely amazed at the German railway network. I saw there was no way we would ever knock out their railway system in the war. Every forest had camouflaged equipment, screw tracks and so on. At this time the air force effort was aimed at wiping them out and strafing trains was common. On Christmas Eve our train was strafed. Our guards jumped from the train and scrambled into ditches. They trained their guns on us while we stayed in the cars. They were especially angry that the Allies had strafed and bombed on Christmas Eve! Finally, we reached Stettin and East Prussia and went on to Stalag Luft I at Barth.'

'Rusty' Lewis arrived at Barth in Pomerania the day after Christmas 1944. The camp held about 10,000 allied prisoners of war in four separate

'Red' Morgan, Medal of Honor recipient, ladles out hot water at Stalag Luft I, Barth. (USAF.)

compounds. Lewis was put into North Compound Three. Perhaps the best known of the bomber contingent at Barth was Lt John C. 'Red' Morgan, who had won the Medal of Honor, America's highest decoration, in July 1943. On 6 March 1944 Morgan was shot down flying with the 385th Bomb Group which was leading the 3rd Bombardment Division over Berlin. Morgan was one of only four men who survived from the 12-man crew after their B-17 was hit by flak. The B-17 exploded and Morgan was pitched out of the bomber still holding his parachute under his arm. He tried to get it on as he fell feet first but the pressure kept pushing it up too high. Then he fell head first and it pushed it past his chest. Morgan finally got it on when he was on his back and a few seconds later he landed in a tree. He fell 30 ft from its branches and was picked up by soldiers from a flak battery. 'Rusty' Lewis passed the time away in PoW camp.

'The old time prisoners thought the war would never

end. We had a radio in the camp and every night someone would come round and give us the BBC news. I remember how joyful we were when the Allies arrived at the Rhine and then for months and months when there was no movement, we got very pessimistic. When we heard troops had crossed Remagen Bridge we were happy again.

'We were now so hungry that we could not keep our minds off food and recipes. We all became expert cooks in our minds and our conversations often centred on food. Everyone got out their little blue Red Cross books and wrote down marvellous menus. Our diet consisted of four thin slices of very black bread, only about an eighth of an inch thick, and a bowl of soup a day. As a consequence, I lost about 45 lb in weight. Lewis later had an operation to remove an ulcer and had most of his stomach cut out because of his PoW diet.

'I saw a cat covered in sores and the thought passed my mind about catching and eating him. He disappeared so someone must have eaten him, sores and all. I also saw a black raven that someone later caught and ate.'

On 1 May scouts from Barth succeeded in link-

Ex-PoWs at Stalag Luft XVII, Krems, Austria, are airlifted to France in B-17s of the 452nd Bomb Group, 8th Air Force. (John Holden.)

ing up with Soviet forces south of Barth. 'Rusty' Lewis recalls. 'On 2 May the Russians began arriving in full force. The first one I saw was part of a bunch of Mongolian paratroops who were terrorising the countryside but when the high echelon troops came through they brought with them a dancing troupe and singers to entertain us. The Russians brought in Red Cross parcels that they had been hoarding, saying that they had been delayed because of transportation problems.'

The Russians' apparent resolve to transport the POWs to Odessa worried Col Hubert Zemke, the SAO. Some POWs succeeded in reaching the American lines to the west and they were promised that the POWs would be flown out. However, some men could not wait for aircraft to arrive so they left the camp, trading with local

people and picking up souvenirs en-route. They finally got through to the Allied lines themselves. Rumours filtered through that some had been shot by the Russians. 'Rusty' Lewis recalls: 'I heard that 26 people who left the camp never made it back.'

On 12 May the Russians finally permitted some Flying Fortresses to fly in over a five-mile wide corridor to airlift the POWs to France and home. Liberations had come at last. However, for thousands like them, still languishing at Krems, it was a different story. On Sunday 8 April about 4,000 American prisoners in groups of 500, were force-marched westwards. On 25 April the column arrived at Braunau; Hitler's birthplace. The prisoners estimated that they had marched at least 400 km from Stalag 17B. They set up camp on the south bank of the Inn river and awaited American Army units to advance towards them. On 7 May the Kriegies were taken to an airfield in Bavaria and C-47s flew the POWs to Camp 'Lucky Strike' in France where they boarded ships for the USA.

Meanwhile, the Red Army had penetrated deep into Poland and were approaching Breslau, about 90-km due east of Stalag Luft III at Sagan. The under-nourished prisoners were force-marched 62 miles in six days through driving snow to Spremberg. Finally, the surviving prisoners were sent by train to Stalag XIII-D, Nürnburg and Stalag VI-A, Moosberg, about 40 km northwest of Munich. On 4 April 1945, with the Soviet Army again very close, the Germans force-marched the prisoners from Nürnburg to Moosburg. The march, which was made in appalling conditions, took 10 days to cover 91 gruelling miles.

Finally, on 29 April, Moosburg was liberated by elements of the 3rd Army. Lots were drawn among the 45,000 prisoners and they were deloused with DDT and transported by road to Landshut, about 10 miles to the northeast, where they were flown out in C-47 transports to France. On 3 May 1,500 prisoners were evacuated and on 6 May 19,500 were flown out from four airfields to Camp 'Lucky Strike' and on to Le Havre for the long sea voyage home to the USA. Their thoughts would never be entirely free of their experiences 'behind the wire'. To quote from a poem written by J. B. Boyle while in POW camp; 'So here's to happy days ahead, When you and I are free. To look back on this interlude And call it history.'

CHAPTER 10

For King and Commonwealth

Although the B-17 proved less than successful during its short career with No 90 Squadron the Fortress was supplied in large numbers to RAF Coastal Command, where it gave sterling service in the Atlantic and Bay of Biscay, and a few to No 100 Group, Bomber Command.

In February 1942 No 220 Squadron received the first of seven ex-No 90 Squadron Fortress Is during the squadron's conversion to the Fortress II. The first of about 200 Fortress II, IIA (B-17E) and III (B-17G) aircraft delivered to the RAF from mid-1942, entered service with Coastal Command in August 1942 when No 59 Squadron began equipping at Thorney Island. Altogether, Coastal Command Fortresses sank 12 German U-boats during World War Two.

RAF Fortress Squadrons
Coastal Command and Bomber Command 1942-5

Date	Squadron	Remarks
Aug 1942	59	Fortress II enters Coastal Command service at Thorney Island
	206	
	220	
	251 (Met)	
	517 (Met)	
	519 (Met)	
	521 (Met)	
Feb 1944	214 (SD)	Fortress II/III enters Bomber Command service (100 Group) at Sculthorpe
Apr 1944	214 (SD)	First Fortress sortie
23 Aug 1944	223 (SD)	Formed at Oulton, Norfolk (B-24s)
Apr 1945	223 (SD)	Converted to Fortress III
19/20 Apr	223 (SD)	First squadron Fortress sortie

Met = Meteorological Calibration

In November 1943, No 100 (Special Duties) Group was formed at Bylaugh Hall, Norfolk for the sole purpose of carrying out radar counter-measures 'jamming' and 'spoof' tactics; tasks which were severely taxing the resources of conventional RAF bombers. Training was provided

Fortress IIA FK186 of RAF Coastal Command. (IWM.)

by the 8th Air Force. In February 1944, No 214 Squadron (Special Duty) was formed at Sculthorpe with Fortress II aircraft. In the spring this squadron received 14 B-17s from the 1st Bomb Division, 8th Air Force.

No 214 Squadron moved to Oulton, Norfolk where, on 23 August, No 223 Squadron was formed with Liberators, specifically for 'Big Ben'

V2 'jamming' patrols. But the V2 proved 'unjammable' and after problems with the B-24, this unit re-equipped with Fortress IIs and IIIs in April 1945. (The role of No 223 Squadron can be found in this author's *B-24 Liberator 1939- 45*, while a superb account of No 100 Group's role can be found in *Confound and Destroy* by Martin Streetley.)

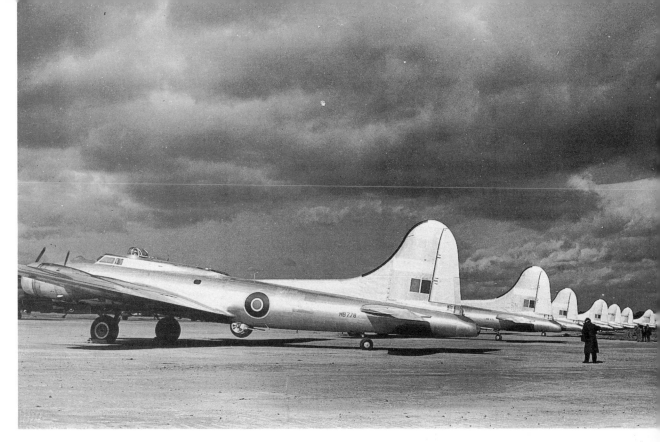

Above: Fortresses for the RAF: the nearest aircraft is HB778. (IWM.)

Below: Fortress IIA FK186 of RAF Coastal Command. (IWM.)

Above: Fortress II of RAF Coastal Command. (IWM.)

Below: Fortress IIA FK184 in flight. (IWM.)

Above right: Fortress BIII of No 214 Squadron shows the plastic nose radome containing an H_2S scanner which was used to aid navigation. (Don Prutton.)

Right: Fortress BIII KJ121 6G-B of No 223 (Special Duty) Squadron at Oulton showing waist position. Note the waist gun interrupter gear used to prevent the tail being shot off at night; the 'Window' chute (underside far left); and the 'Jostle IV' transmission mast (for jamming German R/T transmissions) atop the fuselage. Don Prutton is second from right. (Don Prutton.)

Above: Fortress II FL459 of No 206 Squadron RAF, at Terceira, Azores, in late 1943. (IWM.)

Below: Fortress BIII of No 214 Squadron at Oulton, Norfolk, in 1944. (Don Prutton.)

Above right: This Fortress BIII at Oulton clearly shows the plastic nose radome (fitted to all No 214 Squadron aircraft during June-August 1944). (Don Prutton.)

Right: Photographs of No 214 (Special Duty) Squadron Fortresses – and especially 'Piperack' – are rare. This close-up of Flt Sgt Budge of Flt Lt Liles' crew, shows to good advantage 'M-Mike's' 'Piperack' (Dina II) American-developed radar jamming device. It replaced the 'Monica' tail warning installation when it was found that German nightfighters were able to home in on 'Monica' transmissions from up to 45 miles away. (Geoff Liles via Murray Peden.)

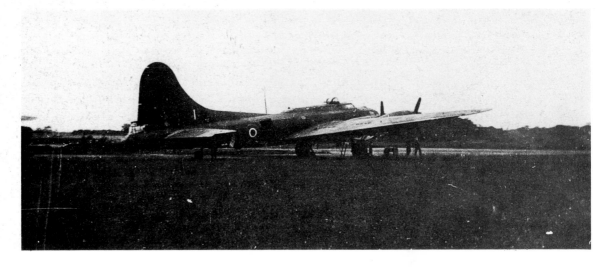

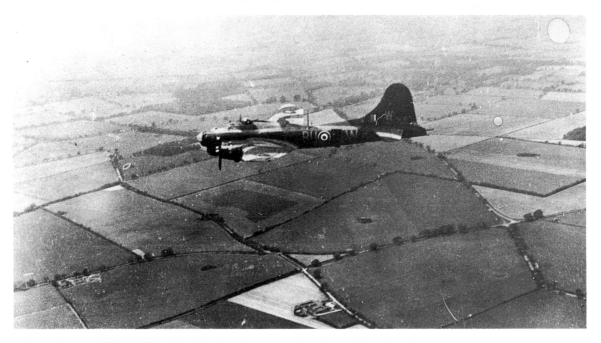

Above: Fortress BIII BU-W of No 214 Squadron over Norfolk in 1944. (Don Prutton.)

Below: Fortress BIIIs of No 100 Group at Oulton. (Don Prutton.)

Above: A Fortress BIII of No 214 (Special Duty) Squadron at RAF Sculthorpe. (Rolly Harrison via Murray Peden.)

Below: Fortress BIII KH999 (B-17G-55-VE 44-8243) 'M-Mike' of No 214 (Special Duty) Squadron at Oulton in the late summer of 1944. (Geoff Liles via Murray Peden.)

No 214 Squadron shouldered much of the work of the Special Duty squadrons at Oulton in World War Two. Flt Lt Geoff Liles and his crew are shown here in front of their Fortress BIII Q-Queenie. Liles is in the centre, front row. (Geoff Liles via Murray Peden.)

CHAPTER 11

All Sorts of Forts

Kampfgerschwader 200 operated a number of captured American aircraft on covert missions. This B-17F of KG200 is hidden under camouflage netting at Wackersleben in April 1945. When Soviet troops neared the base at the war's end, orders were given to fly all aircraft to Fürstenfeldbruck in Bavaria, but in the event only one B-17 reached its destination. (Karl Kossler via Hans-Heiri Stapfer.)

Above left: B-17F-100-BO 42-30336 Miss Nanalee II *of the 385th Bomb Group was used by Luftwaffe fighter units to develop interception tactics against B-17s after it was landed intact by Lt Glyndon D. Bell at Varde, Denmark, on 9 October 1943 after suffering engine failure on the mission to Marienburg. The remaining crew, who had bailed out over the area, were captured. A Danish resistance unit tried in vain to destroy the aircraft. (Hans-Heiri Stapfer.)*

Left: SB-17G-95-DL 44-83706 in Japan during the Korean War 1953-4. (USAF.)

Above: VB-17G-95-DL 44-83798 in Japan during the Korean War 1953-4. (USAF.)

Below: A B-17 at Nicosia Airport during September/October 1948. (Cpl D. S. Mercer, No 32 Squadron.)

Above left: Three B-17s at Nicosia Airport during September/October 1948. (Cpl D. S. Mercer, No 32 Squadron.)

Left: B-17E 41-2401 was modified by Vega to include four Allison V-1710-89 liquid-cooled V-12 engines of 1,425 hp each and re-designated XB-38. It flew for the first time on 19 May 1943 and proved faster than Wright-engined B-17s, but development was cut short when it crashed on 16 June after an engine caught fire. (Lockheed.)

Above: B-17G-110-BO 43-39457 was fitted with a droppable lifeboat for service with the 10th Rescue Squadron based in Alaska and re-designated B-17H, and then SB-17G for Search Bomber when Congress made the USAF a separate branch of the military in 1948. (Boeing.)

Below: In postwar years, PB-1Ws (B-17H) like this one were used by the US Navy for anti-submarine and weather reconnaissance duties. (Boeing.)

CHAPTER 12

Forts Still Flying

The pilot of the B-17 successfully completed his ground run up, testing all four Wright Cyclone engines in sequence. In his earphones he could hear the tower give clearance for take-off. The powerful engines roared as the throttles were pushed forward and the brakes were released. As the large bomber rolled along the runway it seemed just like another take-off, one of several that the crew had made during the last few weeks.

All was well, then suddenly, for no apparent reason, the B-17 swerved alarmingly to the left and the main undercarriage leg began running precariously on the edge of the concrete. Dramatically, the B-17 changed direction again, veering to the right this time, heading off the runway across the airfield. The throttle gates were still wide open because take-off was still a possibility. However, the crew became acutely aware of the trees in the distance. It seemed an eternity as they waited for the bouncing to stop. It did stop and the B-17 began climbing. They were airborne, but only just. Almost immediately there was a loud tearing sound as the No 4 propeller blades ripped through a large mound of gravel, showering the side of the aircraft with a fusillade of stones. The No 4 engine lost power immediately and to make matters worse, the port wingtip hit a tree. By now there was panic and confusion, but one man went back to warn those in the rear of the aircraft.

Meanwhile, the right wing had dipped and for a quarter of-a-mile it cut and swathe through a cornfield. At this point the crew knew they would crash. One of the engineers 'held on for dear life' and shouted 'No! No! No!' above the roar of the engines. The B-17 flew on in an awkward attitude towards a gully where it impacted with an horrendous crunch and slid up the other side. Fire took hold immediately and spread through the bomb bay and cockpit floor. Black smoke was everywhere as the crew scrambled to safety. They fought back the urge to panic. It was every man for himself. The large co-pilot went out the side window while the rest of the crew scrambled to safety through the broken fuselage. 'It was like running through a hot oven of super heated dry air.' There were 1,600 gal of fuel on board and it was 'just waiting to go up'.

Instinctively, seven of the crew just wanted to run from the scene as far as they could but some bravely returned to drag three trapped members to safety. Two minutes elapsed and the centre section was gone. They had never seen metal burn quite like this. Miraculously, everyone escaped with no more than a broken leg, a broken collarbone and 10 shattered nervous systems.

Thankfully, there were no bombs on board and no ammunition either, for this is not an incident from a bomb group log in wartime England, but the sad demise of a B-17G which crashed on 25 July 1989 at RAF Binbrook during the making of a feature film. The aircraft in question was F-BEEA, owned by the *Institute Géographique Nationale*. In June it was flown to England to participate as an 'extra' in a new movie about the wartime Flying Fortress *Memphis Belle*. At the Imperial War Museum airfield at Duxford, Cambridgeshire, F-BEEA was joined by another French-owned B-17, an American based B-17G, and a B-17F belonging to Bob Richardson.

Richardson's B-17F is the oldest surviving Fortress in flyable condition in the world and is based at Boeing Field, Seattle, Washington.

B-17 Sally B *in formation with P-47 Thunderbolt* No Guts – No Glory, *photographed at Duxford in 1991.* (Steve Jefferson.)

Actually a TB-17F, this Fortress has the distinction of being the first Fortress to be modified for aerial spraying and fire-fighting. Richardson's B-17 lost a cylinder en-route; the very same route that thousands of American aircraft used in World War Two as the Atlantic air bridge was maintained to keep 8th Air Force units in Britain at full strength. Appropriately, the second American-based B-17 was captained by Dave Tallichet, who arrived at Duxford via Goose Bay, Labrador, Iceland and Prestwick; the very same route he used in January 1945 when he flew to England to begin 21 missions with the 350th Bomb Squadron of the 100th Bomb Group – known as the 'Bloody Hundredth' because of its high losses.

Just two years before, in 1943, the *Memphis Belle* – one of the 3,400 B-17F models built – graced the skies over Europe and went on to become famous as the star of a wartime documentary. The *Belle* served with the 91st Bomb Group, 8th Air Force, based at Bassingbourn, an ex-RAF bomber station just north of Royston and only a short hop from Duxford. Most importantly, the 91st's base was more easily

accessible from London than most bases in far flung East Anglia with its poor road and rail links.

Maj William Wyler, the famous Hollywood director who had produced *Mrs Miniver* in 1941, was sent to England late in 1942 to make a documentary about 8th Air Force operations, principally for American cinema audiences. Wyler was given a great deal of help by Gen Eaker, Chief of VIII Bomber Command, and his subordinate staff, not least Lt Col Beirne Lay Jr, a Hollywood screen writer with *I Wanted Wings* among his list of credits. Wyler headed for Bassingbourn and was given more help by Col Stanley T. Wray, Commanding Officer of the 91st Bomb Group, affectionately known as 'Wray's Wragged Irregulars'.

Filming for the morale-boosting documentary began early in 1943 after bad weather had delayed its start. On occasion additional scenes were shot at other bases and ground shots were interspliced with real live action over the continent. Dangers were many. Lt Harold Tannenbaum, one of Wyler's original cameramen, and four other combat photographers, were lost aboard B-17s which failed to return from raids over the continent.

In the spring of 1943 several B-17s at Bassingbourn were running neck and neck for the honour of being the first to complete 25 missions (a combat tour for the crews). Those lucky to survive the fatigue, flak, fighters and possible mental breakdown were given a certificate and admitted to the 'Lucky Bastard Club'; this at a time when the average survival rate amounted to no more than a handful of missions. More importantly, they could go home.

One Fortress which caught Wyler's lens more than most, probably because of its emotive and eye catching name, was the *Memphis Belle*. The *Belle* was piloted by Capt Robert K. Morgan of Asheville, North Carolina. During crew training at Walla Walla, Washington, he had met Miss Margaret Polk of Memphis, Tennessee who was visiting her sister in Walla Walla. The romance between the pilot and the Memphis girl flourished for a time and Morgan flew over the French sub pens and German dockyards in a sweater knitted by Margaret. A Hollywood scriptwriter would have had them married and flying off into the sunset but war was no respecter of tradition and Morgan and Margaret later married other partners. The legendary artwork, though, remained indelibly painted on the nose of the B-17 through thick and thin.

Eventually, the finale to the film loomed large as the crew of the *Memphis Belle* neared its 25th and final mission of their tour. Contrary to popular belief, *Memphis Belle* was not the first to complete an 8th Air Force tour, but its 25th mission on 17 May 1943, to Lorient, was duly recorded (using a 'stand-in' B-17F) in 16mm colour and used with great effect in the documentary. Everyone it seemed, wanted to meet the famous 10 men of the *Memphis Belle*. On 26 May they were introduced to HRH King George VI and Queen Elizabeth at Bassingbourn and on 9 June Gen Eaker paid them a visit and then bade them a Stateside farewell to take part in a bond tour of US cities.

What finally emerged in April 1945 was a colourful and exciting 38-minute masterpiece which gave American cinemagoers a timely reminder of the grim reality of the war which was being fought at high altitude in the skies over Europe. By this time a tour of missions had risen to 35 and the chances of completing them were even more remote than they had been in 1942-3.

Britons saw the film for the first time in the winter of 1944-5. By then they had grown accustomed to – though never blasé about – the vast fleets of Fortresses and Liberators flying over the fenlands and flatlands of Norfolk and Suffolk, Essex and Cambridgeshire. Madingley cemetery testifies to their sacrifice.

At Duxford, Cambridgeshire, in 1989 the two American-based B-17s joined B-17 Preservation's *Sally B* and two more flyable Fortresses from France. All four B-17G Fortresses had their chin turrets removed to resemble period B-17Fs and olive drab paint was applied to all surfaces.

The obvious dangers of flying such elderly aircraft were immediately evident. Shooting had only recently begun when over Suffolk, *Lucky Lady* – one of the French-owned B-17s – lost its No. 1 engine. The No. 5 cylinder seized and blew completely off and the cowling furled back like a peeled banana and fell in fields below, but not before it had taken a chunk out of the B-17's tailplane. Stephen Grey, pilot of an accompanying Mustang, did exceptionally well to avoid the flying cowling. *Lucky Lady* returned to the base safely on three engines.

Sally B's nudes gave way to *Baby Ruth* 41-24292 and the call sign 'U' on the starboard side and DF-M 42-22960 *Windy City* on the port side. During filming the serial numbers and nose art were frequently altered to make the B-17 appear as different squadron aircraft. *Sally B* masqueraded as *Memphis Belle* and *Mama's Boys* (DF-P 42-29451). Correctly applied yellow-painted serials and faded blue and white star and bars on the fuselages added credence and credibility. (Later, the harsh staccato of .5 Brownings which emitted long yellow daggers of flame during test firing of the tail guns produced a touch of added realism, even though blank rounds were being used).

Sally B is actually a B-17G 105 (VE). Dave Tallichet's B-17G 85 (DL), which is normally based at Silvermill Museum, Chino, California, was given the honour of portraying the *Belle* and was painted 41-24485 'A' F-BEEA, was decked out as *Baby Ruth* (again) 41- 24292 'U', while

Above right: B-17 Preservation's B-17G Sally B *alias* Windy City *during filming at Duxford in 1989. (Author.)*

Right: Dave Tallichet lands his B-17G, still in its Memphis Belle *film colour scheme, at the August 1989 Geneseo Air Show, New York State. (Author.)*

F-AZDX *Lucky Lady,* owned by Association Fortress Volante, was painted *Mother & Country* 41-25703 'S'. Bob Richardson's genuine B-17F-70 (BO) (41-24335) masqueraded as 'C-Cup' (41-24299 'X') with two large cherry-topped ice-creams on each side of the nose to illustrate the point.

A young dark-haired American lady on the sidelines would have remained in the background had she not been wearing an imitation leather bomber jacket with *Memphis Belle* painted on the back. This 'belle' turned out to be Catherine Wyler, daughter of William and co-producer of the new movie with David (*Chariots of Fire*) Puttnam. When word got around even the most unenlightened of media men were asking Catherine to pose, predictably, under the nose of the 'new' *Memphis Belle.* Cameras turned and shutters clicked like a profusion of clapperboards.

It was Catherine Wyler and the production designer, Stuart Craig, on Oscar winner for *Gandhi* and *Dangerous Liaisons* who, after travelling extensively around the United States scouting locations, decided that the film should be shot in England. Craig has previously worked with Puttnam on *Cal* and *The Mission.* Editor Jim Clark won his Oscar for *The Killing Fields* and also worked on *The Mission* with Puttnam.

The actors chosen for *Memphis Belle* include lead actor, Matthew Modine, who had already seen war film action in Stanley Kubrick's *Full Metal Jacket.* John Lithgow, distinguished start of *The Twilight Zone* and *Terms of Endearment,* played the late Beirne Lay role of PR officer who arrives on the base to orchestrate the return of the *Memphis Belle* and her crew to America. He clashes head-on with the commanding officer (David Strathairn of *Matewan* and *Eight Men*

Left: The ill-fated B-17G-100-VE F-BEEA/44-8846 alias Baby Ruth *during filming at Duxford in 1989.* (Author.)

Below left: Dave Tallichet's B-17G N3703G/44-83546 alias Memphis Belle *during filming at Duxford in 1989 for the movie of the same name.* (Author.)

Below: Preservation Ltd's Sally B *alias* Lady Jane *during filming at Duxford in 1989.* (Author.)

Out) in his passion for his task.

This incident would seem to be based on a real incident which occurred in 1942 when Lay clashed with Paul Tibbetts, then CO of the 97th Bomb Group in England (and who later piloted the B-29 *Enola Gay* which dropped the A-bomb on Hiroshima in August 1945) following the former's request for an awards ceremony to present Purple Hearts to men of Tibbett's command who had been badly injured on a raid on France. The two men lost their tempers but became best friends and later collaborated on an MGM movie about Tibbet's Hiroshima experience called *Above and Beyond*.

Meanwhile, the original *Memphis Belle* has a happy ending. In 1961 all of the *Belle's* 10 crew-members travelled to Memphis for a reunion to see the Fortress. A concerned Memphis doctor had bought the B-17 from the US government for $350 and some enthusiasts went to Altus, Oklahoma and flew it home to Memphis where it remained for a time at the National Guard hangar until the American Legion Post No 1 had the *Belle* moved to her present location. Today the *Memphis Belle* Memorial Association ensures that the legend lives on.

Many of the B-17s that survive today have featured in several war films of the late 1940s, 50s and 1960s like *Twelve o'Clock High* and *The War Lover*. Paul Mantz, the famous film precision pilot, had once owned several hundred Fortresses after buying an entire field of the surplus bombers in 1946 but he later scrapped all but one of them (which he sold). The majority of Fortresses used in the filming of *Twelve o'Clock High* in 1948 were largely QB-17 drones and DB-17 aircraft supplied by the USAF. QB-17s were heavily modified B-17Gs, equipped for radio control by pilots in DB-17P Directors. The unmanned drones were flown through radioactive clouds during nuclear testing at Bikini in the South Pacific to test equipment and gain technical data of the atomic blasts. Later, surviving QB-17s were used as targets for the first air-to-air missiles.

In 1961 the few remaining military surplus B-17s, actually US Navy PB-1Ws, at Dallas-Love Field, were flown to England to participate in *The War Lover*. Also in 1961 Paul Mantz merged with Frank Tallman to form Tallmantz Aviation. The new company was on the lookout for a B-17 and found one, a B-17G, at Norton AFB in San Bernardino, California, where it had

been in storage for years. Tallmantz obtained permission from the USAF to fly the B-17 out but before this could happen a film crew from 20th Century Fox had arrived on the base and had removed most of the cockpit to use it as a mock-up for the *Twelve o'Clock High* TV series! The remains of the aircraft were later used as a prop during filming of the series at Chino Airport.

In 1966 Paul Mantz was tragically killed in an accident during filming but this, and a bad injury to Frank Tallman in a non-aviation related accident which later cost him his leg, did not prevent Tallmantz seeking a B-17 for film use. In 1967 the company leased 44-83525, which the 3205th Drone Squadron at Eglin AFB, Florida, had used as a Director aircraft until it had been retired to the scorching heat of Davis-Monthan AFB near Tucson, Arizona in 1959. After a painfully long restoration to flying condition the old B-17G participated successfully [as *Balls of Fire*] in the *Thousand Plane Raid* which was shot on location in January 1968.

Two other B-17s took part in the filming: 42-29782, a genuine B-17F then operated by Aviation Specialities of Tucson, Arizona, and 44-83684, which had also served with the 3205th Drone Squadron. 44-83684 came from the Maloney collection at Chino and had recently flown as *Piccadilly Lilly* in the television series *Twelve o'Clock High*, filmed at Chino Airport between 1964 and 1967. Today *Piccadilly Lilly* is grounded but is on permanent display at the Planes of Fame Museum at Chino Airport, California.

After filming was completed, Tallmantz did a deal with the owners, the Air Force Museum, swopping two aircraft and a missile for 44-83525. In 1973 Tallman sold his B-17 to Junior Burchinal, curator and owner of the Flying Tiger Air Museum at Paris, Texas. After a cameo role in *MacArthur* in 1976 44-83525 was repainted in the colours of the 93rd Bomb Squadron's *Suzy Q*. Today 44-83525 is on permanent display at the Kermit Weeks' Museum at Tamiami Airport, Miami, Florida.

At the time of writing, only about 14 Fortresses are still in airworthy condition. They can be seen flying on the airshow circuit while static examples are on display the whole length and breadth of the USA in museums and at US Air Force bases. *Texas Raiders* and *Sentimental Journey* are two of the most famous B-17s flying

Above: B-17G-85-DL 44-83525 Suzy Q *pictured at the Weeks Air Museum, Tamiami Airport, Florida, in October 1989.* (Graham Dinsdale.)

Below: B-17G-95-DL 44-83872 Texas Raiders *in flight over Texas in 1986.* (Author.)

today and belong to the Confederate Air Force (CAF). B-17G *Texas Raiders* 44-83872 belongs to the Gulf Coast Wing at Houston, Texas, and is painted in the wartime colours of the 381st Bomb Group, 8th Air Force. It was converted to PB-1W standard and in the 1960s saw service with Aero Service Corporation of Philadelphia and operated on survey work with Aeroflex Inc until it was retired in 1963.

44-83514 *Sentimental Journey*, which was officially added to the CAF collection on 24 February 1978, is operated by the Arizona Wing at Falcon Field, Mesa, Arizona. In March 1945, 44-83514 was assigned to the 13th Air Force, 38th Reconnaissance Squadron, based at Clark Field in the Philippines. Three years later it was used as a 'dumbo' aircraft by the US Navy – a refitted B-17 which carried a lifeboat under its fuselage. In USAF service again it was used as a DB-17 drone controller aircraft until May 1959 when it began 19 years service with the Aero Union Corporation in Chico, California, on fire-bombing duties.

Its silver and blue colour scheme is representative of the 457th Bomb Group – or 'The Fireball Outfit' – which served in the 8th Air Force at Glatton, England in 1944-5. *Sentimental Journey* was suggested as a result of a radio competition to find a suitable name for the aircraft. The shape and form of movie star Betty Grable completes one of the most striking nose art jobs in the CAF.

Hill AFB Heritage Museum, Utah, has a B-17G, 44-83663, on display called *Short Bier* which was airlifted to the museum from Air International Inc, Clearwater, Florida in 1987. It is painted in the colours of the 493rd Bomb Group, 8th Air Force.

The Heritage Museum Foundation's B-17G at Grissom AFB, Indiana, is a former DB-17G which was used from July 1950 until December 1951 as a drone aircraft. In May 1959 it was sent to Davis-Monthan AFB where it remained until July 1960 when it was placed on static display at Grissom AFB. It is painted in the colours of the 305th Bomb Group and is named *Miss*

B-17G-110-VE 44-85828 I'll Be Around *at the 390th Bomb Group Association, Pima Air Museum, Arizona.* (Larry Goldstein.)

Liberty Belle.

Castle AFB Museum at Merced, California, appropriately has a B-17G on display in the colours of the 94th Bomb Group, 8th Air Force and is called *Virgin's Delight.* This Boeing-built B-17 did not see combat during World War Two but was used postwar by the Atomic Energy Commission and the Fastway Air Service before being acquired by TBM, a California- based fire bombing company in 1966. Chico's Aero Union Corporation subsequently bought *Tanker Six One* as it was known and in 1979 the Air Force Museum obtained the aircraft in a swap deal involving a C-54.

The original *Virgin's Delight* was flown by Col (later Brig-Gen) Frederick Castle (after whom the base is named), CO of the 94th Bomb Group, on several combat missions from Bury St. Edmunds (Rougham) during World War Two. Gen Castle was killed leading the 4th Wing on 24th December 1944. He was posthumously awarded the Medal of Honor for staying with the

aircraft to allow his crew to bail out safely (see p129).

Shoo, Shoo Baby is one of the most famous B-17s that can be seen in American museums. This B-17G was assigned to the 91st Bomb Group at Bassingbourn, England, and named by its crew after a popular song of the day. On 29 May 1944 it took Lt Paul McDuffee's crew to Frankfurt on the first of 24 combat missions in which it was damaged by flak on seven occasions. The McDuffee crew completed some 20 missions in this B-17. Its last mission was to Posnan, Poland, on 29 May 1944, when engine problems forced Lt Robert Guenther's crew to make a landing in neutral Sweden.

The Swedish government was officially given seven B-17s as a gift and in exchange American crews were repatriated. *Shoo Shoo Baby's* nose was lengthened by three feet and accommodation provided for 14 passengers and 4,400 lb of cargo in the bomb bay. In 1955, after Swedish and Danish airline service and Danish military

B-17G-85-DL 44-83514 Sentimental Journey *which was completely restored to World War Two flying condition in 1981, the Sperry top turret and operational tail turret 'pumpkin' coming from Art and Birdline Lacey's B-17G which sits atop their 'Bomber Gas Station' in Milwaukie, near Portland, Oregon.* (Author.)

use, the aircraft was bought by a New York company and sold to the *Institute Géographique Nationale* in Paris.

In 1968 *Shoo Shoo Baby* was found abandoned at Criel Air Base in France with its engines missing. In 1971 the French government presented the aircraft to the USAF. In July 1978 *Shoo Shoo Baby* was transported by road to Frankfurt where a 512th Military Airlift Wing C-5 Galaxy flew it to Dover AFB, Delaware, for restoration by the volunteers of the 512th Antique Restoration Group.

The massive 10-year task of restoration to flying condition was completed in 1988 and on 13 October the aircraft was flown to the USAF Museum at Wright-Patterson AFB, Dayton, Ohio, by Dr. William Hospers and Maj Quinton Smith. *Shoo Shoo Baby* flew a farewell flight

two days later before entering the museum. The tyres were injected with liquid rubber and all engine oil was drained and replaced by preservative solution. *Shoo Shoo Baby* is now on permanent display.

The restoration of *Fuddy Duddy*, a B-17G which is central to the National Warplane Museum's collection at Geneseo, New York, is a tribute to the volunteer force at Geneseo who work tirelessly throughout the winter, keeping the B-17 in top flying condition. The B-17G is named for one that flew with the 447th Bomb Group, 708th Squadron, out of Rattlesden, England. First mission for the original *Fuddy Duddy* was in March 1944, when the 8th Air Force attacked Berlin for the first time. *Fuddy Duddy* went on to complete 96 missions without an abort before it was destroyed in a collision

Left: B-17G-35-BO 42-32076 Shoo Shoo Shoo Baby *of the 401st Bomb Squadron, 91st Bomb Group, which landed at Bulltofta, Sweden, on 29 May 1944.* (USAF via Frank Thomas.)

Below left: The restored B-17G-35-BO 42-32076 Shoo Shoo Shoo Baby *which is now on display at the Air Force Museum, Dayton, Ohio.* (AFM.)

Below: B-17s in formation over England for the filming of Memphis Belle *in the summer of 1989.* (Steve Carter.)

B-17G-85-DL 44-83563 in the wartime scheme of 42-97400 Fuddy Duddy. (Armand Miale.)

with another B-17 over Mannheim, Germany, the day before New Year's Eve in 1944. Purchased by the National Warplane Museum in 1985, the second *Fuddy Duddy* is a former water bomber and it has also starred in *The War Lover* and *Tora! Tora! Tora!*.

Another famous B-17 which can be seen regularly in the United States is 44-85740. It was never used as a conventional bomber, having been delivered to the military on 18 May 1945,

too late to see combat duty in World War Two. Postwar the aircraft changed hands many times and in 1954, while in Libya, it performed aerial mapping duties and completed the Shoran controlled magnetometer work begun in 1953. From Libya, 44-85740 flew to Thailand for several months for Far East service before returning again to Libya.

The aircraft spent the next three years in the Middle East on photo-mapping duties and

B-17G painted to represent Heavens Above *in the 388th Bomb Group, 8th Air Force, at Lackland AFB.* (Author.)

B-17G-105-VE 44-85740 Chief Oshkosh *in the wartime scheme of 42-102516.* (EAA Warbirds of America.)

during the Vietnam War in 1958 it carried out all the early aerial photography of Vietnam. In 1966 the B-17 was modified for aerial spraying duties with the addition of a hopper and chemical spraying system. It saw valiant service in the southeastern United States for several years on forest fire-fighting, forest dusting and pest control duties before being bought by William E. Harrison, President of Condor Aviation of Tulsa, Oklahoma.

On 31 March 1981, 44-85740 was donated to the Experimental Aircraft Association (EAA) at Oshkosh, Wisconsin, by Harrison's 'B-17s Around the World' organisation – a group of businessmen who, through lack of funds, were prevented from restoring and maintaining the aircraft in airworthy condition. The Fortress was then known as the *Aluminium Overcast*. The name of the B-17 was changed to *Chief Oshkosh* in 1985 to honour the crews of several aircraft which flew in World War Two under the name of the great Chief of the Menominee Indians. Also, *Chief Oshkosh* is symbolic of this aircraft's new hometown of Oshkosh where the EAA Aviation Foundation maintains the aircraft. Since the EAA acquired the B-17, it has maintained its airworthy 'Limited' classification (cargo only)

and has continued the restoration programme.

Yankee Lady is another B-17 which was restored to flying condition in the late 1980s–early 1990s. *Yankee Lady* is a B-17G built by Lockheed Vega at Burbank which belongs to the Yankee Air Museum at Ypsilanti, Michigan. 44-85829 was purchased and flown to its new home on 2 July 1986 from Mesa, Arizona. Originally, it had been delivered to the US Coast Guard as a PB-1G on 27 July 1945, then it served with the International Ice Patrol in Newfoundland with a home base in North Carolina. Later, the B-17G flew air-sea rescue missions in San Francisco before being surplused around 1960. It began a new career with the US Forestry Department, flying under restricted use as an insecticide and fire-bomber. In 1969 44-85829 starred in *Tora! Tora! Tora!*. Its career with the Forestry Department ended on 22 July 1985 when it sprayed grasshoppers in Oregon. Restoration to wartime flying condition began immediately upon arrival at the Yankee Air Museum and *Yankee Lady* flew again in 1990.

Evergreen International's B-17G 44-83785 was originally sent to the Pacific Theatre in July 1945. Three years later it was converted to a CB-17 and in 1949 it saw service as a VB-17. The

B-17 was retired from the military in 1955 and sent to Kingman, Arizona, for storage. 44-83785 was subsequently purchased by Intermountain Aviation of Marana, Arizona, an aircraft operation with heavy CIA ties. It was during this period that the Fulton 'Skyhook' personnel recovery system was developed using this aircraft. The 'Skyhook' system, designed by Bob Fulton, the great-grandson of the Robert Fulton of steamboat fame, was developed so that an aircraft could fly past a person and snatch him off the ground, after which he was winched up into the aircraft. The last time this system was used on 44-83785 (N809Z) was for the James Bond movie *Thunderball*.

Intermountain then converted N809Z to a fire-bomber. In 1975 Evergreen bought the Marana base and N809Z was part of the acquisition. The registration number was changed to 207EV and was operated until 1984, at which time the Fortress was retired from fire-fighting and placed in storage at Marana.

In 1987, its owner, Del Smith, asked Sandy Ellis to restore the aircraft to as close to the original as possible. The restoration crew replaced the right stabilizer, which was suffering from inter-grannular corrosion and the belly skin panels because of corrosion from retardant. The aircraft was completely rewired and an original design instrument panel fabricated and installed. All new glass and Plexiglass windows were fabricated and installed while the hydraulic pack and the landing gear and actuators were overhauled. New

flaps were fitted and new trailing edges for the wings fabricated and installed. The control surfaces were recovered with Stits Polyfibre and the entire aircraft polished. After two years searching, all the required gun turrets were found and fitted. In deference to its background 44-83785 was re-christened *Shady Lady*, and painted in the colours of the 490th Bomb Group, which served in the 8th Air Force. *Shady Lady* was due to fly again in 1992.

B-17s are still being found and grandiose schemes are in the melting pot to return them to the land of their birth and get them flying again. Until a year or so ago one B-17 was still at large in Bolivia and hopefully it will be brought to the UK for restoration. Two more Fortresses remain, temporarily – if an expedition to unearth them is successful – under a 250-ft deep Greenland icecap. These two B-17s (and four P-38 Lightnings) landed there in bad weather while en-route to Iceland and the UK on 15 July 1942.

Another extreme case concerns an extremely rare and intact B-17E which was located in the wilds of New Guinea in 1972 by a passing Royal Australian Air Force helicopter. The Travis AFB Historical Society plans to return the *Swamp Ghost*, as it is called, to the USA as it is the only B-17 left in the world in its original combat configuration. Let us hope that Fortresses continue to be found and restored to delight future generations of aviation enthusiasts for years to come.

CHAPTER 13

Epilogue: They also preserved

Where once a thousand Wright Cyclones roared now only the chirping of the birds can be heard. A flurry of wind whips the cornstalks beside derelict runways and overgrown hardstands and a rabbit runs for cover as footsteps approach. While walking the now silent 8th Air Force airfields in East Anglia on a peaceful summer Sunday afternoon it is difficult to imagine the cold, dark days of 1943-5 when thousands of American GIs called these desolate and often eerie bases 'home'.

'Home' in fact was normally a forbidding ice-cold corrugated and brick nissen hut located at some far-flung corner of the airfield, miles from the mess halls, briefing rooms and the aircraft at dispersal. Of course almost all B-17 Fortresses have long since been consigned to the melting pot but the memory of young men's raw humour, carefree demeanour and sweat-stained flying suits lives on in the form of cartoons, graffiti and murals which survive in the few remaining briefing rooms, mess halls and barrack rooms of 'Little America'.

During World War Two, East Anglia was dotted with airfields used by RAF Fighter and Bomber Command, but mainly by the fighters and bombers of the US Air Forces. The USAAF originally had 75 airfields in the United Kingdom but the total finally reached 250. These cost £645 million to which the Americans contributed £40 million.

Living conditions were often described as 'rugged' although some Americans were lucky enough to be billeted in ex-RAF barracks at places such as Honington, Suffolk and Bassingbourn, home of the 91st Bomb Group, near Royston, Cambridgeshire. They became known as the 'country club set', one of which even had its own butler! On the more rural bases it was a different story.

As airbase construction reached production line proportions the ubiquitous mud posed problems. One engineer summed up the situation by remarking, 'Where there's construction there's mud. Where there's war there's mud. Where there's both there's just plain Hell!' Passing vehicles showered the men with mud as they trudged or rode their 'GI bikes' to breakfast, usually an uncompromising meal of black coffee, canned fruit, bread with apple butter and 'square eggs' (dehydrated egg powder), which was quite unpalatable.

The accommodation sites were located miles from the airfield and inside the uncomfortable nissens wafer-thin mattresses and coal-fire stoves were inadequate for the 15-18 occupants. During winter, coal was strictly rationed to one of two shovels full daily. Illegal sorties into woods often yielded branches that would burn well. Headquarters tried to stop the practice, worried about the effect it would have on Anglo-American relations. Crews found the blackout and the vast distances between the mess halls, briefing rooms and aircraft dispersals intolerable.

Every day thousands of these young men risked their lives flying in vast Allied aerial fleets against Nazi Germany, using as their launching pad air bases in Norfolk, Suffolk, Cambridgeshire, Huntingdonshire and Essex. Most bases were desolate and away from the main towns, the men's only link with civilisation being the occasional 'liberty run' into nearby towns, or perhaps to London or Edinburgh when a 48-hr pass came their way.

Combat crews' lives were measured in weeks rather than months. Some were known to be flak

Above: Frank Valesh (far left, front row) and crew of B-17G-1-BO 42-31035 Hang the Expense *which, with tailwheel locked, careered off the runway at the start of a test flight on 26 November 1943, hit two trees and demolished a barn. Fortunately, none of the three-man crew and their two American Red Cross girl passengers suffered serious injury. Altogether, Valesh 'lost' five* Hang The Expense *B-17s before he completed his tour on 24 July 1944, including one on 19 May when he crashed taking off from Thorpe Abbotts in thick fog. (USAF.)*

Left: 18th Bomb Squadron insignia painted on a wall at the 34th Bomb Group's base at Mendlesham, Suffolk. (Author.)

happy and continued flying only through extreme personal willpower. Many crews were sent to 'rest homes' but leave policy did not apply to those suffering from operational fatigue or to the ground crews. Missions averaged 17 per month, but higher during prolonged bouts of missions like 'Big Week' in February 1944. The strain was barely tolerable and death not only occurred in combat. It stalked them on training flights over East Anglia and the Fens and on murky, fog-shrouded days when collision was almost inevit-

The outstanding mural of B-17G-100-BO 43-38877 of the 92nd Bomb Group, 8th Air Force, painted on the inside of the old mess hall for NCOs at Podington, Bedforshire, is now on permanent display at the IWM, Duxford. (Steve Gotts.)

able. Memorials throughout the region testify to the grim fact.

But morale never faltered because of the close camaraderie, both in the air, and on the ground. Crews taunted fate by painting mission symbols and wonderful montages on the noses of their aircraft. Most, like *Virgin on the Verge*, *Purty Baby* and *Impatient Virgin* depicted the nude female form. Others had their origins in slightly different circumstances, like the famous B-17 called *The Eightball*. This and its successors crashed so often that the last in the series was called *No Balls at All*. Another series of B-17s, flown by Frank Valesh in the 100th Bomb Group at Thorpe Abbotts, were written off so many times they earned the sobriquet, *Hang The Expense*.

This keen sense of individualism was also evident on the bases. In an effort to brighten their surroundings and remind the men of happier times back home in the states, GT artwork in the form of vivid murals and cartoons, buxom

girls and glossy locations appeared on the walls of the nissen huts, briefing rooms, messes and aero clubs. GI artwork is very evident at many Fortress fields in East Anglia. Bomb logs, sketches, and graffiti survive on barrack room walls throughout East Anglia thanks mainly to altruistic farmers, scrap merchants and residents alike. One of the finest pieces of 8th Air Force memorabilia, a 92nd Bomb Group Fortress flying through a yellow-orange sky with its bomb bay doors open and machine-guns blazing as it dodges heavy flak, could be found on a wall of a piggery at Podington, Northamptonshire, wartime home of the 92nd Bomb Group, until the mural was skilfully removed and put on display at the Imperial War Museum, Duxford, in October 1989.

Ghosts seemed to haunt Podington and other old airfields for, some years ago, a medium photographed the mural at Podington with her Polaroid only to discover that white plumes, like

Above: B-17 mural on the wall of the Red Cross Club in Bedford during the war. (Richards.)

Left: The 388th Bomb Group insignia and 'Gunners Gen' on a wall in the long-since demolished briefing hut at Knettishall, Suffolk. (Author.)

cloud, had found their way onto the developed print. She had also picked up the word 'chow', and being unfamiliar with American airfields was staggered to learn that the building was once the mess hall!

Further examples of GI and Disney inspired cartoons, scenes of American life, movie actresses and squadron insignia, could still be found on crumbling barrack room walls and corrugated nissens as late as the 1980s. To 8th Air Force enthusiasts their finds probably ranked alongside the discovery of hieroglyphics in some ancient Egyptian tomb.

At some locations the old and new happily co-exist. The wartime base of the 95th Bomb Group at Horham, Suffolk has one of the finest collections of murals seen anywhere. The mess had wall-to-wall paintings of medieval scenes including a banquet and a knight on a white charger. Even as late as the 1980s one could still read off the meal times painted in black bold letters on the mess hall doors. At Thorpe Abbotts, which has arguably the finest control tower museum in the UK, one of the old corrugated nissen huts has been re-erected complete with the names of some of the 'Bloody Hundredth's' most dangerous missions in appropriately vivid red letters on the ceiling.

Although a few 43 year old colourful creations still survive at some bases, unfortunately for historians, old airfields make excellent sites for turkey sheds, race-tracks and industrial estates and many murals, cartoons and insignia have long since disappeared at the hands of developers and farmers alike. Never again will any budding Howard Carter be able to step into a time capsule at Knettishall or Deopham Green and discover paintings of 388th Bomb group insignia and briefing notes, or a bow-legged cowboy, six-

Right: A knight on a white charger with the shield insignia of the 95th Bomb Group on a wall at Horham, Suffolk. (Author.)

Below: Meal times had been painted on the doors of the old mess hall at Horham, Suffolk. (Author.)

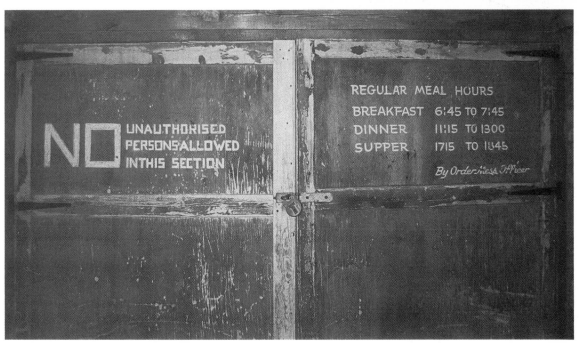

foot high dancing girls and Walt Disney cartoon characters. 'Mickey Mouse' and his pals disappeared when their wall tabloid at the former 452nd Bomb Group base was pulled down. In American parlance 'Mickey Mouse' means 'no longer needed'.

Like the nose-art on the aircraft, barrack room art was never expected to survive long in wartime but the twin enemies – neglect and harsh English winters – have obliterated most of them from the British landscape forever.

Left: The restoration of the Thorpe Abbotts control tower is a fitting testimony to the efforts of the Thorpe Abbotts Memorial Museum. Robert Rosenthal (left, in light suit) takes the salute during a flypast at the 100th Bomb Group reunion in 1986. In peacetime, 'Rosie' was a lawyer and he served at the Nuremburg War Criminals trials. (Author.)

Below: Mission log discovered on a Nissen hut on 8 May 1981 near Thorpe Abbotts, Suffolk, wartime home of the 100th Bomb Group. (Author.)

Above: Despite being ravaged by the passage of time the old Deenthorpe control tower still retained its 'Flying Control' letters as late as the 1970s. (Author.)

Right: A bow-legged cowboy which once adorned the wall of a barrack hut at Deopham Green, Norfolk. (Author.)

Above: Mickey Mouse pictured in 1976 in the now demolished 'Games Room' at Deopham Green, Norfolk. (Marvin Barnes.)

Right: A memorial window dedicated to the men of the 96th Bomb Group, 8th Air Force, at Quidenham, Suffolk, close to their wartime base at Snetterton Heath. (Author.)

Below: The B-17 Fortress 'castle of the air', a cartoon by Col Ross Greening, created while he was a PoW at Stalag Luft I, Barth. (Ross Greening.)

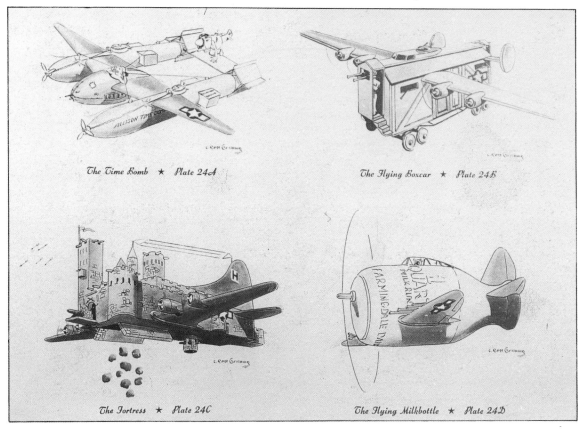

The Time Bomb ★ Plate 24A

The Flying Boxcar ★ Plate 24B

The Fortress ★ Plate 24C

The Flying Milkbottle ★ Plate 24D

Appendices

I B-17 Specifications

Model	XB-17 (299)	Y1B-17 (299B)	Y1B-17A (299F)	B-17B (299M)	B-17C (299H)	B-17D (299-H)	B-17E (299-0)	B-17F (299-0)	B-17G (299-0)
Crew	8	6	6	6	9	10	6–9	10	10
Wingspan	103ft 9in	103ft 9in	103ft 9in	103ft 9in	103ft 9in	103ft 9in	103ft 9in	103ft 9in	103ft 9in
Length	68ft 9in	68ft 4in	68ft 4in	67ft 9in	67ft 9in	67ft 11in	73ft 10in	74ft 9in	74ft 4in
Height	14ft 11in	18ft 4in	18ft 4in	18ft 4in	18ft 4in		19ft 2in	19ft 1in	19ft 1in
Wing Area	1,420sq ft								
Empty Weight	21,657lb	24,465lb	31,160lb	27,650lb	30,600lb	30,960lb	32,250lb	34,000lb	36,135lb
Max Weight	38,053lb	39,000lb	45,650lb	46,178lb	49,650lb	49,650lb	54,000lb	65,500lb	65,500lb
Engines	4x750hp Pratt & Whitney S1EG Hornets	4x930hp Wright Cyclone R-1820-39	4x1,000hp Wright Cyclone R-1820-51	4x1,200hp Wright Cyclone R-1820-51	4x1,000hp Wright Cyclone R-1820-65	4x1,200hp Wright Cyclone R-1820-65	4x1,200hp Wright Cyclone R-1820-65	4x1,380hp Wright Cyclone R-1820-97	4x1,380hp Wright Cyclone R-1820-98
Maximum Speed	236mph	256mph at 14,000ft	271mph at 25,000ft	286mph at 25,000ft	323mph at 25,000ft	323mph at 25,000ft	317mph at 25,000ft	325mph at 25,000ft	302mph at 25,000ft
Cruising Speed	140mph	175mph	183mph	225mph	227mph	227mph	195mph	160mph	160mph
Rate of climb	8min to 10,000ft	6min to 10,000ft	7min 48sec to 10,000ft	7min to 10,000ft	7min to 10,000ft	7min 12sec to 10,000ft	7min 6sec to 10,000ft	25min 42sec to 20,000ft	37min to 20,000ft
Ceiling	24,620ft	30,600ft	38,000ft	30,000ft	37,000ft	37,000ft	36,000ft	37,500ft	35,600ft
Range	3,011 miles	2,400-3,400 miles	2,400-3,600 miles	2,400-3,600 miles	2,000-3,400 miles	2,000-3,400 miles	2,000-3,200 miles	1,300-3,800 miles	1,140-2,740 miles
Armament	5x.30	5x.30 or .50	5x.30 or .50	1x.30 6x.50	1x.30 6x.50	1x.30 6x.50	1x.30 8x.50	11x.50	12/13x.50
Bomb Load	8x600lb (max)	8x600lb (max)	8x600lb (max)	4x1,100lb or 20x100lb	8x600lb or 4x1,100lb or 20x100lb	8x600lb or 4x1,100lb or 20x100lb	4x1,000lb or 20x100lb or 14x300lb	8x1,000lb or any comb to 24x100lb	6x1,600lb and 2x4,000lb

(*war emergency setting)

II B-17 Production Figures

Model	Boeing	Douglas	Vega	Production Totals
Model 299	1			
Y1B-17	13			
Y1B-17A	1			
B-17B	39			
B-17C	38			
B-17D	42			
B-17E	512			F production
B-17F-BO	2,300			3,405
B-17F-DL		605		
B-17F-VE			500	
B-17G-BO	4,035			G production
B-17G-DL		2,395		8,680
B-17G-VE			2,250	
Total	6,981	3,000	2,750	

WW2 Bomber Aircraft Production Totals	
Consolidated B-24 Liberator	*18,188*
Boeing B-17 Flying Fortess	*12,731*
Vickers Wellington	*11,461*
Avro Lancaster	*7,374*
Handley Page Halifax	*6,176*
Boeing B-29 Superfortress	*3,970*
Short Stirling	*2,375*

III 8th Air Force B-17 Order of Battle

Date	Group	Remarks
1942:		
17 Aug	97th	Became Operational. Rouen-Sotteville
5 Sep	301st	Became Operational. Rouen-Sotteville
6 Sep	92nd	Became Operational. Meaulte
14 Sep	97th	Assigned to 12th AF
14 Sep	301st	Assigned to 12th AF
7 Oct	305th	422nd BS first night leaflet operation
9 Oct	92nd	2nd mission, to Lille, then used as Combat Crew Replacement Centre
	306th	Became Operational. Lille
7 Nov	91st	Became Operational. Brest
17 Nov	303rd	Became Operational. St. Nazaire
	305th	Mission debut. Diversion to near Brest
Nov	97th	Departed UK for MTO
Dec	301st	Departed UK for MTO
1943:		
13 May	94th	Became Operational. St. Omer
	95th	Became Operational. St. Omer
	96th	Became Operational. St. Omer
14 May	351st	Became Operational. Kiel
	92nd	Resumed combat missions. Kiel
29 May	379th	Mission debut. St. Nazaire
22 Jun	381st	Mission debut. Huls
	384th	Mission debut. Huls
	100th	Mission debut. Diversion over North Sea
17 Jul	385th	Mission debut, Hannover
	388th	Mission debut, Hannover
12 Aug	390th	Mission debut. Ruhr Valley
15 Aug	482nd	Group activated for PFF missions
27 Sep		Began radar missions for 8th AF
26 Nov	401st	Mission debut. Bremen
24 Dec	447th	Became Operational. 'Noball' targets
1944:		
5 Feb	452nd	Mission debut. Romilly
21 Feb	457th	Became Operational. Brunswick
26 Mar	482nd	Last combat mission before reverting to essentially a 'Mickey' training unit
6 May	398th	Mission debut. Low countries
1 Aug	486th	1st mission after converting from B-24
1 Aug	487th	1st mission after converting from B-24
27 Aug	490th	1st mission after converting from B-24
8 Sep	493rd	1st mission after converting from B-24
17 Sep	34th	1st mission after converting from B-24

IV B-17 Units by Air Forces

1st Air Force	Zone of the Interior	
	1st Photo Group	
	1st Search Attack Group	
	2nd Bomb Group	
2nd Air Force	Zone of the Interior	
	2nd Reconnaissance Group	
	25th Bomb Group	383rd Bomb Group
	39th Bomb Group	393rd Bomb Group
	88th Bomb Group	395th Bomb Group
	304th Bomb Group	396th Bomb Group
	331st Bomb Group	444th Bomb Group
	333rd Bomb Group	469th Bomb Group
	346th Bomb Group	488th Bomb Group
3rd Air Force	Zone of the Interior	
	2nd Reconnaissance Group	
	98th Reconnaissance Group	
	88th Bomb Group	
	396th Bomb Group	
	488th Bomb Group	
4th Air Force	Zone of the Interior	
	34th Bomb Group	504th Bomb Group
	444th Bomb Group	505th Bomb Group
5th Air Force	Pacific Theatre	
	19th Bomb Group	43rd Bomb Group
6th Air Force	Caribbean Theatre	
	5th Bomb Group	11th Bomb Group
7th Air Force	Pacific Theatre	
	5th Bomb Group	11th Bomb Group

8th Air Force	England	
	34th Bomb Group	381st Bomb Group
	91st Bomb Group	384th Bomb Group
	92nd Bomb Group	385th Bomb Group
	94th Bomb Group	388th Bomb Group
	95th Bomb Group	390th Bomb Group
	96th Bomb Group	398th Bomb Group
	97th Bomb Group	401st Bomb Group
	100th Bomb Group	447th Bomb Group
	301st Bomb Group	452th Bomb Group
	303rd Bomb Group	457th Bomb Group
	305th Bomb Group	486th Bomb Group
	306th Bomb Group	487th Bomb Group
	351st Bomb Group	490th Bomb Group
	379th Bomb Group	493rd Bomb Group
9th Air Force	Mediterranean Theatre	
	9th Bomb Group	99th Bomb Group
	97th Bomb Group	301st Bomb Group
10th Air Force	China-Burma-India Theatre	
	7th Bomb Group	
11th Air Force	Alaskan Theatre	
	28th Bomb Group	
12th Air Force	Mediterranean Theatre	
	2nd Bomb Group	99th Bomb Group
	97th Bomb Group	301st Bomb Group
13th Air Force	Pacific Theatre	
	5th Bomb Group	11th Bomb Group
15th Air Force	Mediterranean Theatre	
	2nd Bomb Group	301st Bomb Group
	97th Bomb Group	463rd Bomb Group
	99th Bomb Group	483rd Bomb Group

V B-17 Medal of Honor Awards 1942–4

Date	Name	Group	
7 Aug 1942	Pease, Capt Harl	19th	5th AF Posthumous
18 Mar 1943	Mathis, 1/Lt Jack	303rd	8th AF Posthumous
1 May 1943	Smith, Maynard S/Sgt	306th	8th AF
16 Jun 1943	Sarnoski, Lt Joseph R	43rd	5th AF Posthumous
16 Jun 1943	Zeamer Maj Jay	43rd	5th AF
26 Jul 1943	Morgan, Flt Off John C	92nd	8th AF
20 Dec 1943	Vosler, T/Sgt Forrest	303rd	8th AF
20 Feb 1944	Lawley, 1/Lt William R	305th	8th AF
20 Feb 1944	Mathies, Sgt Archie	351st	8th AF Posthumous
20 Feb 1944	Truemper, 2/Lt Walter	351st	8th AF Posthumous
11 Apr 1944	Michael, 1/Lt Edward	305th	8th AF
23 Jun 1944	Kingsley, 2/Lt David R	97th	15th AF Posthumous
2 Nov 1944	Feymoyer, 2/Lt Robert E	447th	8th AF Posthumous
9 Nov 1944	Gott, 1/Lt Donald J	452nd	8th AF Posthumous
9 Nov 1944	Metzger, 2/Lt William E	452nd	8th AF Posthumous
24 Dec 1944	Castle, Brig-Gen Fred	4th BW	8th AF Posthumous

VI B-17 Bombing Accuracy: 8th Air Force 1st and 3rd Divisions, January 1943–April 1945

Average % of bombs dropped which fell within 1,000ft and 2,000ft, respectively, of pre-assigned MPIs on visual missions under conditions of good to fair visibility

	WITHIN 1,000 ft				WITHIN 2,000 ft		
Period	1st Div	3rd Div	8th AF	Period	1st Div	3rd Div	8th AF
1943:				**1943:**			
January				January			
February	18	—	18	February	36	—	36
March				March			
April				April			
May	13	11	12	May	32	29	30
June				June			
July				July			
August	13	19	16	August	31	48	38
September				September			
October				October			
November	25	27	27	November	46	47	48
December				December			
1944:				**1944:**			
January	34	41	35	January	61	60	58
February	42	46	39	February	76	77	69
March	31	39	31	March	64	70	58
April	34	32	29	April	62	58	55
May	44	33	37	May	68	62	65
June	49	35	40	June	81	65	71
July	42	44	37	July	73	77	69
August	54	42	45	August	84	72	75
September				September			
October	29	46	38	October	61	72	65
November				November			
December	24	25	25	December	54	47	48
1945:				**1945:**			
January	29	24	29	January	59	56	59
February	50	40	49	February	80	69	77
March	40	30	38	March	76	58	69
April	64	52	59	April	91	80	85

VII 8th Air Force B-17 Combat Bombardment Wing Assignments: 1 November 1943

1ST BOMB DIVISION

Group	Wing	Base
91st	1st CBW	Bassingbourn
381st	1st CBW	Ridgewell
401st	92nd CBW	Deenthorpe
351st	92nd CBW	Polebrook
92nd	40th CBW	Podington
305th	40th CBW	Chelveston
306th	40th CBW	Thurleigh
303rd	41st CBW	Moslesworth
379th	41st CBW	Kimbolton
384th	41st CBW	Grafton Underwood

3RD BOMB DIVISION

Group	Wing	Base
94th	4th CBW	Bury St. Edmunds
385th	4th CBW	Great Ashfield
447th	4th CBW	Rattlesden
95th	13th CBW	Horham
100th	13th CBW	Thorpe Abbotts
390th	13th CBW	Framlingham
96th	45th CBW	Snetterton Heath
388th	45th CBW	Knettishall

8th Air Force B-17 Combat Bombardment Wing Final Assignments: April 1944–April 1945

1ST BOMB DIVISION

Group	Wing	Base
91st	1st CBW	Bassingbourn
381st	1st CBW	Ridgewell
398th	1st CBW	Nuthampstead
92nd	40th CBW	Podlington
305th	40th CBW	Chelveston
306th	40th CBW	Thurleigh
303rd	40th CBW	Molesworth
379th	41st CBW	Kimbolton
384th	41st CBW	Grafton Underwood
351st	94th CBW	Polebrook
401st	94th CBW	Deenthorpe
457th	94th CBW	Glatton

*93rd CBW from 17 Feb 45

3RD BOMB DIVISION

Group	Wing	Base
94th	4th CBW	Bury St. Edmunds
385th	*4th CBW	Great Ashfield
447th	4th CBW	Rattlesden
487th	4th CBW	Lavenham
95th	13th CBW	Horham
100th	13th CBW	Thorpe Abbotts
390th	13th CBW	Framlingham
96th	45th CBW	Snetterton Heath
388th	45th CBW	Knettishall
452nd	45th CBW	Deopham Green
34th	93rd CBW	Mendlesham
490th	93rd CBW	Eye
493rd	93rd CBW	Debach

VIII   8th Air Force B-17 Attrition: August 1942–May 1945

Month	MIA	Cat E	War-Weary	Non-op Losses	Net Loss	a/c avail	% loss
1942:							
August						48	
September	2				2	144	1.4
October	6				6	192	3.1
November	9			1	10	288	3.5
December	12	1		1	14	240	5.8
TOTAL 1942:	29	1		2	32	912	3.5
1943:							
January	16			1	17	240	7.1
February	16			1	17	240	7.1
March	13	3		2	18	240	7.5
April	25			3	28	240	11.7
May	61	5		12	78	480	16.3
June	85	8		6	99	624	15.9
July	109	19		1	129	720	17.9
August	107	17		3	127	804	15.8
September	82	17		7	106	804	13.2
October	166	21		15	202	804	25.1
November	65	16		9	90	852	10.6
December	118	30		8	156	900	17.3
TOTAL 1943:	863	136		68	1067	6948	15.4
1944:							
January	142	24		17	183	900	20.3
February	191	30		13	234	996	23.5
March	211	30		7	248	996	24.9
April	233	18		33	248	996	28.5
May	237	27		21	285	1044	27.3
June	116	21	85	76	298	1044	28.5
July	141	36	3	23	203	1044	19.4
August	150	56	14	7	227	1188	19.1
September	198	51	19	8	275*	1284	21.4
October	98	56	6	12	166*	1284	12.9
November	159	88	7	14	265*	1284	20.6
December	83	66	8	17	171*	1284	13.3
TOTAL 1944:	1959	503	142	248	2839	13344	21.3
1945:							
January	93	128	5	11	234*	1284	18.2
February	74	90	6	15	178*	1284	13.9
March	99	98	6	18	209*	1284	16.3
April	102	60	17	24	194*	1284	15.1
May		9	4		1*	1284	—
TOTAL 1945:	368	385	38	68	816	6420	15.9

*Includes repaired war-weary aircraft returned to service

IX Surviving B-17s Around The World

Serial No	Model			Name	Location
40-3097	B-17D		(BO)	*Swoose*	National Air and Space Museum, Silver Springs, Maryland
41-2446	B-17E		(BO)	*Swamp Ghost*	Aggiambo Swamp, Papua, New Guinea
41-2595	B-17E		(BO)		Crystal Lake. Dismantled. Awaiting restoration by M. Kellner
41-24485	B-17F	10	(BO)	*Memphis Belle*	Memphis Belle Memorial Association, Memphis, Tennessee
42-3374	B-17F	50	(BO)	No name	Offut AFB, Nebraska
42-29782★	B-17F	70	(BO)	*Museum of Flight*	Boeing Field, Seattle, Washington
42-32076	B17G	35	(BO)	*Shoo Shoo Shoo Baby*	Wright-Patterson AF Museum, Dayton, Ohio
43-38635	B-17G	90	(BO)	*Virgin's Delight*	Castle Air Museum, Castle AFB, Merced, California
44-6393	B-17G	50	(DL)	*2nd Patches*	March Field Museum, March AFB, California. (Painted 42-30092)
44-8543★	B-17G	70	(VE)	*Chuckie*	BC Vintage Flying Machines, Fort Worth, Texas
44-8846★	B-17G	85	(VE)	*Lucky Lady*	Association Fortress 'Volante'. Jean Salis, Cerny, France
44-8889	B-17G	85	(VE)	No name	Musee De L'Air, Le Bourget, France
44-83512	B-17G	85	(DL)	*Heavens Above*	Lackland AFB History and Tradition Museum, San Antonio, Texas
44-83514★	B-17G	85	(DL)	*Sentimental Journey*	Arizona Wing of the Confederate Air Force, Mesa, Arizona
44-83525★	B-17G	85	(DL)	*Suzy Q*	Weeks Air Museum, Tamiami Airport, Miami, Florida
44-83542	B-17G	85	(DL)	No name	Weeks Air Museum, Tamiami Airport, Miami, Florida
44-83546★	B-17G	85	(DL)	No name	Dave Tallichet, Silvermill Museum, Chino, California
44-83559	B-17G	85	(DL)	*King Bee*	Strategic Air Command, Omaha, Nebraska
44-83563★	B-17G	85	(DL)	*Fuddy Duddy*	National Warplanes Museum, Geneseo, New York
44-83575★	B17G	85	(DL)	*909*	Collings Foundation, Riverhill Farm, Stow, Maine
44-83624	B17-G	90	(DL)	No name	Wright-Patterson AF Museum, Dayton, Ohio
44-83663	B-17G	90	(DL)	*Short Bier*	Hill AFB Museum, Utah
44-83684	B-17G	90	(DL)	*Picadilly Lilly*	Planes of Fame Museum, Corona del Mar, California
44-83690	B-17G	95	(DL)	*Miss Liberty Belle*	Grissom AFB Museum Foundation, Peru, Indiana
44-83718	TB-17H		(DL)	No name	Museu Aerospacial, Rio de Janiero, Brazil (also 44-83462)
44-83728	B-17G	95	(DL)	No name	Musee de L'Air, Le Bourget, France
44-83735	B-17G	90	(DL)	*Mary Alice*	Imperial War Museum, Duxford, England
44-83785★	B-17G	95	(DL)	*Shady Lady*	Evergreen Air of Mt Inc, Pinal Airpark, Marana, Arizona
44-83814	B-17G	95	(DL)	*Tanker 09*	National Air & Space Museum, Dulles Airport, Washington
44-83863	B-17G	95	(DL)	No name	USAF Armament Museum, Eglin AFB, Eglin, Florida
44-83868	B-17G	95	(DL)	No name	RAF Bomber Command Museum, Hendon, London
44-83872★	B-17G	95	(DL)	*Texas Raiders*	Gulf Coast Wing, Confederate Air Force, Harlingen, Texas
44-83884	B-17G	95	(DL)	*Yankee Doodle II*	8th Air Force Museum, Barksdale AFB, Bossier City, Louisiana
44-85599	B-17G	100	(DL)	*Blackhawk*	Texas Museum of Military History, Dyess AFB, Abilene, Texas
44-85718★	B-17G	105	(VE)	*Thunderbird*	Lone Star Museum, Hobby Airport, Houston, Texas
44-85734	B-17G	105	(VE)	*Five Engine*	New England Air Museum, Bradley Airport, Windsor Locks, CT
44-85738	B-17G	105	(VE)	*Amvet*	American Veterans Memorial, Tulare, California
44-85740★	B-17G	105	(VE)	*Chief Oshkosh*	EAA Warbirds of America, Oshkosh, Wisconsin
44-85778	B-17G	105	(VE)	No name	Aero Nostalgia, Stockton, California
44-85784★	B-17G	105	(VE)	*Sally B*	B-17 Preservation Ltd, Horley, Surrey (a/c based at Duxford)
44-85790	B-17G	105	(VE)	No name	On top of a garage, Milwaukie, Oregon
44-85825	B-17G		(VE)	No name	Smithsonian Institute, Washington DC
44-85828	B-17G	110	(VE)	*I'll Be Around*	390th BG Assn, Pima Air Museum, Tucson, Arizona
44-85829	B-17G	110	(VE)	*Yankee Lady*	Yankee Air Force, Ypsilanti, Missouri

(BO) = Boeing   (DL) = Douglas   (VE) = Lockheed Vega   ★ Flying Examples

X Fates of the B-17s: 1945–Present

Serial No.	Type	Last Civil Reg	Last Owner	Career/Fate
41-9210	E	CP-753	Frigorificos Reyes, Bolivia	Crashlanding San Borja 8.76. Being rebuilt at La Paz
41-24434	F	CP-579	Frigorificos Grigota	Crashed Uncio 29.12.58
42-3217	F		Swedish Government	*Georgia Rebel*, 381st BG, landed at Vannacka, Sweden on 24.7.43 and interned. Bought by ABA. Fate unknown
42-3360	F	CP-570	Lloyd Aero Boliviano	Crashed La Paz 21.9.55
42-3470	F	HK-580	Linea Aerea Borinquen	Conv to TB-17F 12.53. Ultimate fate unknown
42-3490	F	SE-BAN	SILA (Sweden International Airline) 'Bob' (10.9.45–5.10.48)	385th BG. Landed at Bulltofta, Sweden, and interned on 21.6.44. Converted by SAAB to 14-passenger airliner and bought by ABA. Broken up 5.10.48
42-3543	F	SE-BAH	A.B.A. 'Sam' (24.1.44–46)	*Sack Time Suzy*, 96th BG, landed at Bulltofta and interned 9.10.43. Converted by SAAB to 14-passenger airliner in 1945. Used for fire practice 9.46
42-5827	F		Swedish Government	*Lakanuki*, 379th BG, landed at Sattarp, Sweden on 1.4.44 and interned. Bought by ABA. Fate unknown
42-6073	F	CP-686	Lloyd Aero Boliviano	Conv to TB-17F. Crashed Trinidad, Bolivia 4.11.6?
42-6107	F	N1340N	Aero Flite Inc, Cody, WY	Conv to TB-17F. Re-engined with 4 RR Darts ex-UAl Viscount after 1968. Crashed Dubois, WY, while fire-bombing on 18.8.70 and destroyed
42-30177	F	F-BGSG	Institute Géographique Nationale, Creil, France (1955)	Served French Air Force as *Charlene*, *Bir Hakiem*, based Wahn, FGR, for French High Commissioner. Damaged and ferried to IGN, France. Used for spares
42-30661	F	SE-BAK	A.B.A. 'Jim' (6.10.44–46)	388th BG *Veni Vidi Vici* landed Rinkaby, Sweden and interned 29.2.44. Was on its 28th mission. Converted by SAAB to 14-passenger airliner. Broken up 12.46
42-30921	F	CP-571	Aerovias Moxos	Lloyd Aero Boliviano in 50s. Crashed Viacha 16.1.62
42-31163	F	SE-BAM	A.B.A. 'Tom' (5.1.45–48)	*A Good Ship & Happy Ship* 388th BG, landed Rinkaby, Sweden and interned 6.3.44. Conv by SAAB to 14-passenger airliner. Crashed Mariefred 4.12.45
42-97115	G	SE-BAO	SILA 'Ted' (26.5.45–48)	94th BG/333rd BS. Landed Bulltofta, Sweden and interned 11.4.44. Converted by SAAB to 14-passenger airliner Wfs, broken up and struck off register 5.10.48
42-102542	G	N5845N	Aero Service Corp, Philadelphia, PA (26.2.55–58)	Conv to TB-17G. Served as memorial at Sioux City municipal airport *Sioux City Sue* 1946–52. Crashed c1958
42-102715	G	N66573	Black Hills Aviation, Alamagordo, NM	Conv to TB-17G. Fire tanker 20.11.61–77. Crashed
42-107067	G	OY-DFE	D.D.L. (Denmark) (3.12.45–30.1.46)	447th BG/709th BS. Diverted to Sweden and

				interned 11.4.44. Converted by SAAB to 14-passenger airliner 19.11.45. Written off in collision 30.1.46. Collided with aircraft landing at Kastrup 30.1.46
43-37650	G	N66570	California Atlantic Airways, Florida	Belonged to 96th BG. Fate unknown after 1952
43-38322	G	CP-936	Frigorificos Reyes (1971–)	Oklahoma Military Academy, Rogers City, OK, in 1946. Crashed La Paz, Bolivia 7.2.65 while serving with Lloyd Aero Boliviano. Rebuilt. Crashed San Ignacio de Moxos 11.2.72
43-38978	G	N4960	Columbia Airmotive, Troutdale, OR	Dismantled for spares in 1950s
43-39304	G	F-BDAT	Institute Géographique Nationale, Creil (12.12.49)	Crashed Niamey, Nigeria 12.12.50
43-39367	G	CP-625	Lloyd Aero Boliviano (11.56–)	Crashed San Lorenzo, Bolivia 17.11.59
44-6332	G	CP-588	Aerovias Moxos	Crashed 2.5.63
44-6556	G	CP-624	Corporation Boliviano de Fomento	Crashed Reyes, Bolivia 23.2.63
44-8990	G	N3678G	Multiple Management Corp, Long Beach (1963–69)	Fate unknown
44-6750	G	CP-597	Lloyd Aero Boliviano (11.52–)	Crashed Trinidad, Bolivia 5.9.55
44-83439	G	N131P	Air Carrier Leasing Corp, Miami, FL (1963–)	Used by Paramount Aquariums Inc, Vero Beach, FL by 1960. Converted for fish transport. Fate unknown
44-83728	G	F-BGOE	Institute Géographique Nationale	Based at Creil, France from 12.7.52. Fate unknown
44-83729	G	F-BEED	Institute Géographique Nationale	*Denise* Creil. Struck off register 1962 and scrapped
44-83750	G	CP-623	Lloyd Aero Boliviano (11.56–)	Crashed La Paz, Bolivia 28.7.58
44-83753	G	NL5024N	A. Schwimmer Miami/Israeli Air Force (9.6.48)	Scrapped in Israel *c*1958
44-83757	G	F-BDRR	Institute Géographique Nationale (25.7.50–62)	Scrapped at Creil *c*1972
44-83809	G	CP-626	Corporation Boliviano de Fomento (12.56)	Crashed Caranavi 25.10.59
44-83811	G	N9814F	Israeli Air Force (9.6.48–58)	Impounded in Algeria en-route to USA 1958. Returned to Israel. Dismantled. Fuselage to Columbia Pictures Corp, UK for use as prop in *The War Lover* 1961
44-83842	G	NL1212N	Charles Babb Inc, Burbank, CA (1948)	A Schwimmer, Miami/Israeli Air Force 6.48. Impounded Azores on ferry to Israel. F.A. Portugal, based Azores. Fate unknown
44-83851	G	NL1098M	Charles T. Winters, Miami, FL	A. Schwimmer/Israeli Air Force 9.6.48. Scrapped *c*1962
44-83858	G	N7228C	Aero Enterprises, Fresno, CA (1966)	Bu77226 (PB-1W). Fate unknown
44-83858	G	CP-742	Comp. Boliviana de Rutes Aereas (64)	Bu77227 (PB-1W). Crashed Santa Ana 21.2.65
44-83859	G	CP-767	Comp. Boliviana de Rutes Aereas (65)	Bu77228 (PB-1W). Last USN PB-1W disposed of from Litchfield Park NAS, Phoenix 1958. Crashed Santa Ana 13.4.67
44-83861	G	CP-741	Comp. Boliviano de Rutes Aereas (64)	Bu77229 (PB-1W). Crashed San Borja 30.10.64
44-83864	G	N73648	Black Hills Aviation, Spearfish, SD	Bu77232 (PB-1W). Crashed Silver City, NM 12.7.72
44-83873	G	CF-JJH	Unknown	Bu77236 (PB-1W). Fate unknown
44-83874	G	N5236V	American Compressed Steel Corp.	Bu77237 (PB-1W). Based at Love Field, Dallas, TX 66/69. Fate unknown
44-83875	G	CP-640	Boliviana de Aviacion (1958–)	Bu77238 (PB-1W). Crashed La Paz, Bolivia 17.8.67
44-83877	G	N5232V	Columbia Pictures Inc (1961–)	Bu77240 (PB-1W). Ferried to UK for *The War*

				Lover. Arrived Gatwick 8.10.61. Scrapped at Bovington 1962
44-83883	G	N5229V	Columbia Pictures Inc (1961–)	Bu77243 (PB-1W). Ferried to UK for *The War Lover*. Arrived Gatwick 8.10.61. Scrapped at Manston 1962
44-85507	G	N5116N	Mark Hurd Mapping Co, Minneapolis (12.6.52–)	Assigned to Esperado Mining Co, Altus, OK for scrapping 25.6.47. Converted to exec aircraft for *Chicago Tribune* 4.2.48. Crashed in Nevada desert 10.11.52
44-83861	G	CP-741	Comp. Boliviana de Rutes Aereas (64)	Bu77229 (PB-1W). Crashed San Borja 30.10.64
44-83864	G	N73648	Black Hills Aviation, Spearfish, SD	Bu77232 (PB-1W). Crashed Silver City, NM 12.7.72
44-83873	G	CF-JJH	Unknown	Bu77236 (PB-1W). Fate unknown
44-83874	G	N5236V	American Compressed Steel Corp.	Bu77237 (PB-1W). Based at Love Field, Dallas, TX 66/69. Fate unknown
44-83875	G	CP-640	Boliviana de Aviacion (1958–)	Bu77238 (PB-1W). Crashed at La Paz, Bolivia 17.8.67
44-83877	G	N5232V	Columbia Pictures Inc (1961–)	Bu77240 (PB-1W). Ferried to UK for *The War Lover*. Arrived Gatwick 8.10.61. Scrapped at Bovington 1962
44-83883	G	N5229V	Columbia Pictures Inc (1961–)	Bu77243 (PB-1W). Ferried to UK for *The War Lover*
44-85594	G	F-BGSQ	Institute Géographique Nationale (28.9.54)	Scrapped at Creil *c*1973
44-85643	G	F-BEEA	Institute Géographique Nationale (12.12.47–)	*Amelie, Chateau de Verneuil*. Destroyed in crash at Binbrook on 25.7.89
44-85728	G	F-BGOE	Institute Géographique Nationale (12.7.52–22.8.67)	Owned by TWA, Kansas City, MO 26.6.46. Exec conversion by Boeing as special Model 299AB. TWA Fleet No. 242 2.12.46. Shah of Persia 4.47. Last flight with IGN 22.8.67. Scrapped 1970
44-85733	G	F-BEEB	Institute Géographique Nationale (20.2.48)	Crashed Yaounde, Cameroun 11.3.49
44-85774	G	N621L	Aircraft Specialities Inc, Mesa, AZ	Lloyd Aero Boliviano 12.56–68. Fire bomber 68–72. Crashed 7.75
44-85778	G	N3509G	Aircraft Component Equipment Supplies, Klamath Falls, OR/Alvin Celcer (11.82–86)	Fire bomber with various companies 1967–77. Fate unknown
44-85806	G	CP-762	Bolivian Air System (12.64–)	Crashed at La Paz 16.12.64
44-85812	G	N4710C	Dothan Aviation Corp, Dothan, AL	Bu77246 (PB-1G USCG). Crashed Blakely, GA 5.8.76
44-85813	G	N6694C	Black Hills Aviation, Alamagordo, NM	EB-17G. JB-17G converted to Model 299Z by Boeing, Wichita. Cont as engine testbed, 5th position in nose. Sold 1981. Struck off USCR by 1984
44-85817	G	CP-622	Aerovias Los Andes (10.56–)	Crashed Laja 18.2.57
44-85821	G	N2873G	Unknown	Bu77247. (PB-1G USCG) until 1959. Fate unknown
44-85824	G	CP-694	Servicios Aereos Cochabamba (1960–)	Bu77250 (PB-1G USCG). Crashed La Paz, 18.12.63
44-85840	G	N620L	Aircraft Specialties Inc, Mesa, AZ (1968–72)	Used by Lloyd Aero Boliviano (CP-620) 11.56. Took part in *Tora! Tora! Tora!* in Hawaii 1969. Scrapped *c*1974
44-?	G	N5225V	American Compressed Steel Corp, TX	Bu77138 (PB-1W) 1963. Fate Unknown
?	F	N60475	Charles Babb & Co, New York (4.1.52)	Formerly used by Sperry Gyroscope Co. Fate unknown

Index